A Completed Life

A Completed Life

Dr Rodney Syme

Title: A Completed Life
First published 2023
Publisher: Dying With Dignity Victoria
Interior and Cover layout Pickawoowoo Publishing Group

A catalogue record for this book is available from the National Library of Australia

ISBN 9780646885353 (paperback)

Every attempt has been made to locate the copyright holders for material quoted in this book.

Any person or organisation that may have been overlooked or misattributed may contact the publisher.

Contents

About Rodney Syme vii

  Andrew Denton viii

Preface ix

  Hugh Sarjeant, President, Dying With Dignity Victoria ix

Foreword xi

  The Syme family: Robin, Bruce and Megan xv

A note from the publisher xvii

  Dying With Dignity Victoria xviii

Contributors xix

Abbreviations xxi

Introduction 1

Chapter 1   The problems of ageing: Who is listening? 9

Chapter 2   Mortality: The grief of death, or the completed life? 15

Chapter 3   The phenomenon of old age: What happened to
the old person's friend? 24

Chapter 4   Aged care: Our second prison system 36

Chapter 5   Remember me, Mrs V? 68

Chapter 6   Dementia: The whole catastrophe 81

The worst disease known to man 107

  Dr Helga Kuhse 107

I'm sorry, Mum 110

  Guy Pearce 110

Chapter 7   A completed life 112

My experience with someone whose life was completed 136

  Dr Nick Carr 136

Everything went quiet   140
    Dr Cathy Henkel   140
Chapter 8   Voluntary refusal of fluids and food   152
Chapter 9   Ending one's own life, or suicide?   169
Chapter 10 Solutions   186
Chapter 11 Conclusions   211

Afterword: Rodney Syme makes us think from beyond the grave   217
    Michael Bachelard   217
Appendix A: Voluntary refusal of fluid and food   221
Appendix B: Advance care directives   225
Informing my Agent   237
References   239

About Rodney Syme

Rodney Syme was one of Australia's most magnificent conundrums: child, and scion, of the medical establishment, but also a law-breaking maverick. For years, Rodney risked his liberty in pursuit of social justice: provoking the law, his fellow practitioners, and the conscience of the nation, to make voluntary assisted dying choice legal. One of Australia's great social and medical reformers, he lived long enough to see voluntary assisted dying become law in almost every state of Australia.

For this, he received the Order of Australia. But, for Rodney, that was not enough.

Now, we see what Rodney was working on till his very last days: a passion (and passionate) project, informed not just by his long years helping, and chronicling, those suffering at the end of life, but also by the loss of his own wife to dementia.

To my mind, there is no more complex subject in medicine than how best to respect the end-of-life choices of those who have become incapable of speaking, or reasoning, for themselves – a complexity made more acute because it potentially asks medical professionals to help end the suffering of someone no longer able to competently communicate that this is, indeed, their enduring wish.

Yet, from my experience over recent years speaking publicly about voluntary assisted dying, I know that there is no end-of-life problem to which more people demand an answer than this. This is hardly surprising. According to the Australian Institute of Health and Welfare, dementia (including Alzheimer's) is second only to coronary heart disease as the cause of death amongst Australian men, and the leading cause of death amongst Australian women; and that the number of Australians with dementia is expected to double by 2058.

I can think of no-one better to help us navigate this medical, ethical and moral minefield than Rodney.

His voice – clear, reasoned and compassionate – will doubtless stir outrage and anger in some, just as it did 40 years ago when he started talking publicly about death with dignity.

Yet, in this, his final work, Rodney Syme once again challenges the nation not to turn away from suffering, but to find a way to act so that people are not forced to endure such suffering needlessly.

Andrew Denton
Founder, Go Gentle Australia

Preface

D r Rodney Syme was a urologist based in Melbourne. He had a long-standing interest in the plight of older people with terminal illnesses and experiencing suffering that could not be relieved.

In 1990 he joined the organisation now known as Dying With Dignity Victoria, one of several such Australian organisations, and pursued the quest for voluntary assisted dying legislation. This initiative was ultimately successful in November 2017. In consequence, similar legislation has been passed in other states, with much less difficulty.

Dr Syme's work, not just as a major force for legislative change, but also as a vast amount of other pro bono work, was recognised in 2018 with the award of an AM (Member of the Order of Australia).

This book presents his views on the plight of people with dementia, and his suggestion for further legislative change. The book's title reflects a life that has been long, and where all that was possible has been achieved – and so is in a sense 'complete'. There follows consideration of the problems that may follow, and what may be a reasonable response.

Hugh Sarjeant
President, Dying With Dignity Victoria

I was pleased to be invited to review the Dr Rodney Syme Book, "A Completed Life". His thoughts on Aged Care, the medical system, the treatment of dementia patients in Aged Care, the great need for Advanced Care Directives and also his approach to the "Completed Life" aspect of dying, are very insightful and a lot of it very similar to my own views on these issues. Dr Syme has accumulated a mass of evidence in support of his views and this forms an important part of the book itself in pointing out the need for change and the expansion of the existing laws. My suggestion would be that the book "A Completed Life" be included as part of the reviews that will be forthcoming on existing VAD legislation in each of the states.

Ian Wood, Spokesperson and Co-founder for Christians Supporting Choice for Voluntary Assisted Dying, Australia

Foreword

It is with a sense of great honour, yet with heavy hearts, that we, Rodney's three children, write this foreword to his third book. It is not yet nine months since our father died of unforeseen circumstances, and we miss him dearly. Yet unforeseen circumstances and the instability of health in old age are our common lot. While most of us may wish for a peaceful death in our sleep, in our own bed, in our own home, it is not often what we get. Only 24 hours before Dad's stroke, he reminded me of his wishes if he should suffer an unforeseen health crisis. These instructions had been well discussed over many years, and his wishes for how he wanted to die, or rather how he did *not* want to die, had been clearly discussed with his family and GP (with all relevant details clearly articulated in his advanced care directive).

As we were growing up, death and the prospect of dying were not a taboo topic in our household. They were discussed as a normal part of life, and, in the case of a serious illness, a blessing. Quality of life was always the counterpoint in our discussion: what makes one's life worth living, and what are the conditions that make it a pointless and intolerable form of suffering. From each of us, contemplating these questions will elicit an answer that is as unique as we are. What is important is that the answers are our own, not dictated by another person, institution or law with a value system different from our own.

As we get older, these questions take on greater relevance, and to consider them seriously we need to be informed. Today in Australia and much of the Western world we are living in a society where the ailments of old age are for the most part hidden from our awareness. Death, illness, advanced dementia, and old age are largely dealt with by institutions. The failings of our aged-care facilities have been, over several years now, made public and the subject of numerous investigations and legal reviews. There is no doubt that for those people who are unable to care for their sick or elderly family members, there is much sadness and trepidation as they leave their loved ones to the care of others.

Today in our affluent Western societies we live in a culture that prizes autonomy and personal responsibility. These are, in fact, defining characteristics of our modern democracy; yet they are exactly what we lose when we become sick, frail, isolated and institutionalised. The voices of sick and elderly people, and therefore their needs, are unintentionally silenced by institutional needs for cost-effectiveness. In this book, Dad looks at the reasons why thinking about and preparing for our death is an important part of living well.

Shortly after Dad's death, as we were sorting through his belongings, we discovered a notebook of poems that he had written in the early 1980s. One of the poems was titled 'Who are you?'. It was a poem about dementia and in it Dad expressed his fear of what it might be like to live with dementia – of what it would be like to no longer recognise your loved ones. We assume that Dad probably wrote this after attending to someone with advanced dementia. It may well have been one of the experiences documented in this book. This was some 30 years before we started noticing changes in Mum's behaviour, and another five years before we understood for sure that she had dementia.

In 2017 Mum and Dad left Melbourne and moved to rural Victoria to live with Robin, their eldest daughter, in a granny flat they had installed on her property. Mum had finally received a confirmed diagnosis of dementia some two years earlier. As we had been expecting this diagnosis for some time, we had spent much time together discussing how we could care for Mum, and what might be required from us. As a family we were in a fortunate situation. Robin and Bruce lived in close proximity, Robin was working only part time, and her daughter was an adult and had left home. These circumstances allowed us to put into action a family-based supportive care plan for our mother. Dad was adamant that Mum not go into care, and he devoted the next four years of his life to being Mum's primary carer, until her death some four months before his own.

The following years spent together were challenging, joyful and frustrating in equal measure, and certainly the frustration masked a deep and abiding sadness. Mum developed what is professionally termed a 'care-resistant' approach to life. Learning to adapt to the constant changes and fluctuations in her functioning capacity was not easy. I think it is possibly only when you are caring for a person with dementia that you truly begin to understand how intricately memory is enfolded into all our daily activities and behaviour, and that the memories we store form our identity and inform our behaviour.

A person with dementia has no choice in which memories they keep and which ones disappear. Dementia affects everyone differently, and we were extremely lucky that although Mum could not say what our names were, or that we were her children – or in Dad's case, her husband – she was able, until the very last, to express her utter joy at our presence. Her love for her family was at the core of her being, and we were all fortunate that this was not stripped away before her death.

Mum died of advanced dementia: she was bedridden, doubly incontinent, and uninterested in food. She experienced almost daily periods of psychosis and agitation, interspersed with more lucid moments of joy. She was extremely distressed by hygiene requirements. The last year of her life required an intense, full-time commitment of care, and we were fortunate that, as a family, we were able to provide this and to support each other in the process. We also had an excellent GP involved and district nursing to guide us in our care efforts. In our current society, it seems that to be able to care for our sick and elderly at home, as is most often their wish, is now a privilege for those families who have the time, space, support and ability to attend to their needs.

After having successfully campaigned for more than 43 years to bring the need for voluntary assisted dying (VAD) for those with a terminal illness into the public sphere for debate and finally legislation, Rodney has, in this book, turned his attention to the plight of those who do not qualify for VAD under the current legislation but for whom life under their current circumstances is no longer desired, as it is only cause for ongoing suffering and misery. In this context he discusses some of the options currently available to terminally ill people who are unable to access VAD.

In this book Rodney draws together stories of his personal experiences working as a doctor and years of personal reading, collating information from medical journals, newspapers and other valid and well-regarded sources to illustrate the tragedy and ubiquity of these cases. He has, clearly, felt impelled to speak out against the injustices to personal dignity and the suffering experienced by those in aged-care facilities, highlighting some of the inconsistencies in our laws and the suffering that they impose.

Dad writes about the critical importance of advance care directives that specifically detail the individual's instructions and wishes for the type of care they want to receive under particular circumstances. He emphasises the importance of these directives, especially for those people with early dementia.

In all these circumstances, what Rodney highlights repeatedly are the necessity and value of clear and respectful communication to achieve a good outcome for the ailing individual. He writes about the ethical responsibility that he believes doctors have, to encourage these conversations between the ailing individual, his or her family members and all relevant medical staff. But good communication on these matters is also required in our broader community, as part of our ethical responsibility towards the aged and dying. Appropriate and respectful language and terms like 'a completed life' need to be understood, so that an individual's experience and wishes can be respected.

Finally, Dad addresses what he sees to be the critical changes required by aged-care facilities in Australia to provide good care that is sensitive to, and informed by, the needs of its residents.

Dad completed the first draft of this book in around 2018. Mum at this time required constant companionship, guidance and support, but she was often happy to entertain herself. This allowed Dad time to write and to collate his thoughts on the further changes that he believed needed to be made to the VAD legislation. During this time, he also continued to counsel many people as they were facing serious illness, death, and quality-of-life concerns. Dad was rarely idle: as Megie has said of our father, 'He rarely let a moment go by without doing something constructive.' He was always reading, writing, researching, listening, supporting, challenging, advocating; he was a strong believer in the importance of having a purpose to provide one's life with meaning and direction. For Rodney, living and acting in a purposeful manner to create constructive change for the betterment of those living and unable to achieve such ends for themselves was a primary goal in his life.

Dad ceased working on this book sometime in 2019, when several chapters were only in their first draft stage. Many thanks to Dying With Dignity Victoria for getting the components combined, and for undertaking a preliminary edit.

We are enormously proud of all the work our father has done to achieve better outcomes for those people facing the end of their lives with a terminal illness, and we hope that this book will further the public conversation on what constitutes a life worth living and what are the humane options available to us when life has no further meaning for the individual other than suffering.

The Syme family:
Robin, Bruce and Megan

A note from the publisher

The author of this book, Dr Rodney Syme MBBS, died in October 2021. However, most of his drafting was finished by 2019, and so some references are now out of date. For example, certain government ministers are either no longer in parliament, or have changed portfolios. In particular, the voluntary assisted dying (VAD) law in the state of Victoria had only recently been implemented, and no other Australian state had legislation. At the date of publication, all Australian states have passed VAD laws.

As Dr Syme had not yet appointed a publisher, Dying With Dignity Victoria (DWDV) has agreed to publish this, his last work. In view of the difficulty in keeping consistency, we have not updated certain references or made other changes in consequence. For the book would then have become in part *our* book, rather than Dr Syme's. We have therefore limited any modifications of his text to typographical corrections and minor editing required for clarity. None of DWDV's small text changes affects the major thrust of Dr Syme's thesis about the concept of a 'completed life', with its notion that at a certain point people might reasonably decide they no longer want to live. Where we considered it important to add a clarifying note to the text, these are introduced by the words 'publisher's note'.

As Dr Syme was based in the Australian state of Victoria, many references may not be familiar to those living elsewhere, and so a list of such terms and abbreviations is included.

When Dr Syme died, he had not completed a bibliography for his book. DWDV has prepared one based on the referencing notes provided by Dr Syme in his manuscript, arranged in chapter order. DWDV acknowledges that, despite our best efforts, this bibliography is likely to be incomplete and may contain unintended errors. We invite any person whom we may have overlooked or misattributed to contact DWDV.

Disclaimer

This publication is for information purposes only, and is designed as a general reference and catalyst to seeking further information about dementia and end-of-life options in Australia. The author, the contributors and DWDV are not responsible for the results of any actions taken on the basis of any information in this publication, nor for any error in or omission from this publication.

Information contained in this publication has been compiled using information from other sources. Any person having concerns about the contents of this publication should refer to those sources for more specialist information and advice. Attribution to sources appears in the text of this publication.

DWDV does not give medical or other advice or services. DWDV – on its own behalf and on behalf of the author and other contributors – expressly disclaim all and any liability and responsibility to any person, whether a reader of this publication or not, in respect of anything, and of the consequences of anything, done or omitted to be done by any such person in reliance, whether wholly or partially, upon the whole or any part of the content of this publication.

Dying With Dignity Victoria

Contributors

Dying With Dignity Victoria gratefully acknowledges the following people for contributing new material, or allowing previously published material, to be included in this book as a complement to Dr Syme's work:

Michael Bachelard (Afterword; Pages 217-219) is a senior writer and former deputy editor and investigations editor of *The Age* newspaper in Melbourne. He has been a journalist for more than 30 years, also having worked for *The Canberra Times* and *The Australian*. He has reported in Canberra, Melbourne and Jakarta, as well as Syria, Iraq and South Sudan. He has written two books, most recently *Behind the Exclusive Brethren*, and has won many awards for journalism, including the Gold Walkley Award.

Dr Nick Carr (Pages 136-139) has been a DWDV board member for seven years, and a GP for more than 30 years. He has been active in supporting those in need of a dignified and compassionate death, both before the implementation of VAD in Victoria, and since. Dr Carr has been influential in assisting with campaigns to get VAD legislation passed in other states. He has a frequent media presence, appearing in weekly radio and television programs.

Andrew Denton (Pages vii-viii) is regarded as one of Australian media's genuinely creative forces, with a career covering radio, television and film. He is the creator of the podcast series *Better Off Dead* (a deep dive into the truths, lies and politics of VAD) and also founding director of the national advocacy organisation Go Gentle Australia.

Associate Professor Cathy Henkel (Pages 140-151) is director of the Western Australian Screen Academy at Edith Cowan University and an award-winning documentary filmmaker with more than 30 years' experience. Her work focuses on inspiring, global stories engaging audiences through cinema, television, online and education platforms. Her films have screened in more than 26 countries, including broadcasts on ABC, BBC, CBC, PBS and HBO. She won the Tribeca Best Feature Documentary Award, SPA Documentary Producer of the Year, an Emmy nomination and numerous festival awards. In 2023 she received the Stanley Hawes Lifetime Achievement Award at the Australian International Documentary Conference. *Laura's Choice*, co-directed with her daughter Sam Lara, is available to stream on ABC iView and listed in *The Guardian*'s ten best Australian television shows of 2021.

Dr Helga Kuhse (Pages 107-109) is an Australian philosopher and bioethicist. She was an associate professor at Monash University's Centre for Human Bioethics, and its director from 1992 to 1998. She has published many articles and books on bioethics and has frequently been consulted by state governments and committees. In the 1980s Helga was president of the World Federation of Right to Die Societies and of Dying With Dignity Victoria. Helga Kuhse is a supporter of voluntary assisted dying.

Guy Pearce (Pages 110-111) is one of the most versatile actors working today. His career has spanned nearly 40 years in film, television and theatre, both in Australia and internationally.

Abbreviations

ABC   Australian Broadcasting Corporation
ACD   advance care directive
AMA   Australian Medical Association
AO   Officer of the Order of Australia (Australian honour, awarded for service worthy of particular recognition)
DWDV   Dying With Dignity Victoria
GP   general medical practitioner, as distinct from a doctor specialising in a particular disease, or part of the body, or type of patient
PAS   physician-assisted suicide
RTO   registered training organisation
VAD   voluntary assisted dying
VRFF   voluntary refusal of food and fluids*

---

* See also Chapter 8 and Appendix A.

Introduction

I am sitting in an old leather armchair in front of my pot-belly stove in my beach 'shack' on Phillip Island. A shack indeed it is. Built in 1949 by a retired merchant seaman, who did most of the work himself, including the electrical wiring, it has many defects. In 2001, I asked the builder of my architect-designed new Toorak house to advise on some minor renovations to the shack. He advised, 'The only sensible thing to do with that place is pull it down and start again.' I ignored his advice and later renovated the kitchen.

My beloved wife, Meg, whose family had long associations with Phillip Island, bought the shack as her bolt-hole from the pressures of city and domestic life, and has turned it into a refuge of tranquillity and beauty. She has filled it with her own artistic creations: paintings, drawings, glasswork, and stone and ceramic sculptures (together with some works by her sculpture mentor, Robert Langley, and a couple of my objects).

Behind the pot-belly, in front of the firebrick, is her magnificent octopus – a 20-tile (each 35 centimetres square) creation in blue, brown and black. The shack is filled with an extraordinary collection of marine artefacts: ship's lights, glass buoys, shells, coral, starfish and seahorses. Everywhere there is something to delight the eye.

I am looking out the large windows into a virtual forest – trees planted and nurtured by Meg over many years. The grey-green olive, the brighter green of the flame tree, and the Australian green of the scarlet flowering gum and the bottle-brush. The *Grevillea robusta* forms a higher canopy before the towering presence at the back of the huge coastal banksias. This place is a veritable paradise of quiet peace, broken only by the sound of the resident birds, were it not for the frequent interruptions from Bach, Handel, Telemann and others.

This environment allows the right climate to distill one's thoughts, sift the dross, and create the plan, the way forward. Often, in years gone by, when Meg was not her usual happy self, I would naively say, 'Why don't you do some drawing, that will make you more content', only to be quickly told, 'You can't just sit down and draw, not if you want to do something good.' There needs to be the right moment, the right mood, the idea, the spark, to succeed. It was only when I started writing that I understood what she meant.

It is here that I retire to write, to the peace and solitude necessary to construct thoughts and ideas, to let them float around, rearrange themselves in a considered way. I have spent this afternoon by the fire and now, warmed by the fire and some fine but not expensive cabernet shiraz, I am expressing some long-held thoughts.

I have had a fortunate life – a very fortunate life. I am reminded of the wonderful book of this title by A. B. Facey. Born into desperate circumstances, he was never discouraged, but worked tirelessly to improve himself and his circumstances. By sheer strength of character, he made a good life for himself, and assisted others to a better life.

Unlike Facey, I entered life with the proverbial silver spoon in my mouth. My grandfather and father were both respected Melbourne surgeons, so there was a sound financial base to our family life. Growing up, my three brothers and I were encouraged to develop self-reliance. After a very brief period of surveillance from my older brother, I took myself to kindergarten by two trams – from the age of four. At other times, my bike was my mode of travel; my parents never drove me to school, not even during the three-month tram strike just after World War II. Twelve years of cubbing and scouting was a wonderful training in resilience and individual responsibility. A fine education at prestigious Melbourne Grammar School created a love of learning, history, books and music, and was a great springboard for self-learning at the university and hospital. I was blessed with a very happy childhood.

But I was blessed with an even greater good fortune – to be born in 1935. This meant that I missed the worst of the Great Depression, was too young for the Korean War, and too old for the Vietnam War. I did live through the Cold War, but was never fearful of nuclear war, because I was sure both sides would not take the disastrous risk. The years after World War II saw the greatest advance of freedom in world history, the collapse of colonialism, the expanse in global wealth, and the creation of an enviable standard of living in Australia. And for a surgeon, this was 50 years of colossal development in medical science and surgical progress. I could not have picked a better year if I had tried.

Now, however, as I move into my eighties, I am forced to contemplate the consequences of the last 70 years of medical progress, together with outstanding changes in public health. Had I been born in 1870, I would have had a good chance of dying by the age of 50. Average life expectancy in 1900 was just that, but a century later it is 80-plus – and rising.

My essential health is excellent: blood pressure is 110/70, cholesterol is up (has been for 20 years), but I choose to ignore that. I do have some emphysema, but my lower limbs, despite some degeneration in the major joints, allowed me to undertake the Oxfam 55-kilometre walk (in 14 hours) through hilly forest north of Brisbane in 2015. My kidneys are sound, as is my liver, despite ignoring medical advice about my intake of cabernet shiraz. I do not have cancer and, as such, the odds of my getting it in a disastrous way are low, although I had lunch yesterday with a very old school friend whose wife was perfectly well three months ago, but is dying quickly now from a brain tumour. Will my good fortune hold?

While my likelihood of an early death is low, I have a number of portents of concern. My emphysema is associated with chronic sinusitis and bronchitis, with annoying sneezing and coughing, and a slowly diminishing breathing reserve. My hips, knees and back are creaking more; this, combined with my respiratory problem, means I could not possibly have done the Oxfam walk in 2019. I am continent, but my prostate tablet will soon be replaced by surgery, which I hope will eliminate my waking at night to pee, and subsequent insomnia. My hearing is good, but there is a background of tinnitus, which I can block out if engaged, but will it get worse? My eyesight is declining due to cataracts, which can be fixed relatively effectively – fortunately, I can hold off on this for now. Finally, I suffer from slowly progressive mild loss of memory: I read a lot of books, but a week later I have difficulty remembering the name of the book or the author. Mild cognitive impairment is its medical name, but it can morph into Alzheimer's disease.

I am sorry to burden you with my many (minor) ailments, but I do so because my situation would be common among my peers. Prime Minister Malcolm Fraser was derided when he said 'Life wasn't meant to be easy.' (He should have said 'Life isn't easy.') If he had said this shortly before he died, with the rider 'for us old folk', he might have been applauded as wise. For it is true that life does become more difficult for everyone as they get older. It can certainly be the case that the ability to take pleasure can diminish, and the ability to be relevant in the world decays. Our world shrinks. But it's not much good moaning – no-one will listen to you. You will be exhorted by younger people to pull up your socks, think positively, or be taken to the doctor to discuss depression. You are advised to 'not do so much; take care, you might fall' – all negatives, to which I reply that if I don't remain active I will deteriorate more quickly. To suggest to family, doctors or carers that your life may be nearing completion, not because of terminal illness, but because of a lack of quality, is to be met with a lack of empathy and denial, by deliberate attempts to shut down the conversation, when all you want is good communication and some recognition of your point of view.

I am now 84. I wake at 3 a.m., due either to my recalcitrant bladder or to bedding that is too warm or too cold. I resist getting out of bed to pee, although I know I will not get back to sleep until I do, and the longer I wait, the harder it will become.

And yet I wait – after all, I am 84, and making decisions has become harder – it is easier to do nothing than to do something. And I know I must take extreme care in getting out of bed, so that I do not stumble and fall. Loss of balance was for me perhaps the first sign of advancing years.

As well as waking my wife, turning on the light only creates another stimulus that will awaken me further, and doom me to an hour or three of fitful wakefulness – during which I think. Wrong: I ponder, have thoughts that are fleeting and ill-formed. Thinking requires time and concentration; it is organised thought, ready to be clearly expressed in speech or word. It is hard work – so hard that some days I stare at my computer, almost in grief for the book I have been trying to write for more than three years, as the thoughts swirl, present but disorganised in my brain.

It is, of course, not just disorganisation, but also lack of energy, tiredness, ennui, or simply just easier to do things that give me some pleasure. This lethargy is complex, both physical and mental, and requires significant determination, mixed with dollops of self-contempt, to overcome.

Then there is the grog, dry reds predominantly, whose merits I enjoy liberally. Their consumption grows as the day advances, and I will continue to imbibe them despite the medical profession's imprecations regarding no more than 'two standard drinks a day' – advice I have ignored for more than 40 years, without ill effect to date. Yet I do recognise the contribution that alcohol makes to this lethargy; as the day wears on, I wear down, finding it easier to do simple tasks, or just watch the fabulous view from my living-room window, than to chain myself to my computer and knock out five hundred words.

However, this effect on output is not obligatory. My hero Christopher Hitchens – the finest writer and commentator of my time – seemed capable of extensive boozy lunches, yet still got his immaculate copy in on time. Having a deadline must help; being retired and not dependent on the publisher's cheque is not a spur to excessive activity. Christopher's plaintive book *Mortality* contains much wisdom about dying, to which I will refer. Neither the booze, radical medical treatment, nor serious ill health stilled his pen, though his treatment significantly quietened his voice.

Since resolving to write this book, collecting material, and organising some thoughts, four years have passed. As a result, I now recognise a number of the facets of ageing based on personal experience, but I am not what one would call frail and elderly. That may yet be to come. However, the frail and elderly are the group about whom I wish to write, and I do so from a close acquaintance and an increasingly intimate experience, as my friends get older, and an increasing number of such people seek my personal advice.

Accompanying loss of energy is a loss of stamina (not the same matter), and diminishing mobility. The temptation to drive to the shops rather than walk has to be resisted at all costs. Balance and stability diminish, falls become an ever-present danger, and the plaints of children 'not to do too much' become harder to resist. Eyesight and memory decline inevitably, often without dramatic cause, and often without remedy. Our ability to use the object that has changed modern living more than any other – the motorcar – diminishes (particularly at night) and is lost. The world inevitably shrinks as one ages. As can one's facility with that other essential modern invention, the computer.

We are all destined to die, in old age, unless some specific illness or accident claims us earlier. The reason is simple: we are genetically programmed to wear out, for our cells to be replaced less often and less efficiently, until degeneration rather than regeneration becomes the norm and we fade away. This applies to brain cells as much as any other, so our memory and intellect diminish, even without the advent of dementia. Most named dementias, such as the commonest (Alzheimer's), are specific diseases, many with specific recognised causes. Alzheimer's disease, although not specifically due to ageing, becomes increasingly common as we age. (Some 40 per cent of 90-year-olds are said to suffer from it.) It is surely the worst disease known to man. As I enter my eighties, my wife, three years younger, has developed Alzheimer's disease. I am steadily becoming her full-time carer. Having studied this disease in the literature, and to a small extent in practice, I am now becoming fully aware of its sadness, cruelty and terror.

As people develop dementia, they lose their 'voice', by which I mean their ability to speak coherently for and about themselves. Not so obviously, so do the frail aged, who, although most can still speak, either cannot make themselves heard, are not listened to, or are ignored.

By coincidence, at about the same time I began planning to write this book, the journalist Michael Bachelard was developing a similar interest, commencing in 2010. He described his journey in *The Sydney Morning Herald* of 23 February 2018. His subsequent investigations and articles, particularly from 2016, have provided a steadily increasing volume of concern about our aged-care system. I believe his work and the response of the public to it have been instrumental in the establishment of Australia's royal commission into aged care.* This will

---

* Publisher's note: the Australian government's Royal Commission into Aged Care Quality and Safety tabled its final report in March 2021.

create an outstanding opportunity for the frail aged and those with dementia to be heard.

This book also attempts to speak for them.

Throughout this book, there are four areas in which I want to clarify my position:

- *Voluntary assisted dying* means the provision of medication by a doctor to a person with intolerable suffering, which they may then self-administer in order to end their suffering by ending their life.
- *Suicide* is not a relevant word to apply to such a well-considered, rational and justifiable action.
- *Euthanasia* means a deliberate injection, usually intravenous, of medications having the effect of causing rapid death. It is voluntary unless stated otherwise. I do not support such action unless a person is incapable of self-administration of medication.
- *Patient* is a word I have come to detest in describing a person seeking medical advice, especially at the end of life. They are a person who is dying, not someone in a doctor–patient relationship in which all the power lies in the hands of the doctor. As Professor Metcalfe stated in the *British Medical Journal* (1998), there exists a power gap between doctor and patient because of the former's 'high social status, expertise, health, territory [...] There is an enormous gap between the power available to the doctor and that available to the patient.' He concluded, 'Perhaps we should grow out of the word "patient" – which divides them from us – and learn to call our fellow-travellers "people."' They are the determinant of their own best interests, and their fully informed, autonomous decisions must be respected. So I attempt not to use the word 'patient' unless the sense of a statement absolutely requires it.

CHAPTER 1

The problems of ageing: Who is listening?

Today I chatted with an ageing man, who was 95 years old, about the end of his life – unusual, because such conversations are much more common with women. I think this is largely because women tend to outlive men by three to four years, meaning they are more likely to spend lonely years in old age, and also are prone to talk more openly.

I had known 'Jack' for about 15 years. He had been an academic philosopher in his professional life, and we met in an educational discussion group on occasions, initially when I was invited to address the group on ethics in relation to choice in dying. Our relationship grew when his wife consulted me regarding her terminal cancer. Her death struck Jack hard; a strong relationship of more than 60 years can create a chasm when it is broken. The support that two ageing people can provide to one another is more than the sum of two: take one away and the sum diminishes to less than one. Jack could not survive alone, and moved in to live with his daughter.

To reach the august age of 95 usually means that one has avoided all the common causes of 'early death'. One has avoided cancer and heart disease, the commonest providers of death, along with stroke and other organ failures. Lucky, you might say, but on the other hand you now face a prolonged period of living with the accompaniments of ageing, with no prospect of a predictable exit.

Some ten years or so ago I responded to a computer program that claimed to provide one with an accurate life prognosis. I entered some medical and family details, and was pronounced viable until I was 98. *Bugger, bugger, bugger,* I said under my breath, because, as an experienced medical practitioner, I knew that I was going to enter the territory that Jack was now in.

As I write, at 83, without any serious illness, I know that the bloody computer was right, and all based on a very simple algorithm. I have just finished reading Yuval Noah Harari's impressive work *Homo Deus*, and my wish to find untenable his argument about the future power of computer algorithms over mankind is shaken, damn it! I shall still, however, retain the choice not to have to travel to Switzerland at the age of 104, like Professor David Goodall, who in many ways is a likely mirror image of Jack.

Jack is not terminally ill. It is not possible to say how long he will live; he may outlive David Goodall, though I doubt it. David kept working academically until he was 102, thus retaining a purpose in life, and some enjoyment – until his organisation kicked him out of his office. His already slowly crumbling physical circumstances lost their foundations, leading him to echo Seneca's wisdom that 'a man should live as long as he ought, not as long as he can'. As a philosopher, Jack understood the meaning of existential suffering, and that quality of life, not quantity – at least for him – was what counted. He was reflecting on David Goodall's decision.

'What is bothering you?' I asked Jack. His answer was not particularly lucid. He did not describe any of the classical physical causes of suffering, such as pain, breathlessness or paralysis. His principal symptom was tiredness, fatigue, but of a degree that limited his mobility, together with some minor joint problems. His appetite was poor; he had little desire to eat. He had lost his driver's licence, which he regretted, although I suggested to him that this was probably wise, for others' sake as much as his (based on my own slowly declining facility). He had no major disease diagnoses, and took no medications except a major antidepressant, the serotonin release inhibitor Pristiq, prescribed by his GP.

I was not surprised to learn this, because I knew that Jack had taken his wife's death very hard. When we had been together with his wife and daughter discussing his wife's distress, despite his support for her, his quietness impressed me. The sadness of a deep love is that the deeper it is, the greater the grief that follows its rupture. This, and subsequent discussions with his daughter, led me to feel that Jack had a strong grief. Grief is a natural response to loss and does not intrinsically cause depression, although if the impacts of grief are prolonged then depression may become an issue. However, Jack was not at all sure whether he felt better on the drug or not. I suggested he discuss this with his doctor. Many an antidepressant, once prescribed, is continued without good evidence of continuing benefit. A trial period off the drug, after a gradual reduction in dose, could do no harm.

Could Jack have multiple reasons for depression? Yes, he certainly could, if we are clear about what depression means. The venerable Dalai Lama, when asked what was the meaning of life, replied that it meant two things: first to have purpose in life ('to do service'), and second to have pleasure in life. These are two intrinsic qualities that are challenged as we age.

In conversation, Jack had all the understanding and careful expression one would expect of an empirical philosopher. Age might have damaged his physical qualities, but his cerebral function was not significantly impaired. I doubt if he could have constructed and delivered an intricate intellectual presentation, but he could still think effectively, and argue on matters of consequence to his values and way of life. He had followed the story of David Goodall with great interest; Jack could have been David, but ten years younger. He understood the problems of ageing and of frailty, and had the same scorn as I did for young journalists, and, believe it or not, for some doctors, who described David as having no serious medical problem, other than a few scratches and bruises after he had fallen over in his flat and been unable to get back on his feet for nearly 48 hours. They said he was merely a little dehydrated – despite being 104 years old and subsequently confined to a wheelchair. It would be my contention that if you asked any experienced general practitioner the 'surprise' question with regard to Goodall, they would have answered 'yes' – the 'surprise' question being: 'Would you be surprised if this person were dead within 12 months?'

Jack was not in the same circumstance as David, and the 'surprise question' did not apply. In summary of his distress, Jack offered the answer that it was largely existential, a summation that a philosopher could come to, but many others would be puzzled by. The Dalai Lama's answer becomes increasingly relevant as we age. I suggested to Jack that he might have a 'completed life'; after a brief interval, he replied very positively. After further discussion it was clear that he was 'ready to die', which meant that he would be content to go to sleep that night and not wake up. He was seriously considering whether it was 'time to die' – that is to say, whether the time for a decision had come. He was not yet sure.

I had helped his wife with terminal cancer a few years before. What could I do, what should I do, for Jack?

'I want to die. Will you help me?'

This profound question was asked of me recently; it is no longer a surprise when people ask me that question, because I have been answering it in a variety of ways for nearly 40 years. But for most people it is a question they have never been asked, and for a somewhat smaller number a question they will probably never ask.

Some doctors are likely to be asked, although perhaps not always so bluntly. Seriously ill people often broach such a confronting matter obliquely – rather like asking someone one does not know at all well whether they would like to have sex. Oncologists and palliative-care doctors are more likely to be asked, because they are regularly face-to-face with seriously ill people, though I know some palliative care doctors who claim that no-one has ever asked them. You need to have good hearing and a receptive mind to hear such questions – and honesty.

Family members are not uncommonly the first recipient of this question, from an aged or very ill parent. The usual reaction is shock, and a negative response, unless this is a family in the habit of honest, open discussion of sensitive matters, and accustomed to future planning. If so, the parent might have appointed a medical treatment decision maker, and created an advance care directive.

If you answer categorically 'no' to this question, because of fear, shock or a sense of inadequacy, you will have lost the opportunity for a deep human experience. If you say 'no' because of fear of legal consequences, or a moral position, your justification is not so valid and you have equally lost an opportunity for growth. You should never just say 'no' to such a question: it is a serious question that deserves a serious reply. Equally, without a great deal of further knowledge you should not say 'yes'. This question is the opportunity to start a dialogue, to find out what lies behind the question. There will be many scenarios, demanding a wide variety of responses, but ultimately one of those responses will be to say 'yes'. Equally, it may be appropriate to say 'no – not now'.

So, at the end, I come to the question: should doctors kill their patients? My answer is *no*, with one exception, which will evolve by the end of this discussion.

Should doctors help their patients to die? My answer is *yes*, in certain circumstances. I use the word 'patient' here, but reluctantly, simply because this is the context in which these questions are usually framed. I will discuss these two questions in two frames: first the competent person and second those who lack capacity.

Doctors have been helping their patients to die for centuries. Prior to the 19th century, they had very few therapeutic tools – believe it or not, patients were deliberately bled to remove 'bad humours', and leeches were applied for much the same purpose. The pain and suffering at the end of life were eased by the use of laudanum, a tincture of opium. Consider the statement of Sir William Osler at the beginning of the 20th century – 'it is the doctor's duty to ease death' – and the judicial utterance of Justice Devlin in 1957, who echoed the same philosophy. With increasing frequency throughout the latter part of the 20th century, doctors have used medications, principally opioids and sedatives, to 'ease death'. Today the 'pump' or syringe driver is frequently used in palliative care to deliver continuous sedation and analgesia to an unconscious patient, without fluids, until death occurs. The incidence of this practice at the end of life in the UK has been reported as being 19 per cent of palliative-care deaths, which is pertinent because the UK is regarded as providing the best palliative care in the world. In the Netherlands it is 12 per cent and in Italy it is 18 per cent. Surprisingly, there are no figures available for Australia, where the process is unregulated. Furthermore, not all of these acts occur with explicit patient consent. (In many cases the patient cannot give consent – they lack capacity.)

In 1991 Dr Timothy Quill, one of my medical heroes, published in the *New England Journal of Medicine* the story of his young dying cancer patient, Diane, whose end Quill assisted. In 2017, when questioned by ethicist Arthur Caplan about the relevance of the Hippocratic notion that doctors should 'do no harm', Quill said:

It would be difficult for me to construe addressing the suffering of a terminally ill patient in some way as a harm. It's really an obligation. The question is how do we respond to those kinds of suffering? We are involved in helping people to die all the time.

When I graduated in medicine in 1959, the phrase 'patient autonomy' was never heard. In the year 2000, Martin and colleagues wrote in *The Lancet*: 'The principle of autonomy is the dominant ethic in health care in North America and Western Europe.' As a consequence, most Australian parliaments have passed legislation giving competent people the right to refuse any medical treatment, even if such refusal should result in their death, and courts have determined that any suffering as a consequence of such a decision should be maximally palliated.

Doctors assist these patients at their death, quite legally in the case of withdrawal of treatment, and quasi-legally in the case of pain relief and sedation (quasi-legal because of a judicial decision in the UK) when there is a necessity to relieve pain and suffering, particularly when there is consent from the patient. Doctors can do this safely, provided they can reasonably argue that it was not their intention to hasten death.

Yes. Doctors do assist in hastening death, but not for the frail aged like David Goodall, or Jack, or those with early dementia who are still competent. Who is listening to them? Who hears their suffering?

CHAPTER 2

Mortality: The grief of death, or the completed life?

In June 2010, Christopher Hitchens woke with extreme breathlessness, without any prior warning of significant illness. Five hours later he was told he had advanced cancer, which was subsequently proven to have arisen in his oesophagus. His father had died of the same condition at age 79, but Hitch was only 61, and at the height of his powers. Hitch died 19 months later.

After much soul-searching, he wrote a number of essays about his illness, with penetrating observations about medicine, religion and dying. He combined these into a book – *Mortality* – in which he describes his 'year of living dyingly'. Although Hitchens was employed by and wrote regularly for newspapers and journals, he was no mere journalist. He was a penetrating analyst and commentator, a philosopher in the classical Greek mould, and a beautiful writer. Simone de Beauvoir wrote a challenging account of her mother's journey with terminal cancer – *A Very Easy Death* – 50 years earlier, but Hitchens tops this because his is a personal account. Such deep personal accounts of dying by laypeople are uncommon, and *Mortality* has much to teach us about the cost of modern cancer treatment, of dying of cancer, of hope and of 'letting go'. I hope his close family and friends will forgive me for using *Mortality* as a basis for discussing some essential human issues. My own view, without having met him, is that he would have allowed it, but would have wished to be present to engage in argument.

Hitch showed enormous courage. A few hours after receiving the chilling advice of his advanced cancer, he fulfilled two speaking engagements before large audiences. He describes in painful detail his phlebotomist puncturing him 12 times before obtaining a blood sample, all the while encouraged by the sufferer. His wife, Carol Blue, makes clear his constant and optimistic engagement with friends and, even near the end, a plan to write another book. I admire and applaud his decision to share his diagnosis and progress with friends and colleagues (the public too, in his case – but most of us don't have such a platform). Such openness allows honest communication, and expression of important feelings, thoughts and values that are not shared when secrecy and silence rule the day, and are commonly accompanied by depression. Good, open communication is one of the most important components of a good death.

Christopher sought widely for advice, including from the renowned cancer researcher Francis Collins, who gave him frank if disappointing guidance. Not so some others, who suggested a 5 to 20 per cent chance of cure, and so he embarked on a program of chemotherapy followed by radiotherapy.

Of his intravenous chemotherapy, he observed that as the 'venom sack' was administered, 'you feel swamped with passivity and impotence: dissolving in powerlessness like a sugar lump in water'. His loss of hair is noted, as is – especially – a continually runny nose. More distressing, 'the immediate loss of Eros is a huge initial sacrifice'. And there was a loss of 7 kilograms of weight.

Then, suddenly, probably due to nerve involvement by the cancer, he lost his voice. Richard Dawkins described Hitch as the 'finest orator of our time'. Hitch wrote of this that 'to lose this ability is to be deprived of an entire range of faculty: it is assuredly to die more than a little'. At this point he uses the phrase 'year of living dyingly', and indicates that his chief consolation had been the presence of friends. Unable to share in eating and drinking, they offer the 'blessed chance to talk', which he had lost – in his words, 'the freedom of speech', in a literal sense.

Then began his radiotherapy. After one month of ultra-aggressive irradiation which left its evidence on his skin, he wrote of his

> struggle to convey the way that it hurt *on the inside*. I lay for days on end, trying in vain to postpone the moment when I would have to swallow. Every time I did swallow, a hellish tide of pain would flow up my throat, culminating in what felt like a mule kick in the small of my back. [...] If I had been told about all this in advance, would I have opted for the treatment? There were several moments when I bucked and writhed and gasped and cursed when I seriously doubted it.

His only consolation is his acute observation that 'it's probably a merciful thing that pain is impossible to describe from memory'. And he observed that, following all this treatment, he was enormously weaker than before it started.

While contemplating Friedrich Nietzsche's oft-quoted statement 'whatever doesn't kill me makes me stronger', Hitch quotes medical professor Sidney Hook, who 'concentrated his attention on the way in which each debilitation builds on its predecessor and becomes one cumulative misery with only one possible outcome'. Hitch acknowledges this feeling, describing how 'the annihilating fatigue that came over me in consequence also contained the deadly threat of surrender to the inescapable: I would often find fatalism and resignation washing drearily over me as I failed to battle my general inanition.' Hitch would probably also have been aware of Nietzsche's statement:

> To die proudly when it is no longer possible to live proudly, death of one's own free choice, death at the proper time, with a clear head and with joyfulness, consummated in the midst of children and witnesses: so that an actual leave-taking is possible while he who is leaving is still there.

Unfortunately, we do not know Hitch's view on this profound comment.

Oh, and the regular painkiller, although Hitch found the wait for the next fix unjustly long. It is only at this point that we learn he has lost one-third of his original weight, despite being maintained by a feeding (PEG or percutaneous endoscopic gastrostomy) tube. We also learn that his voice has recovered somewhat by injections into his vocal cords, but he is now battling pain and weakness in his arms, hands and fingers, which threaten his ability to write. Faced with this, he reports that 'I feel my personality and identity dissolving as I contemplate dead hands and the loss of the transmission belts that connect me to writing and thinking'.

Finally, after two bouts of hospital-acquired staphylococcal pneumonia, which nearly proved fatal, he is admitted to hospital in Houston, where he coughs up some blood. Despite being terminally ill, he is subjected to a bronchoscopy and is intubated, having been given the 'good news' that the bleeding was not due to cancer. He subsequently died, as his wife wrote, 'unexpectedly'.

What to make of this poignant story? I have only Christopher's and Carol's words to go by, so I seek forgiveness if I have misconstrued some aspects.

In Hitch we see a relatively (in modern terms) young man, at the height of his powers and success, achieving great public recognition and financial rewards, and I am sure he felt that there were mountains yet to climb, and that he could climb them; in short, he had a great sense of purpose in his life. As to pleasure, he was a notorious bon viveur, with a very wide circle of like friends. Before his diagnosis, Hitch had both purpose and pleasure in spades. Eighteen months later, he was without energy, emaciated, tube-fed, in constant pain, suffering from 'chemo-brain' (dull, stuporous), struggling with both speech and writing, and recurrently undergoing hospital treatment. The only pleasure he had, I presume, was the ardent support of his wife and friends. His purpose was all but gone, although his last jottings spoke (rather optimistically) of another book. Yet those last jottings, probably created while he was wafting between opioid bliss and numbing pain, coherent though they are, stand in stark contrast to his normal lucid prose, and are to me an indication of his physical and mental state.

Speaking of opioids, Hitch, in his characteristically penetrating but oblique way, when alluding to medical euphemisms mentioned: 'Have you met our pain management team yet?'. One has to ask what does 'pain management' mean? Treatment, minimisation, alleviation, reduction, temporary, intermittent or permanent, elimination or oblivion? All important questions, but what place does the person with pain have in the discussion? Hitch doesn't say so, but nevertheless you feel that although the 'pain management team' cannot measure your pain, they, not you, will make the decisions as to its 'management'. They never seem to give quite enough relief, or give it sufficiently frequently.

Hitch's own story leads me to believe that at the end he had great suffering, certainly of a physical nature, but ultimately all suffering is in the mind, and he might have argued with me about my conclusion. Previously, I might have used the word 'distress' to describe his situation, but he, when discussing his experience of water-boarding and the not-too-subtle association with torture, compared that sensation with the aspiration of bronchial secretions in a medical scenario. He wrote that the 'aspiration' of those secretions can trigger a flood of panic. Essential though such a medical procedure is, it is often performed on conscious but incommunicative persons.

I wonder how many nurses or doctors are aware of such 'distress' (or torture as Hitch might have described it). He says that 'Any discomfort?' is a common medical question, and he places 'distress' as a word high on the medical euphemism scale. In his mind it did not come anywhere near to describing his experience. I hope to avoid using it in the dying context in the future (another lesson I owe to Christopher).

It was clear that he was dying, but he maintained a will to live, as most of us do in the face of death. He had considered the alternative. When discussing Professor Hook, he wrote: 'So we are left with something quite unusual in the annals of unsentimental extinction, not the wish to die with dignity, but the desire *to have died.*' Later he wrote: 'Only two things rescued me from betraying myself and letting go: a wife who would not hear of me talking in this boring and useless way, and various friends who spoke quite freely.'

What made Hitch's end so difficult, and most might say tragic (as I do)? If I might be bold, I would say it was because he did not have a completed life. What makes for a completed life? This is a complex question, worthy of discussion.

A completed life could be defined as one with no further meaning, as indicated by the Dalai Lama, or more specifically one associated with such intolerable suffering as to crush any pleasure or purpose. In coming to such conclusions, most people will need accurate and honest medical information. They may not get it, unless they ask for (demand?) this information, which should include an honest if difficult prognosis and which will need updating as the disease progresses.

They have a right to it. They have a right to medical reports about scans, biopsies and treatments, and to second opinions.

What did Christopher get? According to Carol Blue, he was told that he had a 5 to 20 per cent chance of cure, depending on the physician advising him! Even the lower figure is wildly optimistic, and given more in hope than reality, or for other reasons. In 2010, the five-year survival rate for stage 4 oesophageal cancer was no higher than 3 per cent (and that is survival, not cure).

The decisions people make about treatment of serious illness around the end of life depend greatly on the medical advice they are given. They have a right to accurate advice, and to a readily accessible second opinion, when making serious treatment decisions. Remember, a doctor is actually in business, and the difference between a consultation fee and the fee for a large procedure is significant.

This dilemma was the most difficult ethical problem I ever faced as a surgeon. My observations from when I worked in the USA indicated that it was a significant problem there. Doctors everywhere face a constant ethical problem when dealing with seriously ill people: the battle between extinguishing hope and providing reality. In my view, the doctor should provide critical reality, and then allow the individual to impose their view of hope on the outcome.

What does hope mean, and on what factors does hope depend? Let us confine the discussion to terminal illness with no probability of cure. Despite Carol Blue's statement regarding prognosis, and Christopher's never specifically acknowledging it, that ultimately was his circumstance. Who wouldn't, in his situation, hope for another day, week or month? But if, like his father, he had been dying of oesophageal cancer at 79, would he have had the same approach? He had considered 'letting go'; in that changed circumstance might he have done so? Who knows – when it comes to an individual facing his or her own mortality, the outcome is totally unpredictable, despite any earlier assertions. Facing one's own mortality honestly is one of the hardest things one can contemplate.

Is hope a religious concept? Many who believe in God accept that they will die when God decides. And if they believe in salvation, and an afterlife, they face great anxiety as to their judgement: heaven or hell? Educated as a weak Anglican, I had no concepts of such torments, until I listened closely to Elgar's *Dream of Gerontius*, which places Catholic concepts of heaven, purgatory and hell dramatically before the listener. I am not sure how valid these concepts are in today's diminished Catholicism, but no doubt they are still important to some.

Is hope a medical concept? It should not be. When I graduated in 1960, there was still a quite prevalent tendency to withhold unpleasant diagnoses from patients, on the basis that, armed with the truth, they would lose hope. Indeed, I do remember a 40-year-old man, physically well, who presented with a localised lump on his back. On removal it proved to be metastatic stomach cancer. It fell to me as the intern to give him this bad news; clearly, I did it badly, as he turned his face to the wall and died within four days, for no explicable reason.

Despite that experience, I firmly believe that people should be told the truth; to do otherwise is to lose trust, a far more important medical tool than false hope. Without truth and trust, the best medical decisions cannot be made.

Letting go. In his last section (VIII) of *Mortality*, which the editor describes as fragmentary unfinished jottings, Hitchens makes reference to Ian (possibly his editor) remarking that a time may come 'when I'd have to let go'. What does this ambiguous statement mean? Letting go of writing commitments? Letting go of active medical treatment? Letting go of futile medical treatment which did not seem to apply in the performance of a diagnostic bronchoscopy for a dying person? Letting go of hope and letting nature take its course, or even something more active? It could mean any or all of these things, and only careful open communication will reach the answer. Hitch mentions 'letting go' in section VI, but says Carol will not hear of him talking 'in this boring and useless way'. Did they discuss it at a later stage? I am sure they discussed many things that Hitch did not write about. Carol described his death as unexpected, so I wonder. Why would a wife so devoted to such a dedicated, charismatic, attentive and exciting husband not want another day or week, or whatever, of shared life? How could you bear to lose a jewel like Hitch?

Letting go, by which I mean ceasing all active treatment, other than palliative, can be one of life's hardest decisions. Nevertheless, sometimes the greatest gift a loved one can give is permission to 'let go'. Sometimes, until that permission is given, the sufferer will continue the fight at great cost. Encouragement to continue may be encouragement to continue suffering. Once permission is given, a peaceful calm can replace the anguish. Finding the proper moment is a difficult task.

How hard it is depends on your age, your illness and its prognosis, your suffering, and your values, all overlaid by the values of those who love and care for you. It is ultimately resolved by open discussion, commencing early in the course of the final path, once that is recognised.

I hope my comments have not offended anyone close to Christopher. His death is a tragic loss, for his wife and family, friends, the world of letters, in fact the whole world. I did not know him personally, but felt a bond with him through his words. I can say I have not felt so keenly the loss of any other person I have not known.

Is there tragedy in death? Of course, because there is potentially huge loss, but it varies enormously according to circumstances.

An expected death allows some time for adjustment. My father taught me this. At 74, dying of pancreatic cancer, he refused futile palliative surgery, was completely open with everyone about his situation, and had a constant stream of his friends and colleagues, for a cup of tea or a glass of whisky, to share reminiscences from their shared lives. He had ample time to say goodbye to all who mattered to him. I cherish my last words with him, which I still fully remember. He personified openness of communication, the acceptance of death, and the ability to face one's own mortality.

My mother had died four months before, of chronic respiratory failure from emphysema. While she would have passed the 'surprise' test for at least the previous two years, her death was for me anticipated yet unexpected. I saw her on Thursday morning and she seemed no different from usual. She went into hospital later that day, and died 36 hours later, peacefully in coma. In a way, I had been saying goodbye for some time.

Thus my father had recently lost his partner, was dying by wasting and the terrible itch of jaundice (fortunately he had no pain, due to an effective nerve block), and thus he saw his death as welcome. As did I and his other sons. There were loss, sadness, but also a sense of relief. What I believe diminished any sense of tragedy was that our parents had brought us all up to be highly independent, so that their deaths did not leave us bereft of advice or solace. This can be entirely different for close partners of longstanding and deep love. There can be added tragedy through the strength of the bond.

However, a sudden death, unexpected and unnatural and without blame on the deceased person, as in a hit-and-run by a drunken driver, a terrorist bombing, an air or car accident, or particularly what is called suicide, leave enormous grief, and are tragedies of the worst kind. The death of any child preceding their parents' is exceedingly tragic, as are myriad other circumstances.

The manner of one's dying, the degree of associated suffering, not just of the physical symptoms – prolongation of dying with its associated psychological and existential suffering – can have a profound effect on the tragedy of dying, on the extent of grief, and the pain of lingering memories.

Family, cultural and religious values can all increase, or sometimes diminish, the tragedy of death.

But in relation to all, age is an exceptionally important component in the tragedy of death. Christopher Hitchens, at 61, had an indomitable will to live (at least intermittently, as his end-of-life jottings reveal). Again, had Christopher been dying of oesophageal cancer at 79, like his father, I would venture the view that the tragedy of his death would have been diminished. His life then may well have had a sense of completion, and he may have welcomed death. Many older people can see their death approaching and are not alarmed; some welcome it, but we do not make it easy for them to do so. There is the world of difference between a hard early death and one at the end of a long and complete life. Compare the circumstances of Jack (mentioned in chapter 1) and Hitch. We would find it easier to support them if we understood 'the completed life'.

In 2011, the eminent medical editor of the *British Medical Journal*, Richard Smith, published an editorial entitled 'Death can be our friend'. He noted an increasing number of people dying in intensive care units, and quoted an intensivist: 'I'm running a warehouse for the dying.' Smith wrote that 'because too many doctors have forgotten that death is a friend, people are kept alive when all that makes life valuable is gone'. The secret to avoiding this catastrophe is good, open, honest communication both ways – doctor to person, and person to doctor.

Smith was echoing the classical Roman rhetorician Seneca, who said: 'Death is a punishment to some, to others a gift, and to many a favour.' He was also echoing Socrates, who, according to Plato, said that 'those of us who think that death is an evil are in error'. Socrates seemed to have accepted his own death with equanimity.

CHAPTER 3

The phenomenon of old age: What happened to the old person's friend?

Have you noticed the wrinkled skin and thinning, lustreless hair (or lack of it), the stooped posture, and the shuffling, unsteady gait of many older people? The watchful eye of family members, friends or carers, the stick, four-point aide or walking frame, or eventually the magnificent motorised wheelchair — all considered necessary to avoid the catastrophic fall and resulting fracture, which can signal the beginning of the end.

As a child, I delighted in attempting to build a house of (playing) cards. Getting to two stories was usually possible, three was exceptional, four almost impossible and doomed to crash quickly. All it took was for one card to collapse and the whole house would come crashing down. This analogy has some resemblance to the problems of old age.

What we see in my introductory image is simply the obvious external appearance of ageing. All the tissues of the body atrophy (waste or weaken) as we age. Our skin is an important external and visible organ which protects us from the environment and, in conjunction with all the other organs of the body, declines with age. The tone and vibrancy of skin depend on the elastic tissue in the underlying layers, and the depth and strength of the superficial cells. As we age, the cells are replaced less quickly and effectively, and the skin becomes thin. The elastic tissue, as in your socks, loses its zip, and the skin sags. Supporting fibrous tissue behaves similarly. Hair follicles fail to produce robust — or any — hair, and we bald. Ageing skin may look unpleasant, but also, if damaged, is slow to heal and may result in painful ulcers.

The stooping referred to above is due to changes to the musculoskeletal system: our muscles, ligaments, tendons and joints, which hold us erect and enable us to move. With age, our bones thin and weaken (osteoporosis) and we often shrink in height, and stoop. The cartilage and lubricating membranes in our joints wear out (like an engine without oil). This can have a major effect on our weight-bearing joints in the lower limbs, reducing mobility, but arthritis in the small joints of the hands can devastate our dexterity for simple but critical manual tasks.

Our muscles weaken and we can no longer run 100 metres in 13 seconds or better, and it is an exceptional physical sportsman who can still excel over the age of 35. Typically, we lose muscle mass and power, though much can be done with exercise. (Remember the 60-year-old potato farmer Cliff Young, who won the 1983 Sydney-to-Melbourne ultra-marathon, though he did it not by speed, but by determination, shuffling continuously while his competitors slept.) Our tendons and ligaments, made of fibrous tissue, decline, stretch and even rupture; joints wear out (arthritis) and, together with the other musculoskeletal problems, lead to pain and loss of mobility and stability, one contributor to the prevalence of falls.

Our bowel is a very important organ, but is essentially a muscle, which also weakens with age, hence the common development of constipation with ageing, which may cause secondary effects on the bowel, such as diverticulitis. It is also an absorptive (of fluids) organ, and a minor excretory organ (of digestive enzymes), so variations with diarrhoea can occur.

The bladder can be more of a problem, designed as it is to work more frequently than the bowel. It is also a complex muscle, designed to store urine and empty completely at controlled voluntary intervals. A weak muscle can lead to incomplete emptying, and thus more frequent evacuation, and perhaps kidney failure; however, for largely unknown reasons, an overactive bladder can lead to very embarrassing frequency and urgency, which at its extreme leads to uncontrollable urge incontinence, surely one of the most distressing symptoms of old age. For women, pelvic-floor damage due to childbirth can lead to additional problems of stress incontinence. Our essential sphincters are also muscles, and weaken as we age. Few body failures lead to greater loss of dignity than incontinence.

A huge US study of 57,753 older persons with heart, respiratory or renal failure, or frailty, found that nearly 70 per cent felt that bowel and bladder incontinence was the 'same or worse than death' (Wachterman et al., 2016).

Our kidneys do shrink with age, and their function diminishes, but having two is a benefit. Without some extraneous damage, age alone will not impair our kidneys to any significant extent. The liver is another large organ with very significant reserves, and unless there is some extraneous influence, liver failure simply from old age is unknown.

The heart and blood vessels are very interesting. The blood vessels, although containing elastic tissue, can survive extremely well into old age, their condition depending more on diet and the ravages of high blood pressure. The heart is also a muscle that can weaken with age, but if this is accompanied by diminished demand, as is commonly the case in old age, it can do surprisingly well. The outstanding Australian long-distance runner Ron Clarke stressed his heart to such extremes that he required a heart transplant in his fifties.

As age destroys our mobility, so our social potential withers. As we are increasingly confined to home (especially with the loss of a car licence), our entertainment is largely confined to music, reading and television. These require good hearing, clear vision, and a functional intellect, all of which can be diminished by ageing. I am still quite mobile and drive a car, but my life without music or books would be a desert. Degenerative conditions in both eyes and ears are common, and although modern treatments can be excellent, if unsuccessful they result in existential disaster. As noted in *The Gerontologist* in 2011, 'in addition to directly contributing to higher depressive symptomatology, subjective vision contributed to depressive symptoms indirectly by predicting more physical limitations and feelings of social isolation, that, in turn, contributed to more symptoms of depression.'

Loss of mobility further limits exercise, which further reduces muscle quality – a vicious circle. Less time outdoors, less sun, less vitamin D, more osteoporosis, and a greater tendency to fracture from simple accidents, and so the house of cards becomes wobblier.

There is a common reduction of appetite in old age. Living alone certainly inhibits the desire to prepare nutritious food. Malnutrition, loss of weight, and further muscle loss are all consequential. Not surprisingly, iron in the diet may be deficient and anaemia occurs. Finally, the lack of dietary protein has a profound effect on the immune system, and the body's defences to infection are seriously impaired, which is why pneumonia (once called 'the old person's friend') is so common in the aged as a potential cause of death. Sir William Osler, professor of medicine at Harvard and Oxford at the end of the 19th century, said, 'Pneumonia may well be called the friend of the aged. Taken off by it in an acute but not often painful illness, the old man escapes those "cold degradations of decay".' Pneumonia in 2019 is a very different disease from that of 1900. However, because of the advent of antibiotics, dying from pneumonia without medical intervention to prevent death is difficult, even though doctors have better tools to effectively palliate people dying of pneumonia, if they are prepared to use them.

Hearing and vision are probably our most important senses as we grow older. They are both seriously threatened by ageing, but fortunately excellent remedies are at hand for many people. Effective and relatively simple cataract surgery, artificial lenses, and modern hearing aids keep many in touch, but macular degeneration has no cure, and neither has tinnitus. Severe loss in either modality can lead to loss of independence, isolation and loneliness.

The ability to drive a motor vehicle safely is a subtle combination of skills, some or all of which may decrease in old age, thus making us dangerous to ourselves and/or others. Declining eyesight is worse at night, or in bright flickering light; good hearing makes us subtly aware of other and adjacent vehicles. Good neck movement is essential for quick observation to the rear and side, quick muscle and joint movements operate controls, while the brain controls judgement of distance and coordination of all other actions. It is no wonder that driving skills diminish with age.

Finally, we come to nerve function, which can affect the periphery, but predominantly affects the brain and its extraordinarily complex networks. Our peripheral nerves make us aware of touch, position and temperature – essentially, of our environment and our safety in it – and decline with age, nutritional deficiency and diabetes. Although it is believed that nerve cells, once destroyed, do not regenerate, we do know that the brain has an extraordinary reserve of circuits and remarkable plasticity, and so can replace many lost functions. There is a progressive loss of brain function with age, described as mild cognitive impairment, but not specifically related to dementia. Its cause is unknown, although it is clearly related to age, and may well be associated with the gradual loss of brain cells. It has particular characteristics such as loss of memory for names, and of recent simple events, such as where one left one's keys or specs, or whether one took one's tablets this morning. Memory impairment alone is not sufficient for a diagnosis of Alzheimer's disease. It may be an early precursor of Alzheimer's disease if time allows, but I can safely say that no human has more brain function at 90 than they had at 25.

The relationship between ageing and Alzheimer's disease is intriguing. There is no doubt that the incidence of Alzheimer's rises with age. Dementia expert psychiatrist Professor Constantine Lyketsos acknowledged in 2009 that age is a precursor to dementia. If you live beyond 85 you will have a one-in-three chance of getting dementia, and a one-in-three chance of caring for someone with dementia. It is established that the brain disease that causes Alzheimer's develops years before diagnosis. Its cause is unknown, so it is possible that some environmental factor, combined with a genetic factor, may be significant. This is why a very high proportion of aged-care residents have severe dementia, and a proportion of those placed there because of frailty in older age also have indications of cognitive impairment. It profoundly affects their care and prognosis, but not in an easily predictable way; each person with dementia runs their own particular journey.

My years in medicine, and of studying ageing, have led me to describe the 'Six Horsemen of the Ageing Apocalypse': loss of sight, loss of hearing, loss of mobility, loss of continence, loss of cognition, and – the result of any one or combination of these five – loss of independence.

There is no doubt that many environmental factors accelerate these deteriorations: sun on the skin, excessive noise on the ears, bright light on the eyes, excessive stresses and injuries on skeletal structures, diet on the blood vessels, smoking and the quality of air on the lungs, alcohol and drugs on the liver, and chemicals on the kidneys. It is not simply ageing that causes decline, for these other external factors are relevant, usually accelerating the process.

It is beyond dispute that these acquired conditions accelerate ageing. A University of Adelaide report has confirmed that 'the proportion of baby boomers (born 1946–1965) with three or more chronic conditions is 700% greater than the previous generation'. However, overlying all these environmental threats is the steady, programmed decline in repair of the body over time. One hundred and twenty is our probable maximum age. Few reach 110, although more people are living to 100, largely due to medical technology and improved living circumstances. But there is a limit, I sincerely hope, otherwise we will destroy this already overpopulated world.

We will all die – if not of one of the recognised and described diseases such as cancer, heart failure, stroke, breathing failure, or kidney or liver failure (all due to myriad factors), we will succumb to the inevitable degeneration of vital functions. It reminds me of the very clever advertisement for long-life batteries, where a rabbit powered by a particular battery beats a drum while all its competitors stop. We all gradually lose power and stop. Yet there are, believe it or not, researchers out there attempting to reverse this process of ageing, to allow us to live longer and become more useless in an overpopulated world. Why? Could monetary reward have more influence than common sense?

The consequences of this lack of repair and regeneration are the frailty associated with old age. Professor John McCallum found that the hazard of nursing-home placement increased significantly with age, urinary incontinence, impaired respiratory function, physical disability and depression, but this hazard was diminished significantly by moderate alcohol consumption and being female.

The picture I drew at the start of this chapter was of a frail person, who is usually elderly. That state is usually due to a combination of the ageing changes I have described, and it is an inevitable state as we age, sooner or later, if we do not die of a specific disease before then. The term 'frail aged' is in common use, but while it is a condition we can recognise, it is very hard to define in medical terms. It is a descriptive term, rather than a diagnosis.

In 2006 the Royal Australian College of General Practitioners (RACGP) reported on the medical care of older persons in residential aged care facilities:

> Older people in residential aged care are the sickest and frailest subsection of an age group that manifests the highest rates of disability in the Australian population. The prevalence of chronic conditions among residents in high care is estimated to be 80% sensory loss, 60% dementia, 40–80% chronic pain, 50% urinary incontinence, 45% sleep disorder, and 30–40% depression. Annually 30% of residents have one or more falls and 7% fracture a hip.

Do you want me to repeat these figures! They did not include a 40 to 50 per cent incidence of dysphagia (difficulty in swallowing), not uncommon in stroke, Parkinson's disease and dementia. This problem can lead to dehydration, malnutrition and aspiration pneumonia – all potentially lethal complications. Frailty may not be a diagnosis in its own right, but as a descriptor of a terminal state, it ranks highly.

Given that many of these residents have a terminal condition, it is surprising that, in a 55-page document, there is only one-third of a page devoted to advance care planning, and no discussion of palliative care. Still, this was published in 2006, and I would hope that a new edition would have a different emphasis – one based on the residents' directions with regard to life-prolonging treatment and the provision of palliative care. The provision of adequate pain relief and sedation is well within the province of a well-trained general practitioner.

The Royal Australian College of General Practitioners might also note Victoria's *Medical Treatment, Planning and Decisions Act* of 2016, which gives statutory recognition to advance care directives, and Victoria's *Voluntary Assisted Dying Act* of 2017, which allows competent terminally ill people to request assistance in dying.

Professor Linda Fried, director of the Centre for Ageing and Health at Johns Hopkins School of Medicine, acknowledged that frailty was 'a kind of pre-death phase', based on the research discussed on ABC Radio's *Life Matters* program in 2003. People should think about frailty as equivalent to substantial disability and dependency. She described frailty in older persons who were 'perhaps losing weight, perhaps were getting weak, perhaps had some problems with falling, maybe reporting problems doing the things in their life that were important, because they didn't have the reserves they used to have'. My own observation is that loss of balance is also very significant (one of the earliest symptoms that I noticed as I aged), and that loneliness, social isolation and a natural consequence of depressed mood are common features – but they are hard to change. A short weekly visit from a relative hardly cuts the mustard.

People who were frail had at least several of the following characteristics: weight loss; loss of muscle mass and strength; slowing down physically, in the sense that they didn't walk as fast, or they couldn't do tasks as quickly as they were used to doing; reduced appetite; low physical activity; and a sense of exhaustion, or low reserves to draw on. This could be a purely physical syndrome. But there might also be a component of what people are starting to call 'cognitive frailty' – perhaps some decreased ability to learn new things, some decreased ability to organise tasks. This is a chronic, progressive condition. They may feel reasonably well, until a significant illness or stressor occurs, and a crisis follows. People who are frail 'might be slow to mount a response to an injury or an infection, or some other kind of stressor', starting or slowing the immune response. The 'house of cards' collapse can begin.

Professor Fried acknowledged that when we talk of frailty, maybe it is the end stage of life, and the end stage of ageing, which is probably a pre-death phase, the end stage of life for many people who don't die abruptly. Other researchers have documented the consequences of frail ageing as falls, increased injuries that are slow to heal, more acute illnesses, disability, dependence, increased hospitalisations, institutionalisation and death.

There are no laboratory tests specific to frailty. Researchers have been attempting to develop frailty scales which have predictive value. Rockwood and colleagues have done much excellent work – their scale accurately predicted that no-one with an index of less than 0.46 per cent on their scale survived past 90 days. However, frailty is not recognised as a cause of death for death certificates, although it is a frequent accompaniment of death in the elderly. Doctors recognise it when they see it, and they realise its importance. It has a significant effect on the outcomes of surgery and medical interventions, and it influences the outcomes of stroke and heart attack. It is one of the commonest reasons for placement in a nursing home.

Most laypeople can recognise a frail aged person. It is a physical rather than a mental state. They typically lack energy and mobility – they move slowly, often with aids, and are prone to falls. They have poor appetite and often have lost significant weight, and sleep poorly, even though they spend much time immobile. If they are unable to care for themselves, or do so with great difficulty or danger, they are almost certainly frail unless these difficulties are due to cognitive decline as in dementia – although most dementia sufferers become frail in the late vegetative state.

American president and noted humanitarian Thomas Jefferson wrote, 200 years ago:

> The powers of life are sensibly on the wane, sight becomes dim, hearing dull, memory constantly enlarging its frightful blank and parting with all we have ever seen and known, spirits evaporate, bodily debility creeps on paralysing every limb, and so faculty after faculty quits us, and where then is life?

He had no trouble recognising frailty.

The *Medical Journal of Australia* recently announced that Australians with advanced disease, which certainly includes the frail aged, will average eight hospital admissions in their last year of life – and face a 60 to 70 per cent chance of dying in a ward (even though 90 per cent say they would like to die at home). Dr Robert Cushman, chief executive officer of a Canadian local health-care network, observed: 'We're talking about the frail elderly. And we have too much emphasis on the cure when the returns for the cure can be very low. I think we need to respect seniors' independence and their dignity.'

Intensive care specialists Charlie Corke, Ken Hillman and Peter Saul have railed for some time against the futility of admitting the frail aged, with what are probably irreversible complications, to their intensive care units – or in many cases, to an acute hospital – particularly from aged care. It is all too common that such patients either have an advance care directive which is ignored, or have not completed one, or the opinion of the informed GP is not provided. In an after-hours crisis, the GP is often not available, so the institution calls an ambulance and off to casualty we go (sometimes yet again), or a locum is consulted, who makes the same decision.

All too often, the emergency staff provide treatment by default (unaware of any other directives, or ignoring them for fear of medical or family censure – less trouble if you treat than if you don't, is the classic medical default position). Admission commonly follows, with an upward journey to intensive care, because no-one seems prepared to make a tough decision, the obvious clinical decision, and to sit down and talk realistically with the patient and family about the futility and burden of further treatment.

Substantiating this view is the 2016 paper of Cardona-Morrell and colleagues, who analysed 38 studies and found that 33 to 38 per cent of patients near the end of life received non-beneficial treatment (treatment with little or no hope of it having any effect – largely because of the underlying state of the patient's health and the known or expected prognosis regardless of treatment). This situation has a direct connection to my decision to talk about Christopher Hitchens, of the treatment advice and prognostic information he was given. There is a crying need for a more open and honest communication between doctors and the people they treat.

A very recent Queensland study showed that nearly half of doctors will not tell patients how long they have to live, whereas more than 90 per cent of elderly and terminally ill patients would like their doctors to give them an honest prognosis as to the amount of time they have left. That time is precious, and people want to be able to plan their future, complete projects with more urgency, arrange their affairs and make their goodbyes.

Charlie Corke's intensive analysis of more than 1,000 people found that 61 per cent of those aged over 75 strongly opposed any intervention that prolongs life in poor health, or results in poor quality of life. Corke was well aware of the 2004 Canadian study of the cost of dying which found that 1.1 per cent of the population consumed 21.3 per cent of the health-care budget. Of the 'oldest-old studied (those aged 85 years or older), 48% of costs were for hospital care with 41% being for long-term institutional care'. According to the authors, this 'high cost of dying' stems from 'frail individuals with heavy needs for extended periods'. Philip Nitschke, commenting on this paper, cited people like his own mother, who was 'trapped in a nursing home, well beyond, in her words, "her use-by date"'.

Hannah Carter and colleagues reported in 2017 on the incidence, duration and cost of futile treatment for end-of-life conditions. Their analysis involved a retrospective multi-centre cohort study with a clinical audit of hospital admissions in three Australian public-sector tertiary hospitals. Included in the audit were adult patients who died while admitted to one of the study hospitals over a six-month period in 2012. The incidence rate of futile treatment in end-of-life admissions was 12.1 per cent across the three study hospitals (range 6.0 per cent to 19.6 per cent). For admissions involving futile treatment, the average length of stay following the onset of futile treatment was 15 days, with 5.25 of these days in the intensive care unit. The cost associated with futile bed days was estimated to be A\$12.4 million for the three study hospitals using health system costs. The overall consequences were substantial in terms of both the bed days and cost incurred. An increased awareness of these economic costs may generate support for interventions designed to reduce futile treatments.

What such situations need is a half-way house between standard high-level aged care and acute hospital emergency – a small aged-care acute palliative section, with trained staff, access to immediate palliative phone advice, and, if needed, specialist palliative nurse attendance. Residents who have made a prior decision for no life-prolonging treatment, and palliation only, could be moved there, be well palliated – and avoid hospitalisation. An added expense for aged care? Yes, but a huge saving to acute hospitals, which could allow reimbursement to the aged-care and palliative-care industry.

All of the above demand relatively simple yet challenging communication. The proposal does not work without this, but with it there are huge benefits to patients, families, institutions, hospitals and the community.

Yes, communication. Conversation. Talking. It's not difficult, we do it all the time, but for many it's the subject that seems difficult. Philippe Ariès observed in *The Hour of Our Death* that 'when death really began to be feared, it ceased to be talked about'. So when dying became more drawn out and uncontrolled, and removed from the home in the 20th century, conversation dried up. And that was not only for patients and families, but also for most doctors. For doctors, there is an added problem relating to the difficulty and perhaps lack of familiarity with the topic, and that is time. Such conversations cannot be conducted in a 5 to 10–minute consultation. Although it is fundamentally the doctor's responsibility to begin the conversation when they can see that the situation needs it, this does not excuse patients from starting it, if it is in on their minds. In particular, the patient can commence a conversation with their family. After all, the individual alone is fully aware of the extent of his or her suffering and feelings about their situation. If they don't speak up, they can readily find themselves on a medical conveyor belt to a long, unwanted, lonely and painful journey to 'the bourn from which no traveller returns'.

At the start of my medical career, I found doctors to be exceptionally patronising (they were mostly male), and patients very quiet and afraid to ask questions; they did as they were told. I am pleased to say that there has been a steady and progressive change on both sides. More women in the profession has helped, but there has also been a profound change in recognition and respect for the autonomy of patients – that is, their right to be fully informed and make their own decisions.

Further progress is needed. There is now no reason for a patient or family member not to seek further information or advice. Don't be bashful or frightened – ask if you don't know, don't worry that you are taking too much of the doctor's time (you're paying for it), but be aware that these conversations about end of life take time, so book a long consultation.

Both you and your doctor gain, in an eventual crisis, if both of you know what you do or don't want in terms of treatment.

CHAPTER 4

Aged care:
Our second prison system

I n our society we maintain a prison system, in which we incarcerate citizens who have seriously offended against our laws and social norms. This system exists as a deterrent against breaking those laws, as a punishment to those who do, as a protection for the community against further harm, and – it is hoped – as a means of reformation of unwanted behaviour. Such systems have been in place in Western societies for hundreds of years.

To imprison someone restricts their freedom, and this occurs entirely against their wishes. No-one seeks imprisonment. What is more, in our prisons we restrain people together in large numbers, for reasons of cost and efficiency. We confine together people of different views, values, temperaments, ages and crimes. Some are recidivist villains, some unfortunate victims of a moment of indiscretion. Do prisoners make friends under these circumstances? Possibly more acquaintances than true friends, and then for mutual protection and some company, but they are not living among people with whom they have chosen to reside. If they find a genuine companion, they are probably extremely fortunate.

Their lives become regimented with regard to meals, sleeping, work and other activities, with an almost total lack of privacy. The people controlling the inmates' lives have primarily a disciplinary role, but also, in the best institutions, a rehabilitation role. Could these controllers be called 'carers'? Yes, they could in a sense, but control comes first. They do have an important role in preventing prisoners from harming themselves and other prisoners, and in being aware of the feeling in the environment in order to forestall trouble. They need to be aware of the mood of the institution and its inmates. But do prison officers actually care for their prisoners in the best sense of that word, or are they simply doing a job? And if the latter, probably not a job that many people would wish to do. It probably calls for workers of a particular temperament.

So, a prison is an institution that incarcerates large numbers of people against their will, restricts their freedom, regiments their lives, destroys their privacy, and aggregates them with unknown 'neighbours' who may be unfriendly or even hostile. Some of these prisoners will have only temporary restrictions of freedom, but some are there for the rest of their natural lives.

A few years ago I was asked to give a talk to a group of social workers, which I titled 'Aged care: Our second prison system'. This was not meant to be insulting to social workers or workers in aged care, but to be provocative, and to stimulate thought about the system. Let us consider some of the comparisons. To do this, let's dissect the conditions surrounding aged care. We must recognise the individual forms of aged care, ranging from care in the home, low-level care (essentially board and lodging with minimal physical care or nursing assistance) and high-level care. It is effectively the high-level care that I am discussing.

Who is placed in high-level aged care? Research shows that 45 to 60 per cent of these people have moderate to advanced dementia, most commonly Alzheimer's disease or vascular dementia, as the primary reason for placement. The outstanding characteristic of this group is that they have lost mental competence, or decision-making capacity. This is a critical difference from the following groups who, while possibly having some cognitive impairment, are assumed for the purpose of this discussion to retain decision-making capacity. The second group is the frail aged, which includes people who enter directly from hospital after treatment has failed to restore their ability to care for themselves, while others are placed from their own home. The third group is patients with terminal illness (commonly cancer) who are either not close enough to dying for inpatient hospice, or who have outstayed their allowance of time there (usually 30 days). Finally, there is a further group: seriously disabled persons who cannot care for themselves unaided, but who are neither necessarily frail nor aged. These are commonly people with neuro-degenerative conditions such as multiple sclerosis, motor neurone disease, Parkinson's disease, stroke, or spinal cord damage. The critical characteristic of all these people is that they can no longer sustain themselves in their own homes, either unaided or with the maximum aid that can be gathered to help them. They have reached the end of the road of independent living, and it is their diminished health that has brought them to this pass. Further discussion in this chapter is confined to the frail aged who retain mental capacity for decision-making.

Think of yourself in this situation. What choices do you have at this point? Sadly, in our society, only one sanctioned choice: to enter institutional care – a residential nursing home – and be cared for by others. Does this sound reminiscent of a serious criminal, sentenced to incarceration? No choice but to enter a large institution in a community with people you have never met, nor have made any choice to be in company with? Although you may be fortunate enough to have your own room, you have limited privacy; staff can enter at any time, as may other unwanted residents. You will suffer other regimentations to suit the efficiency of the institution: when you are woken, when you are fed, what you can eat, when you will have your medications, when you will be bathed and dressed, and when the lights go out – not in a total or absolute sense, but close to it. You can't run a home for a hundred or more people without regimentation, and homes of fewer than 60 beds are not financially viable.

Such circumstances cause people to lead restricted lives, to experience social isolation, to be discredited, and to feel that they are burdening others. What is the effect of institutionalisation on the socialisation of elderly people? Buckwalter and colleagues found that it devalues the existence of old people in our community at large, and that once help is required to meet basic needs the health-care system does its best to finish the process of reducing our elderly people to non-people. These are the characteristics of a 'loss of self', which Professor Charmaz describes as a fundamental form of suffering in the chronically ill.

Barbara Spriggs, testifying at Australia's royal commission into aged care, stated that Oakden care facility in South Australia, where her husband died, was 'like a prison'. Ian Yates of the Council of the Ageing, also a witness at the royal commission, pointed out that 'with older people, we bracket them off into the aged care system, which, I might say, apart from prisoners, is the only institutionalized system we have left'.

On 17 May 2019, Professor Henry Brodaty of Dementia Australia gave evidence to the royal commission of residents regarding themselves as 'prisoners'. He cited two residents, one with Parkinson's disease, the other having suffered a dense stroke, who were depressed – fundamentally because they were in the nursing home, and did not want to be there. They felt that they were prisoners, actually saying to him, 'I'm a prisoner here.'

Further testimony was given to the royal commission by 84-year-old Merle Mitchell AO (as reported in *The Age* on 11 May 2019): 'I live in an institution. No matter how many times they tell us it's our home, it's not. [...] This is where I live but it's not a home.' Her husband fell in January 2016, entered an aged-care facility and died roughly six months later. Merle also fell, fracturing her back, and joined him in care. They had to quickly find a facility: 'It was terrible. There was the shock of loss. There's not enough recognition of this: loss is not just death; it is the loss of your way of life.' After her husband died, she said, 'There's just that feeling that this isn't a proper life – that the quicker it's all over the better it is for everybody.' Merle concluded, 'I'm in an institution. I have to follow what the institution wants – the time to get up, the time to have meals. You lose your choice totally, and that's one of the things that needs to change.'

What this highlights is that living in old age with one's partner in one's own home is very special. Losing a part or whole of this is a huge existential loss, which is almost impossible for aged care to replace. Merle Mitchell highlighted the totally inadequate staffing, but noted that, even if this were corrected, there would always be an impersonal relationship in the care. Merle alerted me to the importance of counsellors in aged care who would help to navigate this sense of loss to some extent.

The carers in our prison system (we call them warders) are a special breed (they need to be tough but fair). So too are the carers in our aged-care system, but they are dealing with a very different clientele. They require very different virtues and values and training, but nevertheless are still responsible for maintaining control of some residents who can be angry or violent. Carers in this situation require considerable patience, and virtues of compassion, which are very difficult to test for in an interview. They require skilled training to do an effective job, much of which should be 'on the job', hands-on apprenticeship, but the skilled nurses who should supervise them are excessively busy with obligatory administrative tasks. This caring role is very poorly paid ('you can earn more at Aldi') for relatively skilled work, and commonly attracts immigrants from a culture different from the residents', which can result in difficulty in communication regarding care needs, pain and suffering.

What is more, unlike most criminals, you will be entering this circumstance for the rest of your natural life. Once you enter aged care, you are probably trapped in this environment for the rest of your life, without the privacy of home, surely one of your most prized assets, unless your family can somehow rearrange their circumstances to bring you home. A few people enter care homes temporarily for rehabilitation or respite, and in my 25 years of counselling in this area, it is almost without exception that people who have had a spell in aged-care respite are determined never to go back. However, the vast majority who enter are destined never to leave, except in a box. These homes are not called 'warehouses for the old' or 'God's waiting room' for no reason. Coarse judgements perhaps, but true. The survival statistics of aged-care residents have been analysed by Professor McCallum and colleagues, who found that 'the median time to death in a nursing home [in high-level care] was 10.5 months for men and 9 months for women'. Would it be unreasonable to consider a significant proportion of these people as terminally ill? McCallum emphasises that the large group with dementia take longer to die, because they are cognitively impaired but not necessarily physically impaired. They, and some of the chronically disabled, skew the figures for the survival of the competent frail aged.

The short survival of many entering aged care indicates that they are terminally ill. Terminally ill people have significant requirements for palliative care, which is seriously lacking in aged care. The typical response is to send dying residents to acute-care emergency departments, where they receive either unwanted or non-beneficial (futile) treatment and die after some days of expensive care. With appropriate palliative care it should be possible to manage their dying in their care home – or even, if sufficiently important, to go home with expert home care to die with their family.

About four years ago I received the following letter from a woman, describing the lonely death of her 96-year-old mother in her nursing home:

> She had had a stroke 11 days prior and refused food for several days and since then had persistently expressed her wish to die and had asked me to help her. Her doctor and the nursing home however felt she still had several days to go and may indeed rally. For this reason palliative care assessment was delayed. My instinct all along was to arrange for palliative care from the day after her stroke, but as it turned out she died before an assessment was even done. On her last day she was in delirium, very agitated and in considerable psychic pain. Naively believing the advice of the nursing home that she had several days to go, I left around 5 pm, intending to return the following day, but she died around midnight. The decision to take no immediate [palliative] action meant she had endured 11 days of needless acute suffering and she died alone and in torment. What that must have been like has haunted me ever since.

I am compelled to ask why the attending GP could not provide palliative care. The relief of suffering and ensuring a peaceful dignified death are not rocket science, and should not be beyond a reasonably experienced GP, with specialist advice needed in uncommon circumstances only. This is the problem with establishing medical specialties: they become the authority without which less-specialised medics are loath to act, particularly in sensitive areas such as dying. Specialist palliative care will never be adequate to serve the needs of our growing population (there are fewer than 400 palliative-care specialists Australia-wide). Satisfactory provision of palliative care will occur only when there is an adequate body of palliative-trained GPs who are prepared to apply their skills without specialist referral. Even after such a referral, fear by doctors, nurses and home managements of criticism for over-aggressive medication often inhibits effective care – usually resolved by good communication.

Professor McCallum has stated that about a quarter of Australians who live more than 85 years can expect to end up in a nursing home, but 'few regard this as their preferred option'. McCallum was the lead investigator of the 14-year

'Dubbo study' of elderly Australians, and found that 'there is a higher rate of [hospital] admissions just prior to death, which indicates a major role for these institutions in palliative care as well as a dominant role in dementia care'. Is palliative care closely integrated with aged care? Certainly not, but it should be, as a matter of urgency.

And now consider this: who makes the decision to send someone into aged care? A judge, a jury? You, the person who is entering aged care? No, usually anyone but that person. Commonly it will be the doctors in a hospital who have been unable to fully rescue you from a heart attack, stroke, serious trauma, or cancer (or in fact a multitude of other events) who decide they can do no more, and that you must be moved (usually as quickly as possible) to another place to 'free up' an acute bed. It costs the state government $1,000 to $1,500 a day for a hospital bed, whereas the federal government pays $173 per day for an aged-care place, and as a result the family and social worker are forced into top gear under great pressure to find a – suitable, one hopes – residential-care bed. You, the damaged person, are rarely consulted. Whose end of life is being considered? Whose journey is being influenced? Many of these decisions are an abuse of personal autonomy, and are made out of necessity and lack of any other option.

I have been counselling people about end-of-life concerns for more than 25 years, in recent years seeing two or three people a week. When I analysed the relevant data, I discovered that 32 per cent of requests were from cancer sufferers (not surprising), but what astonished me was that 20 per cent were from the frail elderly. This should not have been a surprise, because when I asked my audiences at lectures or workshops, 'How many of you are looking forward to entering a nursing home?', rarely did one hand go up. Some of these people had practical experience of a friend or family member living or dying in such a situation, but more simply had a philosophical horror at the state of frailty that would necessitate such a move, and at the loss of independence and control it would involve.

I did recently have a conversation with a woman who had been living alone without much family support, and who thought she would be better off in low-level aged care. She entered voluntarily and had been there for five years. When I asked her how she liked it, she replied vehemently that she hated it. A large number of the residents spoke no English, but she was not advised of this when signing up.

Another woman, Lynda, was told, after her father had been admitted to hospital following a debilitating stroke, that he should be admitted to a nursing home: 'The hospital began to pressure my emotionally and physically exhausted family to do the impossible and find him a bed. Fourteen weeks after entering hospital, my father contracted bedsores and died as a result of septicaemia' (*The Age*, 19 November 2007).

I can fully understand the family's distress at this outcome. Nevertheless, some, including me, and perhaps her father, might have considered it fortunate – he might have lived 14 months, or even years, in aged care, and perhaps resenting every minute of it. I have heard of people surviving for 20 years in aged care after a stroke. My cousin told me of her elderly mother who suffered a profound stroke and was completely paralysed on one side, confined to bed, incontinent and unable to speak. She entered aged care, and every day when her daughter visited her, she drew her mobile hand across her throat, indicating her deep desire to die, which did occur after seven gruesome months.

Family members making these decisions are often utterly distraught at being put in this position, and suffer lifelong guilt as a result. Freelance writer Avril Moore belatedly recognised this. She wrote in *The Age*: 'Having been complicit in urging my own elderly parents to leave the family home of 50 years and enter a "lifestyle" facility touted as "safe, sanitary and supervised", I have, since they passed away, regretted this decision.' There is a collective anxiety when it comes to witnessing the physical decline of elderly people, especially that of our own parents. The current obsession with moving them at a time in their lives when remaining in familiar surroundings is their last hope of independence, let alone dignity, is just plain cruel.

Almost 25 years ago, a literature survey published in the *Journal of Advanced Nursing* investigated the effect of institutionalisation on socialisation in elderly people. The answer was that we seem to devalue the existence of old people in the community at large, and once they require help to meet basic needs, the health-care system does its best to finish the process of reducing our elderly people to non-people.

Another daughter (*The Age*, 25 November 2000), asked for the umpteenth time by her mother to take her home from the nursing home where she was locked up (her 'prison'), reflects on the six years during which she *did* look after her mother with no help. The daughter could no longer cope with the stove being left on, the midnight wandering, the urine-soaked lounge chairs, the faeces-smeared face-washers stuffed down the toilet bowl. She could not cope with the isolation, and placed her mother in care. It was an alternative that satisfied nobody, but there was no alternative. The daughter's story was told by a self-confessed 'burnt-out aged care manager at 37', ending 'I hope never to manage an aged-care facility again.' There is little if any evidence of change.

If the decision is largely medical, the family member is just as vulnerable to the system as is the patient. If the decision is initiated by family because of the increasing vulnerability of their loved one – often after a tooth-and-nail, bittersweet struggle to stay at home – the sense of failure can be enormous, and this can follow a prolonged period of burden through home care.

Nurse Rhonda Nay, now a professor, found in her research in 1995 that:

> The aged people who participated in her research felt that they had no real choice; they had to enter a nursing home and that was that. For them, entering a nursing home meant losing everything. They had lost everything and felt compelled, albeit for good reasons, to enter into a situation and status that had no value. Consequently, they felt devalued as individuals. They had come to the end of the line, here was no future.

The National Health and Hospital Commission assessed in 2009 that, given the choice, most frail and aged people would prefer to die at home among loved ones.

Michael Bachelard clearly exposed that stress and guilt when he reported the story of Jyl Stephens in *The Sydney Morning Herald* on 23 September 2017. This elderly lady, who had been living alone in her own home and garden, had two serious falls, with leg fractures, within 12 months. After the second fall, hospital staff recommended full-time residential care, and without delay. Her son Daryl said, 'I felt like we were being swept up in this vast machine.' He described a sense of powerlessness. His mother had no desire to go; the thought terrified her. She essentially did not make the decision – it was forced on her and her son. She would have to sell her home to fund her placement in a local nursing home. The 'vast machine' included an extraordinary, almost-immediate, sales pitch from six care homes. Jyl had a stroke and died before she entered the home. She may not have felt that she had a completed life before her second fracture, but might soon have felt so after a short time in residential care. Consider also the guilt that would have been engulfing Daryl and his brother as they faced this decision. They faced complex decisions under time constraints with little information, decisions affecting their mother, whom they loved dearly and about whom they were gravely concerned.

Make no mistake, Jyl would have been entrapped if she had entered the nursing home. She would have found it almost impossible ever to leave, both for financial and health reasons. In high care you do not even have control over any personal medications, such as making a decision about pain relief, and pain is something that only you can measure.

An entirely different situation from this rather acute decision-making is the more considered situation of an elderly person, usually living alone, but sometimes with a partner who is also ageing and becoming frail; they are struggling to look after themselves, and gradually becoming an unmanageable problem for their partner or family. There is no doubt that, where competent people have time to consider the question of such a change, they are implacably opposed to nursing home placement. A survey by the Combined Pensioners and Superannuants in 2015 found that 95 per cent of people wanted to receive care in their own homes. Twelve per cent of Australians were recorded as 'informal' carers.

The Australian Government Productivity Commission (*Caring for Older Australians*, 2011) stated: 'Older Australians generally want to remain independent and in control of how and where they live; to stay connected and relevant to their families and communities; and be able to exercise some measure of choice over their care.' It continued:

> A number of participants presented their visions of a future system of care and support for older Australians. While the visions varied, they had many common themes including that: the focus should be on well-being; services should promote independence; and people should be able to make their own life choices, even if it means they accept higher levels of risk. Older people should be treated with dignity and respect

and should be able to die well. Carers of older people should be adequately supported [...]

There is strong empirical evidence that consumer choice improves wellbeing, including higher life satisfaction, greater life expectancy, independence, and better continuity of care [...]

Many, especially those not suffering from dementia, are deferring entry into residential high care until they reach greater frailty.

The essential message in this report is of the importance of independence and choice: do people who are facing placement in, or who are currently living in, aged care have this independence and choice? No, certainly not.

Jacob M. Appel (bioethicist and medical historian) wrote in *HuffPost* in 2009:

I'd sooner be dead than live in a nursing home [...] Such facilities impose grave limits on human autonomy [...] As a personal matter, I find the prospect of relying on another human being to change my clothing or to empty my bedpan incompatible with the minimum level of human dignity that I ever wish to endure. When I can no longer manage my activities of daily living at home, I am prepared to conclude my life with the same dignity that I hope I have displayed during my life. I prefer a timely death to a lengthy sojourn in a human warehouse.

John Bell, actor and director of Bell Shakespeare, said in 2012: 'I don't want to reach that stage of being incontinent, helpless, totally dependent. It's a dreadful way to end a life that's been a very happy and blessed one.' He said that often children of parents are particularly torn by how to care for their dying loved one. 'They often feel guilty about wanting the parent to go, and therefore not being able to let them go and not knowing how to do it.' He would have been well aware of the Bard's lines from *As You Like It* describing the seven ages of man:

The last scene of all, that ends this strange eventful history,
Is second childishness and mere oblivion,
Sans teeth, sans eyes, sans taste, sans everything.

Sharon M. Valente wrote in *Cancer Nursing* in 2004:

> family members experience significant burdens and guilt when they decide to place a loved one in an extended care facility. Often, they have exhausted all other options before placement and feel this may be the most difficult decision they have made, a decision accompanied by feelings of loss, pain, regret, and fear of the future. Often, the family members cannot imagine the loved one's death and are torn between the notion that death may be a blessing and a tragedy. They felt angst at watching their loved one decline.

Sociologist at the University of Melbourne Leah Ruppanner and Assistant Professor Georgiana Bostean described in 2015 how most aged care is actually provided by unpaid family members (2.7 million in 2012), in the older person's home or in the carer's home. They indicated that such care can be stressful and damaging to wellbeing, which may have severe health consequences: 'With approximately 12% of Australians providing care the current system is unsustainable.'

Catherine Thompson, a research fellow at the University of New South Wales, wrote: 'Research suggests that the provision of unpaid care can have a profound impact on a carer's participation in employment and education, on their incomes and retirement incomes, on their social relationships and on their health and well-being.'

Echoing this sentiment were M. W. Rabow and colleagues, who in 2004 described the 'five burdens of family caregiving – time and logistics, physical tasks, financial costs, emotional burdens and mental health risks, and physical health risks'. Caregivers who suffer high levels of chronic burden or stress tend to have the most severe health consequences. What is more, 'laborious care-giving is often performed by people who are themselves elderly, ill and disabled'. A Griffith University study found an 'alarming' one-quarter of people caring for a family member with dementia have contemplated suicide – these people suffer higher levels of burden, anxiety, depression and dysfunctional coping strategies.

Where do Australians die? Fifty-four per cent die in hospital and 32 per cent in institutions. Research shows that only 1 per cent wish to die in an aged-care home. Ninety per cent of aged-care residents die in residential care, the other 10 per cent after a transfer to hospital. Swerrison and Ducket for the Grattan Institute (2014) documented that most want to die at home, supported by family and friends and the services they need.

Why doesn't this happen? If you are going to die at home, you need a doctor to make home visits, home-nursing services, and a supportive and available family, because dying at home can take some time. Unfortunately, few GPs now make home visits, and home-nursing services are costly if prolonged. Sixty years ago, doctors looked after many people dying at home, but that culture has changed. If a person is dying in aged care today, their doctor, commonly an out-of-hours doctor who has never met the dying person before, will refer them either to an emergency department, or to a specialist, with much the same outcome: hospital admission to manage (medicalise) the process of dying. There is an abysmal lack of communication about the fact that the person is dying, and of discussion as to how they would like it managed.

Apparently, those in general practice no longer have the inclination or the skills (the expertise and experience) to manage dying at home. What a catastrophe: before acknowledging the reality of dying, the hospital makes one more futile attempt to 'cure' them. This is not simply me saying this – ask intensivists of their experience. Our acute hospitals should be specialised institutions for effective treatments, not places where people go to die. Specialist oncologist Robyn Ward, discussing the practice of admitting dying people to hospital, said: 'My personal experience with [dying] patients is that it's very traumatic for them. Hospitals are terrible places at that time of life. They don't cater for lots of family and friends being around. The patient is taken out of a familiar setting.' They should be at home with palliative care or, if not possible, in a palliative-care hospice.

So much for where aged people prefer to die; where would they prefer to live? An Australian Government Productivity Commission report in 2015 found that 83 per cent of people aged over 60 preferred to continue living in their own home, compared to 1 per cent in a residential aged-care facility. In 2012 Council of the Aging Australia facilitated a series of public 'conversations' between then Minister for Ageing Mark Butler and 3,400 older citizens and their carers. This revealed a 'strong-held belief that they want to stay at home'. It also showed that 'many older Australians [argue] that they should be able to control the way they die. Many said they wanted to die at home, with support also for euthanasia. Having control over your own death was raised in every conversation.'

Research in 2007 by Professor Mari Lloyd-Williams and colleagues shed some further light. They conducted in-depth interviews with 40 individuals aged in their eighties and living alone at home. The results revealed that concerns associated with end of life included fear of how they would die; fear of becoming a burden to others; wanting to prepare for, and have a choice in, where and when they die; and issues related to assisted dying.

A person who has terminal cancer is very difficult to effectively palliate at home if their cancer illness is prolonged. Inpatient palliative care is funded for about one month only, so some people who enter there but do not die in that period are transferred to aged care. They are usually so weak and debilitated that they have no say in the matter. When they have been asked (Linda Foreman et al., 2006) 58 per cent of 2,052 residents expressed a wish to die at home, but only 14 per cent did so. The preferred places of death were home 70 per cent, hospital 19 per cent, hospice 10 per cent, and nursing home 0.8 per cent. Consider that: only 0.8 per cent would prefer to die in a nursing home, yet 30 per cent actually die there! A number of people changed their minds about dying at home when they realised how prolonged and difficult that might be. I am provoked to ask: *why* should it be so prolonged and difficult to die at home from cancer?

Palliative Care Australia investigated this problem in 2004. It found that at-home carers in general, but especially those caring for terminal cancer patients, experience difficulty in maintaining employment, and are forced to give up work and rely on government assistance, which is frequently inadequate in the light of increased expenses such as drugs and equipment hire. Carers experience an increase in adverse health effects related to stress, weight loss, and disturbed sleep leading to fatigue. There are reduced opportunities for social and physical activities, further reducing their own wellbeing, which can lead to social isolation, even to the point of becoming homebound. Carers often diminish the importance of their own needs; lack of respite care and other support services leads to social isolation, exhaustion, illness and negative feelings towards the dying person. Carers report feelings such as guilt, fear, frustration, anger, resentment, loss of control, and a sense of inadequacy, which is why we desperately need more palliative-care nursing at home.

Are nursing homes a nirvana, a utopia, that ageing people no longer capable of looking after themselves aspire to enter? The evidence is an emphatic *no*.

Notable Melbourne journalist Jill Singer wrote in the *Herald Sun*:

> It is no measure of a nursing home's success if it is full of old, frail and demented people who linger on for decades thanks to the 'wonders' of medical science. I've spent more time than I care to remember in various nursing homes, and even the good ones are depressing places, full of elderly confused and incontinent people, often agitated and who are spoon-fed mush.

This is not a universal opinion by any means. Joyce, aged 86, has spent two years in Inglewood aged care and 'loves her life in the hostel and is very happy', as does Joan who has spent ten years in Inglewood after breaking her hip at 71, and is 'very happy living in the hostel'. Joan is fortunate, as 5 per cent of people who break their hip die in hospital, and up to 25 per cent will die within the year as a direct result of their injury.

Researchers G. Salkeld and colleagues reported in the *British Medical Journal* (2000) on the attitudes of elderly women towards the outcome of hip fracture (20 per cent are dead within a year). They found:

> Nearly all women would trade off almost their entire life expectancy to avoid the state of being admitted to a nursing home. Eighty per cent of respondents said they would rather be dead [...] Any loss of ability to live independently in the community has a considerable detrimental effect on their quality of life [...] The single most important factor (threat) seems to be the loss of independence, dignity, and possessions that accompanies the move from living in their own homes to living in

a nursing home [...] Respondents often commented that they were living on borrowed time and that they had lived a good or fair life (a 'fair innings') [...] They did not want to live on borrowed time at the expense of younger people [...]

At their age, death was expected and preferable to a state of health that meant losing their home, their independence, and their normal quality of life [...] Among older women who have exceeded average life expectancy, quality of life matters. Older women place a very high marginal value on their health. Any loss to living independently in the community has a significant detrimental effect on their quality of life.

But such outcomes are not always predictable. A daughter, talking of her frail aged parent who was failing to cope after being widowed, said: 'When I first became Mum's carer, I felt like the role was thrown on me.' Her mother was living alone but adjacent to her daughter. She added that 'there were a couple of times I nearly cracked with all the pressure, but I knew if I wasn't going to care for Mum no-one was'. She had times when she wished her mother would die. Eventually her mother had to be moved to aged care and was very angry about it, but in time she said she 'loves it'.

What is the experience of living and dying in a nursing home? Barbara Fiveash made a study in 1998 of the articulate resident's perspective of nursing home life. She wrote:

All people need freedom and choice; it is a basic need. This society uses segregation in the form of imprisonment to punish people for their crimes. Older sick and disabled people are aware that they have been segregated from the mainstream culture and some view themselves as being imprisoned or inmates. They are unaware, however, of what crime they have committed except to be old and to have difficulty looking after themselves.

An ethnographic nursing home study from 2002 by J. Kayser-Jones in *The Gerontologist* found that research on the experience of dying was limited. The study concluded that lack of attention to cultural needs, cognitive status, inadequate staffing, and inadequate and inappropriate communication between health-care providers and nursing-home residents and their families were the predominant factors that influenced the experience of dying. A Mari Lloyd-Williams study also demonstrated that questions relating to the end of life are a major concern for older people, but are seldom addressed by professionals.

Listening to and understanding the views and experiences of the older age group regarding end-of-life care are needed if adequate, person-centred care is to be provided to this ever-growing group. Lloyd-Williams and colleagues found in 2007 that 'a common fear was not of death itself but the mode of death [...] The fear of a long and debilitating fate and the burden of such a fate on family [...] was a major issue.' They noted that 'many believed they had lived a long and good life and that death was inevitable' and 'many wished they would not have to move from their current home before dying'. Further, 'the greatest fear was of a chronic life-limiting illness, for example stroke, which would mean that they would require full-time nursing care in a nursing home and thereby have to give up their own home. Cancer was not an illness feared by participants in general.' They summarised: 'It appears that a good death for this population would be death that involves the minimum amount of physical or mental dependency/ disability, the minimum burden to others, and one that involved staying in their own home.' In conclusion, the study found:

> The assertion that, at a societal level, dying and death are managed very well, generally having little or no impact on its smooth and productive running, does not appear to be true. It is clear that death and/or dying is a major factor in the lives of elderly people and our study challenges the suggestion that many people are unable to talk openly about death.

Research by Singer and colleagues in 1999 identified five important domains that affected quality of life:

1. adequate pain and symptom management
2. avoiding inappropriate prolongation of dying

3. achieving a sense of control
4. strengthening relationships with loved ones
5. relieving burden.

Observations on dying in aged care in Australia suggest that these are not being universally achieved, and points 2 and 3 require a change in the law for implementation.

Jaci, a 61-year-old resident of Inglewood aged care facility, was diagnosed with chronic emphysema about five years ago, and given two years to live. Living in a nursing home, she is on oxygen 24 hours a day, seven days a week, and is 'endlessly' in pain. 'It's like someone putting a block of concrete on your chest all day and all night', she said.

Professor Peter Saul reminds us that 'we need to understand that our deaths will not be with a bang but with a series of diminishing whimpers' (*The Conversation*, 29 April 2013).

Here is a personal note I received:

> My 98 year old cousin, who did her nursing training at the Alfred hospital and was a nurse through WW2. She is now in a top Aged Care facility in Melbourne. Her brain is still 'spot on' but her body is a wreck. She is completely incontinent, has ulcers on her leg, and has no balance at all. Her dignity and desire to continue living has gone. In the Aged Care facility there are nearly 300 patients, and on the first floor where my cousin lives with 96 people, there is only one person she can communicate with. This intelligent cousin of mine has lost the desire to continue this way of life.

This comment takes my mind back to Jane, whom I discussed in chapter 13 of my book *A Good Death*. Suffering from chronic disability (multiple sclerosis) for 12 years, Jane was incarcerated in a nursing home for two years. She was among another 100 residents, but could converse with only one other person – if he spoke and she listened! I mention her now because she was able to end her life by ceasing ingestion of fluids and food, a subject I will address later.

In 2012 Naomi Richards wrote in the *International Journal of Ageing and Later Life* that 'there is a paucity of sociological and anthropological literature on dying in old age, particularly within the gerontological field', a fact supported by a 2013 Swedish survey which found only 33 studies across the world of the views of death and dying among older people. Given the size of the problem, this astonishingly small volume of research reveals the shameful lack of interest and concern for these abused senior citizens with completed lives.

Jane Fleming of Cambridge University carried out further research in 2016, particularly into the 'older old' (95-plus). Most felt ready to die, and some even welcomed it. Others were more desperate to reach the end: 'I wish I could snuff it, I'm only in the way.' Others begged not to be left to live until they were 100, saying that there was no point to keeping them alive.

Completed lives? No doubt, and if we only bothered to ask, we would discover many more. When people who are aged and frail contact me for end-of-life advice, I ask them if they consider they have a completed life. The answer is almost universally 'yes'.

A study into depression in residential care published in 2013 by the Australian Institute of Health and Welfare found that just over half (52 per cent) of all permanent aged care residents had mild, moderate or major symptoms of depression. This contrasted with estimates of around 10–15 per cent of older people living in the community. Further, this study found that:

> About 45% of residents admitted to permanent aged care for the first time between 20 March 2008 and 31 August 2012 had symptoms of depression. About 22% had mild symptoms, 13% had moderate symptoms, and 11% had major symptoms [...] Over this period, the rate of symptoms of depression in newly-admitted patients increased 21% (from 40% in July 2008 to 48% in June 2012).

The authors concluded that these were likely to be underestimates, and that 'nearly one-third of permanent aged care residents with symptoms of depression did not have a medical diagnosis, nor was one being sought'. This brought forth a letter to *The Age* on 18 October 2013, headed 'Curse of care': 'It is no surprise to read that "Depression hits half of those in aged care". Some of us in this workplace already know the three plagues of residential aged care are boredom, loneliness and hopelessness.' She could have added unrelieved pain, incontinence and lack of mobility.

This type of depression is now being described as an adjustment disorder – it is due to external circumstances, and unless those circumstances can be altered, the mood disorder is extremely hard to influence. It is a natural human response to the situation. It is not primarily a psychiatric disorder. Professor Julian Savulescu has described it as one example of a condition that could be considered a normal variation of mood, but is treated as a disease.

What are the results of treatment of this situation? A Cochrane review (the most prestigious treatment analysis research group) of five trials comparing antidepressants to placebo in patients receiving palliative care found no difference in efficacy after 6–12 weeks. No trial showed any benefit to quality of life. These were trials for cancer patients, but there is little reason for belief that depressed persons in aged care with severe medical problems would achieve a benefit.

Pain is a critical issue for the frail aged. The pain of chronic musculoskeletal damage due to osteoporosis and degenerative arthritis is common in the frail aged person, and is recognised as being under-recognised and under-treated. Pamela Melding, chair of the Faculty of Psychiatry of Old Age at the University of Auckland wrote in 2002 that 'chronic pain can be an unfortunate consequence of several degenerative diseases associated with ageing, such as vascular insufficiency, sensory neuropathies, osteoarthritis, osteoporosis, spinal stenosis and vertebral collapse. Depression and poor psychological adjustment are also more prevalent in older people who are in pain.' Moreover, depression appears to heighten the suffering caused by pain. Predictably, the prevalence of chronic pain is high in nursing-home residents.

Chronic pain can be of two patterns: persistent, steady, chronic pain (relatively easy to manage with regular maintenance medication which prevents the pain) and/or sudden, acute 'incident' pain due to a particular incident or circumstance. The latter commonly involves movement, as in turning, lifting, moving joints as in bathing or changing clothes, or in changing dressings. If such pain can be anticipated, pain relief before the incident can be effective. In surgery we provide pain relief *before* we make an incision.

There is a strong swing among pain specialists away from opioids for chronic pain (defined as pain persisting for more than two or three months), because of lack of efficacy, and harmful long-term consequences, but the latter concern makes little sense for the frail aged person who has a short life expectancy. They are in a palliative category and every effort should be made to ensure they do not die with inadequately relieved pain. Yet at the 2015 Victorian Parliamentary Inquiry into End of Life Choices, palliative care specialist Michelle Gold stated that sometimes pain relief was withheld or given in lower doses than ordered because hospital staff were scared of being reported. Professor Bill Silvester said he knew of doctors afraid to prescribe medications such as morphine because they thought the patient may die and they would be at risk of prosecution.

I hear this again and again from relatives requesting increased pain relief for their parent – they are told 'we cannot give more, as it might hasten death'. Is it so difficult to discuss such an option with an ageing patient and their family, to ask if the risk is accepted in exchange for good pain relief? If the answer is persistently affirmative and recorded and witnessed, then the provision is ethical and legal in this context. The Guidelines of the American Geriatrics Association state that 'it is the responsibility of physicians to relieve pain, especially when the prognosis is poor; pain relief may be the most important thing physicians can offer their patients'.

The final, but often unexpressed, fear is that of residents and their families who are afraid of being discriminated against if they complain of inadequate doses or frequency of doses, or make any complaint at all. Theresa wrote this to *The Sydney Morning Herald* in response to Bachelard:

> My mother has lived in a nursing home since June 2016. In mid-2016, the management contractor brought in new managers, the first aim being to introduce 'additional fees'. In June 2016, my mother had a fall, she fractured her left forearm which remained undiagnosed for five days. During those five days, she was toileted, dressed and she was in pain, as was detailed in the clinical notes. The nursing home's explanation was

that my mother didn't want to go to hospital. My mother is fearful of any complaints being lodged, she fears the repercussions.

Stories abound of residents being frightened of making complaints – simply locally, or more generally to management or authorities. If mention is made of end-of-life ideas, threats of psychiatric assessment or mandatory sectioning are made – rather like a threat of solitary confinement for a recalcitrant prisoner. Therese has a similar story:

> I have been trying to get best care practice for my parents, what a joke that is. Mother has been told several times to just 'go' in her pants as that is what they are there for … Two weeks ago she buzzed for assistance, waited for as long as she could, my father was helping her as she couldn't hold on any longer, she had a fall and has broken pelvis. … I was visiting her this week, she needed the toilet, is unable to mobilise … the nurse's response was, and I quote, 'Well you will have to buzz and wait as the girls are busy', she then walked out of the room. I am afraid of repercussions if I challenge this, as I have seen adverse repercussions when I complained previously.

Charles Sturt University's Associate Professor Maree Bernoth, herself a former nurse, states that many people are frightened to make a complaint. It takes a lot of courage and determination to take on these large organisations, which are backed by lawyers and money and experience. They have formal advice from lawyers as to how to deal with 'difficult families'. It can be a David and Goliath exercise, requiring careful record-keeping, photographic records of injuries, and – one hopes – support from a staff member (unlikely when their job is at stake). The obstruction, obfuscation and delay will sap the patience of most complainants, who are also usually dealing with significant grief.

One in six Australians is now aged over 65, and this is projected to rise to 25 per cent of the population by 2096. Remember that now about a quarter of those over 85 will require aged-care assistance. Who will care for them? In 2016 almost a quarter of a million people were in residential aged care, a rise of 31 per cent in ten years. Quite apart from finding appropriately trained carers, the cost will be considerable, estimated to be about 6 per cent of Australia's gross domestic product by 2060. Public health provision of aged care is declining, opening the door for private investment in what is now called an 'industry'! Where there's a buck to be made, as they say, the bees will swarm around the honey pot, which inevitably brings motives of profit into conflict with best care. Thus what was once an aged-care system has now become an industry. Almost 40 per cent of Australian nursing homes are run for profit, and the most 'efficient' managers take up to $25,000 profit from each occupied bed per year – a profit margin of 20 per cent! Only 5 per cent of homes are government run; the remainder, approximately 55 per cent, are so-called not-for-profit, yet these often mimic the practices (and financial results) of the for-profit sector.

The community is heavily indebted to Michael Bachelard and his investigative team from Fairfax, and the Australian Broadcasting Corporation, for their extensive research and revelations into the aged-care industry. I have relied heavily on this work. The cumulative effect of this investigation, and the subsequent response from the public, have been largely responsible for the Australian government establishing a royal commission to investigate quality and safety in the industry.

On 29 May 2017 *The Age* published 'Aged care: Preventable nursing home deaths on rise'. Michael Bachelard and Rachel Browne wrote: 'Australia's nursing homes are increasingly deadly places for their residents, with a 400 per cent increase in preventable deaths over the past decade despite billions of dollars of federal and private money being spent on them.' Falls, choking and suicide were the main causes of preventable deaths, according to research by Monash University researcher Joe Ibrahim. In response to Michael Bachelard's series of articles in September 2017 there was a tsunami of public letters to the editor. Two caught my eye, and supported my contention regarding a 'prison system'. Marie Claire wrote in *The Sydney Morning Herald* on 29 September 2017 under the heading 'A resident's lament':

I live in a big not for profit home. Mentally I shouldn't be here, but physically, my body needed help, which I thought I was going to get when I came here. Slowly I have been educated about what aged care is really about.

I was here for two weeks when someone told me not to bother pressing the buzzer, because they never come. It's like being imprisoned and there's no way out.

[...] When I complain, the frustration is terrible – the denial is unbelievable. They say they'll 'look into it'. They treat you like a nuisance and they make you feel like an idiot.

Carol was even more pertinent: 'Old people would be better off committing a crime and going to jail for the rest of their lives. Aged care is a disgrace.' Michael Bachelard (*Sydney Morning Herald*, 1 May 2018) wrote:

The big for-profit nursing home companies are using the same 'tricks and schemes' as tech giants to minimise the amount of tax they pay, even though the vast majority of their funding comes from the public purse.

[...] Between them, the six largest for-profit companies were given over $2.17 billion in government subsidies – 72 per cent of their total revenue – and made profits of $210 million per year between 2016 and 2018.

A recent report by Adjunct Senior Professor Jason Ward from the University of Tasmania stated that 'I was a bit surprised to find the extent of tax avoidance from companies that are providing a public service.' The Australian Nursing Federation states: 'Our members tell us that the money is being spent, but not on care [...] they impose restrictions on goods like continence pads.' And they certainly do not spend it on food. The most profitable homes spend just $6.08 per day per resident on food!

The accounting firm Stewart Brown provides a 'benchmarking report' for homes in which a 'care result' does not refer to the amount or quality of care but to profit per bed; the most profitable homes spend less on nurses and chefs, have higher occupancy rates, higher accommodation deposits, and are city-based.

Staff working in aged care responded to Bachelard. A former national operations manager wrote:

> As a recent corporate employee of one of the listed companies mentioned, I could not agree with you more. It is a national disgrace and the sooner something is done the better.
>
> I left the industry for all the reasons you mentioned in your article … I was always being asked to cut costs and raise revenue.
>
> In the end I said to the board, I'll just offer bread and water and charge the residents more – that should keep the shareholders happy!
>
> I miss looking after these vulnerable people. I wish I could go back but, alas, it is as you say, 'all about the money'.

Arlo stated, 'I quit working in aged care as I just couldn't stand these massive companies making millions in profits. The chief management even came in to gloat how much they had made that year!!!' An aged-care worker from Tasmania responded (*The Age*, 19 January 2019):

> Every aged care facility I ever worked in was staffed by a caring, well-trained, underpaid and overworked skeleton crew. Many more staff are needed to monitor residents who are a danger to themselves and others.
>
> [...] The central problem of the aged-care industry is money. Not enough comes from governments, not enough goes to workers and too much goes to the profiteers. Fix that, please, Mr Wyatt.

A telling anonymous response (indicating the fear of reprisal if one speaks out) recorded:

> I'm a trainer/assessor of future aged care workers, working within a private RTO [registered training organisation]. It's hard to articulate to students the absolute greed of service providers within the industry purportedly cloaked in care and special attention, but revealed to you as callous, exploitative and profit making.

My father, 92, late Alzheimer's and palliative bowel cancer, is in a residential aged care facility and I despair for his treatment. He is my litmus test for my students – would I let them anywhere near him? Only if I'm satisfied that they have the skills and compassion to work with old people do I submit a satisfactory assessment of skills and training. But I get a lot of pressure put on me by my RTO employer to tick and flick students through, because funding has to be repaid by any RTO who enrols a government funded student who doesn't complete or qualify.

One writer to *The Age* (26 February 2001) asked the carers of her father in aged care the same question: 'Would they want to finish up in a home?' There were no takers. And her observation of his 'home': 'There's no point in applying the rules of your own world to this one.'

I have a mass of files on excruciating aged-care behaviour. The daughter of a 77-year-old man said he was being tube-fed, unable to speak and for about five years could only move his eyebrows, yet the health-care operator claimed he was verbally refusing care and was verbally disruptive. Such a descriptive might have gained more government funding, at a time when the home was unprofitable and about to close.

GP Professor Dimity Pond said of residential homes in 2009, 'It can be a very deprived environment', citing one British researcher who described the social interactions in a nursing home as being on the level of those between people in a laundromat line (McCredie, 2009). However, Pond's professional experience in aged care didn't make it any easier when her father told her he felt as though he was back in his World War II prison camp. Psychogeriatricians are in the unfortunate position, on occasions, of giving people advice that they don't really believe.

And it was not just the for-profits that came in for a belting. Another anonymous response in 2017 from the not-for-profit sector:

I currently work in a not-for-profit aged care facility as a Registered Nurse.

Last week I had to work an evening shift 2:30pm to 11pm followed immediately by a night duty shift from 11pm to 7am the next morning.

This happens regularly in my facility. At the end of my double shift I'm so tired that I can hardly think, let alone make critical clinical decisions around care needs. On the night duty shift I have 150-plus high care residents to care for and on the evening shift I have 75 plus.

In looking after this many residents I have to rely on non qualified carers and an occasional Certificate IV carer to feed information back to me.

I have worked in nursing homes all over Sydney in the last ten years plus ... I have recently taught clinical nursing care in a Sydney University.

I do not want to become a resident, ever, of any Aged Care Facility I have worked in.

It is not just carers who have problems. The Royal Australian College of General Practitioners stated in its 'silver book' on residential aged care of 2006 that 'general practitioners working collaboratively with other health providers play a key role in delivering high quality primary care to older people living in residential aged care settings'. The spotlight is rarely thrown onto the medical profession, who actually have a critical role in assessment of pain, depression, and ultimately attitudes and directions of residents. The ABC's *7.30 Report* of 8 August 2018 reported that GPs were turning their backs on aged care, and that 'alarm bells' should be ringing. The work was described as challenging clinically and ethically, and poorly remunerated.

Astonishingly, it is not just the for-profit area that is involved in care versus profit. A Christadelphian not-for-profit group reported a $14.5 million surplus in 2016. Professor Gillian Triggs reported in 2018 that the Human Rights Commission had found that faith-based bodies provided about 64 per cent of aged-care facilities for older people. Presumably the remaining 36 per cent are operated for profit.

I am not economically qualified to discuss nursing home bonds (refundable accommodation deposits), but I think I can smell a racket from a mile off. In 2016 such bonds averaged $377,000 across Australia, but one was $2.7 million for residence in Neutral Bay.

How is it that a facility that only 1 per cent of Australians wish for is so profitable?

Meanwhile, running parallel with the aged-care industry is the anti-ageing and life-prolonging industry, which reached a net worth of $88 billion in 2013 and is predicted to grow quickly to more than $300 billion worldwide. Despite there being no evidence that medicine can alter the process of human biological ageing, university-funded research is occurring. This at a time when we are struggling with gross world over-population stimulating climate change. Well, there's a buck to be made, isn't there?

Lest you assume that I am fundamentally opposed to aged care, let me state that I believe it is an essential public health service, and that it is a government responsibility to provide an effective, cost-efficient system. Aged care does an essential job with inadequate support, and is subject to much unjustified criticism. The nature and difficulty of its task are enormous. Its staff work in difficult, provocative and sometimes dangerous circumstances. But it should be provided to those who want it.

However, it has grown like 'topsy', in a very uncoordinated and catch-up fashion as the problems have evolved. Starting with home-nursing services in the 19th century, benevolent societies and religious bodies opened residential facilities in the early 20th century. Nursing homes can be seen as a cultural creation of the fragmentation of the extended family. Governments gradually entered the fray as the costs became excessive with the increasing size of the problem. Australian Prime Minister John Howard introduced the *Aged Care Act* in 1997 with the intention to regulate, scrutinise and hold providers to account, but assessment and accreditation systems were unsatisfactory. The sector has been grossly under-resourced, and is now being overwhelmed by demography.

Faced with a massive predicted future cost ($31 billion over ten years), the Liberal–National government accepted the recommendation of the Productivity Commission for a competitive market with reduced regulation. Imagine that, for an essential public health service! The predictable result occurred: as Dr Sarah Russell wrote, 'Private equity firms, new foreign investors, superannuation and property real estate investment trusts entered the aged care market in large numbers.'

Under a self-regulated system (so favoured by conservative governments, and so frequently found wanting in capitalist societies), fiscal accountability was missing. Under current arrangements, providers of care do their own assessments for government subsidies. These are not based on external medical assessment, but on the opinion of the provider that would reap the subsidy. Sarah Russell states that 'government subsidies in aged care often serve the interests of the provider more than residents. When a resident is reclassified as requiring higher level of care, the provider receives the money from the government. However, staff levels rarely change nor are extra services provided to the resident.' The Aged Care Funding Instrument is used to calculate funding for residents in aged care, but it found that one in eight claims for increased funding in 2014–15 were incorrect, leading Michel Pascoe to ask, 'Where's the dividing line between systemic fraud and innocent mistakes?' in the aged-care sector.

Transparency in care was also lacking, a matter acknowledged by Aged Care Minister Ken Wyatt, who has said that 'confronted with complaints, some homes have pulled down the shutters and not dealt with it; that's when people get angry and become frustrated'. It's not just about complaints: important data on nurse-carer to resident ratios, bedsore rates, falls, and incontinence pad changes are simply not available or provided.

At the same time that the federal minister Ken Wyatt says we have a 'world class system', Victoria's Minister for Ageing Martin Foley says the aged care system is 'broken'! Guess who pays for, and is responsible for, aged care. It is not as though this is a problem that has suddenly appeared. In July 2013 the ABC's *Lateline* presented a program headed 'Aged care crisis', stating that 'A critical lack of staff and training in some nursing homes means that many elderly people are being left to die unnecessarily or are in great pain without proper palliative care', and backed this assertion with powerful interviews, including of one woman with an undiagnosed thigh bone fracture who was forced to walk for five days. Unforgivable, and I am personally aware of a similar event.

It is not as though this is a sudden discovery. The Office for Senior Victorians produced a report in October 2005 about the Elder Abuse Prevention Project. Jane Lee reported in *The Age* in April 2016 that Health Department figures showed that the proportion of registered nurses in aged care fell by nearly 30 per cent between 2003 and 2012. In the same time, unregulated 'personal care attendants' grew from 57 per cent to 68 per cent. The Australian College of Nurse Practitioners told a Senate inquiry that registered nurses were 'not seen as cost effective', and claimed that some residential aged-care facilities are 'employing minimal staffing numbers to maximize profit margins'. Personal care attendants are not regulated. Many are not qualified to do more than bathe, feed and change the elderly residents. This information was being heard at the same time that the Turnbull federal government was cutting aged-care training programs by nearly half a billion dollars over the next four years.

Aged Care Insite reported in 2019 that Australia's ageing population will cost the federal budget more than Medicare in a decade. The Parliamentary Budget Office (2019) showed that this will subtract 0.4 per cent from annual real growth in spending (a cost to budget of $36 billion by 2028). The Parliamentary Budget Office stressed that this was already affecting economic growth. With a significantly rising aged population, is anyone prepared to bet on a sustainable improvement in care?

In 2013 Greg Evans, co-author of a report on Australia's looming aged-care challenges, said in an interview with Michael Short that there was a need for a revolution in the way Australia's aged-care services are designed, funded and delivered. He stressed the looming need for a huge expansion of the number of people working in aged care:

> Right now, the aged-care workforce is made up of about 240,000 direct caregivers. That is around 2 per cent of the Australian workforce. By 2050, the aged-care workforce will need to quadruple to meet the demand, and this will happen while the number of people participating in the work force is in decline.

Would anyone like to predict improved aged care in 2050, let alone 2020?

Doctors, nurses, care managers and governments have been aware of these problems for more than a decade, but the problem is getting worse, not better. Thankfully we now have a royal commission to throw much-needed light onto this disastrous system. Its early findings are confirming the appalling staff ratios and the consequences for care.

Both palliative care and aged care deal with terminally ill people. Generally, those in palliative care are clearly close to death, while most of those in aged care are not imminently dying. Palliative care has resident specialist doctors, trained specialist nurses and significant government funding. Australian aged care has no resident doctors, and is not a popular medical environment. Bachelard writes: 'There is no minimum legal ratio of staff to residents, no minimum training requirement and no statutory requirement to have a nurse on duty at all times. The only legal requirement is the unenforceable rule that staff numbers are "adequate".' The Australian Nursing Federation maintains that there are minimal trained nursing staff, and inadequate training for low-paid assistant carers. It is no wonder there are incidents from time to time of inadequate or abusive care.

Monash University Professor Joe Ibrahim (*Sydney Morning Herald*, 24 September 2017) foresees a time when a big law firm takes on some cases:

So potentially you'd end up with Slater and Gordon, pro bono, taking on a case of false imprisonment for a number of cases for a nursing home listed on the stock market, so you have a law firm worth billions fighting listed aged care worth billions fighting out on human rights.

A circumstance like that detailed by Peter would be relevant. He wrote:

After trialling several facilities in Sydney's southern district, we settled on [a for-profit home] for my mother, Rosemary. Like most, they promised the earth.

The reality was inedible, cold and unnecessarily pureed meals. Response to calls for help often took over an hour, and were sometimes met with 'what do you want this time?' or 'why are you ringing again?'

Rosemary was there from July 2012 to June 2014. She was blind, immobile and needed help to eat and drink. Often her food and drinks were just left there, so she was often hungry and thirsty.

Within months a serious pressure ulcer, roughly 1cm across had developed on Rosemary's buttocks ... All we got were more verbal promises and an explanation that the budget was very limiting.

Rosemary had a high intellect and active mind, so she enjoyed word games and quizzes but was rarely moved to the common room to participate in them. Instead, she was often wheeled into the company of dementia patients.

Alternative to a complaint of abuse of human rights would be one of incompetent care. Bedsores are regarded as a preventable medical complication, given adequate nursing care. They are due to sustained pressure on bony prominences (such as the sacrum, heel or hip) due to lack of movement, and are more likely when skin is damaged by unchanged incontinence pads. Leaving someone in a sodden nappy for hours is asking for trouble. Bedsores are a particular risk in spinal cord–injured patients, and turning teams are employed to prevent them. They are also a considerable risk in late-stage dementia patients. The reported incidence (Department of Health) of pressure sores in Australian aged care is between 26 per cent and 42 per cent of residents (in a similar group in the USA it is 6.2 per cent, according to Dr Michael Wynne). The prevention of bedsores depends on good nursing; their occurrence suggests the lack of same, particularly for a competent person.

So, what is my response to the possibility of a legal case about incompetent care or abuse of human rights in aged care? Bring it on! Such an action would have a dramatic effect on the overall level of care.

The very nature of the system that has evolved has aspects of inbuilt abuse. The whole basis of the aged-care system needs to be addressed. In reality, homes are increasingly required to deal with the multiple ailments of ageing, then – ultimately – palliative care and death. More than 80 per cent of residents are high care; one-third of them will die each year.

HOW DO THEY GET AWAY WITH IT? SIMPLY BECAUSE THERE IS NO ALTERNATIVE, NO CHOICE.

I will return to this matter after dealing with the dementia catastrophe.

Chapter 5

Remember me, Mrs V?

A woman lies in bed, facing the wall, her legs and arms drawn up to her body in a position I often adopt when preparing for a comfortable sleep.

She is not in her own bed.

I am sitting in a dark corner of a room observing this woman, whose sparse grey hair suggests she is elderly.

She is only 61.

It is 9 am, and I am expecting her to stir and wake to eat.

She does not move; she cannot move, and she does not eat.

People come into the room, and speak to her, loudly, as they move about, preparing to wash, dress and feed her, but she does not respond.

She cannot talk.

These people, her carers, are kind and attentive, remarkably jolly considering their work. They do not ignore her as a person, which they could be excused for doing, but attempt to communicate with her. Her name is Marie.

She appears not to acknowledge them.

Tom, her husband of 39 years, who has seen this scene many times, approaches his beloved wife, and expresses his love and continued devotion.

There is no glimmer of recognition.

The carers have now turned her onto her back, and I can see that her limbs remain drawn up close to her body. They do not stretch out as mine would do after a long, comfortable sleep.

They cannot move.

Her limbs are contracted into a foetal position, flexed and contorted, her fingers curled into her palms, her fingernails difficult to trim and in danger of lacerating her palms. Her seemingly spastic flexor muscles cause this apparent fixed position, although perhaps there is an element of defence about it, of primitive protection.

She cannot express what she fears or what she feels.

I can now see her face, and it reminds me of something I have seen before. Her mouth is slightly agape, but my attention is drawn to her eyes. They are both wide open, staring blankly into the distance, apparently not focusing on anything. The impression I feel is one of terror, of someone being in a place where they are in peril, where they do not want to be, but cannot express this fear, this profound existential suffering. Now I recall where I have seen this expression before: it reminds me of Edvard Munch's painting *The Scream*. And I remember seeing this same wide-eyed look of trapped fear and distress when I visited 'BWV' in her nursing home, suffering in a vegetative state from dementia due to Pick's disease, some seven years before.

This haunting visage does not change in four hours of continuous observation, except—

The woman is now lying on her back. Suddenly her face contorts, and she raises her body such that it forms an arch, based on her shoulders and her heels, with nothing else touching the bed. She repeats this grotesque movement quite frequently while she is being washed, and her clothing is changed. It transpires that she has a serious bedsore, the size of a small plate, eroded down to the bone. She is clearly trying to relieve the pain caused by lying on her back.

Not so long ago, experts said that persons in end-stage dementia could not feel any pain nor be aware of suffering.

Now the carers are gently removing the woman's night clothing and reveal her incontinence apparel. An unpleasant odour of stale urine and faeces becomes apparent as they change this incontinence device. She has had no control over her body's excretory functions for many months. This is partly responsible for her bedsore, the other reasons being her immobility and wasting. She has not been capable of any voluntary mobility for many months, and has been confined to the position in which she is placed by her carers, either in bed or in a chair. She makes the transition from one to the other by way of a hoist, a mechanical device for transporting immobile human beings from one place to another. Somehow it reminds me of a device from the Middle Ages, from the Inquisition.

Some Catholic theologians say there is inherent dignity in all human life, no matter the circumstances.

As the carers remove the woman's clothing, wash her and redress her, they cannot avoid stretching her contracted limbs. Her arms and legs have been in this position for many months due to lack of use, lack of movement, and now the more powerful flexor muscles have overcome the weaker extensors, and the contracted posture developed. As the carers stretch these contracted joints, the woman's face distorts, grimaces and reddens, and short groans and squeals of distress are emitted. These are the only sounds she makes in the four hours of observation: sounds of pain and distress. They are her only ways of communicating.

They fall on deaf ears.

Her carers are not nurses; they are barely trained at all, but are actually doing a splendid job, within their limits, of tending to this unfortunate woman. She cannot express to them verbally how much pain and distress their ministrations are causing. Her facial and body language, and her vocalisation, are the clues to this, but the carers have not been trained to recognise this. It goes unreported, and, as a result, when a palliative-care specialist reviews the woman's paltry pain relief and observes her sitting (apparently) comfortably in her special chair for a few minutes, she finds no reason to alter her pain medication. *Steady as she goes* is the advice, much to the distress of the woman's GP, who was hoping for some support for an increase in her pain medication.

It is no surprise that pain and distress in end-stage dementia patients are badly under-recognised and under-treated. It takes time and skill to do otherwise.

Now it is time for the woman to be fed. She is placed in her hoist and transported into her tub chair, her tiny frame swinging from side to side in the air. It reminds me, on a smaller scale, of sacks of wheat being transferred from the wharf to the ship's hold of cargo. That's a gross thought, you may say, but I have never before seen a human being manipulated in this way; it may be better than physically lifting her by human hands, with the risk of breaking bones, stretching joints and causing pain, but it does not seem like a way to treat another human being. It is a way of dealing with a problem. It is dehumanising.

Yet, after time, doctors and staff in these places become dehumanised to the suffering that surrounds them. They cease to see it.

It is now apparent just how wasted her body is. She has lost more than half of her normal body weight. Food and fluid have been placed in front of her for some years, but she became unaware of their meaning and ignored what once she would have enjoyed. She is spoon-fed – wearing a nappy – unable to talk. At least as a baby she opened her mouth at the sight and smell of food. Now her carers place the mush in a spoon under her nose and hope she will open her mouth and swallow it. Lately, she has ceased doing that, and the carers tap the spoon against her lips, forcing her mouth open, so they can deposit the mush in her mouth. This is what neurologists call a 'snout reflex'. There the mush seems to sit, some of it dribbling out down her chin to be gathered up and forced back again. Some of it is eventually swallowed after sitting in her mouth for some time. This is a laborious and time-consuming process. The carers are only too happy to have a family member who is willing to do this regularly. The relatives find a sense of comfort in caring for their loved one. Why then is she losing weight so steadily?

Well, despite this intense effort, love and devotion, ultimately this feeding process, which most of the time can be seen as forced feeding, is simply inadequate to provide sufficient caloric intake to maintain weight and health. The woman has ceased to have any interest in food, ceased to have any enjoyment in food, ceased to have any understanding of the meaning and importance of food. Her body no longer wants it, her mind no longer craves it. What is more, her ability to even swallow has been jeopardised. This oral-assisted, or spoon, feeding has become a futile exercise – a futile medical treatment.

Surely feeding a vulnerable person is not a medical treatment, but is a basic human act, an act of love?

Many would say so, but do they stop to think of the consequence of this futile attempt at feeding? Does it achieve its aim: to maintain weight, nutrition and health? No, it does not. It fails so badly that it led to a vogue for tube (PEG – percutaneous endoscopic gastrostomy) feeding, where a feeding tube is placed through the person's abdominal wall into their stomach, bypassing their mouth, and saving the time taken to laboriously hand-feed. All that was required was to place a bag of mush on a pole and let it run into the body through the tube. LET IT RUN INTO THE BODY THROUGH THE TUBE. INTO THE BODY. My mind imagines a feedlot or a battery chicken farm. How dehumanising.

We must maintain the body, even if there is nobody home.

For some years in Australia, tube (PEG) feeding was commonly employed because nursing homes and hospitals were afraid they would be found negligent if they allowed people to die naturally in end-stage dementia. They felt that a lack of feeding was a lack of care. But they failed to understand two important things: first, that people die naturally from dementia because they lose any interest in or need for food and fluids; second, that such feeding by tube or spoon might prolong people's lives but, more importantly, it prolongs their suffering.

Here we have an image of a human being in a nappy, unable to communicate, unable to move, and being spoon-fed. Does this ring any bells? It should, for those of you who have borne and raised children. It conjures up the image of an infant, totally dependent on its mother and father for care. And they give it unstintingly because the infant has the promise of a full and exciting life ahead. But this human being I am describing is not an infant with a full and exciting life ahead – she is a person who we would hope has led a full and exciting life, even if cut off in her prime. Did she ever envisage that she would end her life in an infantile manner? Would she have regarded that as a dignified way for her life to end? Would you?

Do we know what Marie felt about her gradual descent to oblivion? Alas, not in specific terms of decisions taken against a background of concrete information. As for most people who develop dementia, the disease's gradual and insidious onset occurs against a background of ignorance and fear as to what is taking place. By the time the diagnosis has been made, the opportunity for understanding and expressing firm views regarding the future may well have been lost. Lacking any understanding of what lies before them, such people rarely have the opportunity to consider whether certain circumstances that they may confront would constitute for them a time to die. The idea that they might put in place protections when that time occurs, to prevent prolongation of their life of suffering, is unlikely to have occurred to or been suggested to them. As such, they become trapped in incompetence, and destined to suffer to the very end. Without the opportunity to contemplate the very end, they are unable to refuse treatments that prevent natural dying.

Tom certainly knew that Marie detested what was happening to her, and he knew that she was aware of her loss of connection to her family. He does recall occasions when, in extreme distress, she expressed a wish not to continue living in such circumstances. Eventually, by virtue of their long marriage, he had an intuitive understanding that her time to die had come, but he did not have an explicit direction as such. This crushing dilemma caused him great distress, as he grappled with the conflict between relieving suffering and hastening death.

Unfortunately, this conflict is exceedingly common in the end stage of dementia.

Fortunately, Tom Valenta recorded his thoughts about his wife's illness in the following article published in a UK magazine, and in more detail in his book *Remember Me, Mrs V?*.

Tom's story

This story is about a woman I once knew. Her name is Marie and for over 39 years she was my wife.

She died on 14 October 2009 aged 61 after being diagnosed with Alzheimer's disease nearly 7 years before. Alzheimer's cruelly and stealthily destroyed the woman I once knew.

At the time of diagnosis, she was 54 years of age, a healthy, happy, active and intelligent mother of three. She looked after herself, didn't drink, didn't smoke and was rarely sick.

After the diagnosis, her deterioration was rapid. For reasons that nobody can explain, Alzheimer's is often more aggressive in younger people.

She remained at home for four years after the diagnosis and her decline over those years was dramatic and deeply distressing to the entire family.

Looking back, I can trace not only her decline but the corrosive change in our relationship, and her relationship with the rest of our family. Proud, independent and courageous are words I often used to describe her. She had always been fiercely protective of her family and all those she loved, until Alzheimer's struck.

An equal partnership at home and in business began to fall apart. The relationship that had endured for more than three decades was changing so quickly that I barely understood what was happening to us. All those years before the diagnosis we had shared everything that happened in our lives – the good, the bad, the wins and losses. Our partnership extended beyond parenting. Our bank accounts were in joint names. The business we started in 1994 was jointly owned – everything was T & M Valenta. She was strong where I was weak, and my strengths covered her weaknesses. Even when we fought, it was toe to toe, eyeball to eyeball.

Alzheimer's changed everything and Marie soon became a dependent, defenceless person.

From soon after the diagnosis, her ability to hold a conversation deteriorated rapidly, and simple tasks such as laying a table, counting out five dollars in coins and following a street directory all became monumentally difficult. In the first year, she gradually cut back on her work hours as she realised that her ability to function normally was declining. By the end of the year she had ceased working altogether.

The changes seemed to come in bursts. In the early days, if people asked her how she felt, she would say, 'nothing hurts'. She would try to maintain some semblance of competency but it became a struggle and, at that time, she was well aware of what was happening to her.

From mid-2004 the shock of growing dependence, non-communication and strange, unpredictable and erratic behaviour was beyond my comprehension. Could this really be the person with whom I had spent more than half a lifetime?

It was in June 2005 that our neurologist told me that I should think of Marie as a five-year-old child. Would I, asked the neurologist, leave a five-year-old child at home alone? Of course not. So instead of an independent equal, I had the equivalent of an infant living with me. And infants require constant care and attention.

By late 2005, she needed help with such basic tasks as showering, dressing and feeding. Around that time there were the first ominous signs of incontinence – which destroyed her self-esteem. A once proud and independent woman had become highly dependent.

Her dependence in 2006 was so great that had she not been fed by me or one of our carers, I suspect she would have starved. Her reluctance to drink fluids led to several urinary tract infections which added to her distress. In late 2006 she was diagnosed with depression and psychotic paranoia. Her moods became erratic, and looking after her that year was so stressful that I lost more than 10 kg in weight.

Because of her paranoia she would imagine that there were other people in our house; she would become angry and abusive towards me and hostile towards carers who she once liked. The once calm and logical person had disappeared to be replaced by a volatile, unpredictable and irrational one. At one point she accused me of stealing our daughter's jewellery. Our daughter had not lived at home for some 10 years and by that time had a family of her own.

Finally on medical advice I placed her in a nursing home – just before Christmas 2006. It was the hardest decision of my life. She was 58 at that time, and I believe, the youngest person in the home.

In the second half of 2007 I began to suspect that she didn't know who I was and the same seemed to be true of our three adult children and two baby grandsons. She could barely speak or communicate in any way. Until then, the sight of her grandsons would bring an instant smile. From mid-2007 she would stare blankly and even wander away when they came to visit.

At first she constantly paced around the corridors of the nursing home. One day in July when I went to the home to take her out for a walk, I stood talking to a male staff member as I waited for her to complete a lap of the corridor. As she came towards us I called her and put out my hand. Instead of coming to me she went to the staff member. The shock of not being recognised was heartbreaking and troubles me still.

Just before Christmas 2007 she collapsed while pacing the corridors and never walked again. From that time she was heavily medicated and was asleep more than awake. A wasted body, hollowed cheeks and wispy hair made her look much older than her 60 years.

Within six months or so of losing her mobility, Marie's responsiveness diminished rapidly so I had no way of knowing whether she was in any way aware of my presence. Perhaps my greatest sorrow over this time was that I was unable to offer any comfort to her. Touching her hand or kissing her cheek yielded no response. I have heard theories about dementia patients retaining 'an inner consciousness' but have seen no scientific evidence to support the belief. Very occasionally there seemed to be a flicker of recognition but it never lasted for more than a second or two.

From the time Marie entered the nursing home, the separation of late 2005 had become much more like a bereavement. By the time she lost all mobility and responsiveness there was still a heart beat but little else. Medical science would say that she was alive but this was hardly living.

For the last six or nine months of her life she did appear to suffer from time to time. Her deterioration seemed to outpace the effectiveness of her medication. Her face would contort and she would squirm in her bed or daytime 'tub', a hospital recliner. Occasionally she would whine like a puppy in pain. When this occurred, her medication would be increased and suffering would subside.

The end seemed a long time coming. I was placed in the excruciatingly difficult position of begging for treatment that I knew would lead to her death. Was I doing it for her or myself? I will never know the answer but would like to think that I was asking for us both – and the rest of the family. Finally she developed a chest infection that mercifully ended her life three or four weeks after it was first detected.

As a carer once remarked, 'for dementia sufferers, heaven's gates open very slowly'.

This is why I call her 'a woman I once knew'. In less than seven years she became a shell of who she had once been. From not very long after the diagnosis, Alzheimer's relentlessly took her away from me and our family.

Alzheimer's took far more than her memory and cognitive abilities. It took her independence, her self-esteem, her dignity, her personality and her identity. It took her ability to give love and accept love; it took away her place in her family and her community. It took everything that she once treasured.

Then it took her life.

Some weeks before I visited Marie, Tom had gone to her caring GP and said, 'It's time.' The doctor agreed. What they understood was that her suffering was unacceptable, and that more aggressive palliation was necessary, even if it had the likely effect of shortening her life. This was 'the excruciatingly difficult position' Tom refers to above. Relieving her pain with higher doses of analgesics, and her mental anguish with sedatives, would cause her to sleep more, be more inert (if that were possible), and be likely to lead to a chest infection. And be less able to feed – or be force-fed. Whichever way one looks at it, diminishing or ceasing spoon-feeding would lead to a more rapid decline.

The GP sought advice from palliative care, believing that more aggressive palliation was appropriate, but wanting a confirming second opinion. She wanted protection from any allegation that she was negligent, was deliberately hastening death, and was concerned about referral to the Medical Practitioners Board. Although she knew she could defend such claims, she did not want the stress, and distraction from her practice.

A very experienced palliative-care expert visited Marie, spent ten minutes with her while she was sitting in her tub-chair, and stated that her care was appropriate, and that no change was necessary. She was apparently unaware of the state of her bedsore, or perhaps that she had a bedsore. All this reveals is that a short visit at a particular time does not properly allow a full assessment of a dementia patient's distress, or perhaps a disinclination to advise palliative care that might have the effect of hastening death.

Tom was dissatisfied with this consultation, and asked for my advice. He and I visited Marie, and I observed her behaviour for four hours, which I describe in the introduction to this chapter. Tom asked me to speak with her GP, which I did, relaying my observations, and recommendations for more pain relief and sedation. She welcomed the conversation, and agreed to act. As Tom describes, Marie became more relaxed and peaceful, and died not long after of an untreated (but palliated) chest infection.

The big question is this: Is Marie and Tom's experience with dementia exceptional?

In December 2010, journalist Clare Halliday wrote in *The Weekly Review* about two families in which the husband suffered early-onset Alzheimer's disease:

> 'One of Garry's greatest fears is wondering what's going to happen to him,' says Mandy. 'It's one of my fears too. Will I get to the point where I have to relinquish care of my husband? That does my head in, thinking about it.'
>
> Garry (47) is scared, he says, matter of factly. 'I get really scared. It keeps me awake at night. Sometimes I'm just in bed, staring at the ceiling, and this voice in the dark will say, 'I know you're awake'. And it's her [...] and I won't answer. I try to breathe slower, quiet.'
>
> Mandy knows because it keeps her awake, too, sometimes grappling with her own fear that comes from a different perspective – watching someone you love disappear. 'It's such a treacherous, revolting thing that robs you of the person's very existence' she says.
>
> Trevor was diagnosed at 57. Today, at 62, the progression has robbed him of his memory and his ability to engage in meaningful conversation. 'Communication is his biggest enemy' says Sandra. The strain on Sandra is obvious, despite her stoic exterior. She is unable to leave her husband alone without respite care. What she misses most is intellectual stimulation – those endless conversations the pair would have.

In 2001, Dr Joan Teno and colleagues reported the results of a nationwide US study on pain in nursing home residents. They found that 14.7 per cent of nursing home residents, on two consecutive assessments, were in persistent pain, and that 41.2 per cent of residents in pain at the first assessment were in severe pain 60–180 days later. They believed that their results underestimated the true burden experienced by nursing home residents, because the data were reported by nursing staff rather than by patients. They concluded that untreated pain resulted in impaired mobility, depression, and diminished quality of life.

In 2000, Drs Morrison and Siu, reporting in the *Journal of Pain and Symptom Management* on hip fractures, found that advanced dementia patients received one-third the amount of morphine (or equivalent) received by cognitively intact patients with the same injury. This was in addition to the evidence that the cognitively intact patients themselves were under-treated: 44 per cent of the latter individuals reported severe to very severe pain pre-operatively, and 42 per cent reported similar pain post-operatively.

In 2003, Paolo Manfredi reported in the *Journal of Pain and Symptom Management* on clinicians' observations of pain during dressing changes for ulcers. Such changes have long been known to cause significant pain in cognitive patients. He assumed that such changes would be capable of causing pain to severely demented patients. On making careful observations, he found that facial expressions and vocalisations were indeed an accurate means of assessing the presence of pain in such patients, but not necessarily an indicator of pain intensity in patients unable to communicate verbally because of advanced dementia.

In 2007, the Mayo Clinic reported that in the United States the Alzheimer's Association Ethics Advisory Panel suggested that efforts to prolong life in the advanced stage of Alzheimer's result in unnecessary suffering for people who could otherwise reach the end of their lives in relative comfort and peace. In the ethics panel's view, antibiotics given to treat infections are considered life-extension efforts. So are invasive technologies such as cardio-pulmonary resuscitation, dialysis and tube-feeding. At the other extreme, people with end-stage Alzheimer's often receive too little pain medication because they can no longer communicate the fact that they are in pain. A sudden increase in disruptive behaviour, such as shouting and striking out at caregivers, may be a sign of inadequate pain control.

There is thus, both from a research and an experiential aspect, evidence that persons with dementia suffer significantly, from the moment of diagnosis to the end stage and until death. The early suffering is predominantly psychological and existential, is recognisable and can be described by the sufferer. It is exceedingly difficult to palliate. In the late stage, relievable but unrecognised physical suffering is regrettably very common, but in addition quality of life is negligible in most people's estimation. It would not be surprising that some people in early dementia would find that their 'time to die' had arrived, nor that many more in that late stage would agree, if only they could say so.

Dementia is a terminal illness without any cure. Surely it is reasonable to say that by the time they could no longer recognise their close family, no longer communicate and no longer feed themselves these people had reached a completed life. If we know that this outcome is predictable and certain, should we not inform them in a sensitive way, and give them an opportunity to have some control over that outcome? This is not an easy discussion, but the early preparation of an advance care directive to prevent the unnecessary and unwanted prolongation of suffering is the most important measure that can be taken, and these people deserve that protection.

CHAPTER 6

Dementia: The whole catastrophe

The worst journey in the world

From time to time in my urological career I was asked to consult about a person in a nursing home with dementia-associated incontinence. Essentially there was no effective treatment other than diligent nursing and incontinence pads or catheters. The person would usually be sitting in a chair, the conversation very one-sided, as they had little to say. In this stage of their moderate dementia they can still communicate in response, but rarely communicate spontaneously or express an opinion. Specific urological diagnosis was impossible due to lack of symptom description.

Walking through the high-care unit, I would see others sitting quietly in their chairs, or I might come across a person shuffling, mute, along a corridor, and see them again shuffling along the same course as I left. The staff assured me they were not suffering, and it was possible to believe them, as I did not see those who were confined to their rooms by immobility – until I met 'BWV'.

In June 2002 I received a counselling request from a man whose wife (known as BWV) had suffered from an uncommon form of dementia known as Pick's disease. I described her story in some detail in chapter 10 of *A Good Death*. BWV's dementia had progressed slowly over 15 years. After eight years she lost the ability to swallow. She was still mobile and living at home and having some quality of life, so a PEG tube was placed (requiring a surgical procedure), but her disease progressed and she had to be moved to a nursing home.

There BWV entered a vegetative state (mute and immobile) with significant distress. Her husband and family wanted the tube-feeding to cease, as they were all convinced that was her wish in those circumstances. I talked at length to her husband, and then visited BWV in her institution, and found her to be in a vegetative state with obvious and considerable suffering and pain. Every few minutes she would grimace, go red in the face, and groan.

I found her tube-feeding to be futile, and simply prolonging her suffering. Her husband and I approached the home management and her doctor, seeking to have tube-feeding ceased, but they refused as, at that time, it was not clear whether this could be done legally. I believed that the PEG was unwanted medical treatment and could be refused, but, despite my intervention, it remained. I advised BWV's husband to take the matter to the Public Advocate.

After confirmation of my view by the Victorian Civil and Administrative Tribunal, and a judicial decision from Justice Morris in the Supreme Court, it was established that PEG tubes were medical treatment and could be refused or removed. BWV died a short while later in palliative care. PEG tubes are now used infrequently in dementia aged care.

In 2002 I began holding workshops for members of Dying With Dignity Victoria (DWDV) regarding end-of-life matters: medical enduring powers of attorney, advance care directives, the law, palliative care, and negotiating with the medical profession. These were interactive sessions, and it soon became apparent that dementia was a condition that caused great anxiety to our members and to the public generally. As a result I did extensive research into dementia, and developed a specific workshop and advance care directive for dementia. Ultimately it became obvious that dementia was the most important condition for which one needs an advance care directive (ACD): a written statement of explicit directions for treatment if one has lost the ability to communicate – one of the symptoms of dementia that almost inevitably occurs.

From 1992 I had been providing counselling about end-of-life matters to DWDV members and the general public. A proportion of these requests (about 7 per cent) were from people with early dementia, or the relatives of people with advanced dementia. Two experiences involving advanced dementia made a huge impression on me. The first was BWV and the second was Mrs V (Marie Valenta), described in chapter 5.

With Marie Valenta, I was again involved at the request of a very concerned husband. Tom Valenta had been closely associated with Alzheimer's Australia (Victoria) (now Dementia Australia, with an office in each state), and I joined this organisation and had discussions with the executive staff, and attended some of its meetings and conferences. I was aware of the statement by the US Alzheimer's Association Ethics Advisory Panel that 'efforts to prolong life in the advanced stage of Alzheimer's result in unnecessary suffering for people who could otherwise reach the end of their lives in relative comfort and peace'.

The notice for the 2012 annual general meeting of Alzheimer's Australia (Victoria) asked for questions for discussion. I suggested that advance care directives be developed and promoted. To my surprise, this was taken as a motion, and I was given five minutes to present a case. Before any debate began, the president announced that the board did not approve of the motion. I pointed out that Alzheimer's Australia (at the national level) had in 2006 commissioned a research paper that recommended 'the use of formal advance directives as soon as possible after diagnosis', and that a further commission from ethicist and academic Emeritus Professor Colleen Cartwright of Southern Cross University advocated for advance directives. I quoted Professor Cartwright who, in her role as chairperson of the association's ethics committee, said, 'I felt there was a lot of emphasis on the early and middle stages of dementia but little information on the late stages of dementia especially dying. People diagnosed with dementia cannot exercise their rights if they do not understand what those rights are.' Despite the president's comments (unethical, in my view), the meeting voted 50 per cent in favour of my 'motion'. But no action followed, as it needed 75 per cent of votes to be adopted.

Even to this day it is extremely difficult to find a useful advance directive on this organisation's website.

Stephen G. Post, professor of biomedical ethics, published the second edition of his acclaimed book *The Moral Challenge of Alzheimer Disease* in 2000. He began by stating:

Seldom does human experience require more courage than in living with the diagnosis and gradual decline of irreversible progressive dementia. [...] It is easy to understand why many fear dementia as much, or even

> more, than cancer, for with cancer self-identity is not at stake and physi-
> cal pain can in most instances be controlled without compromising
> mental lucidity. A person with cancer will retain his or her autobiog-
> raphy, or life story, and the sense of temporal continuity between the
> past, the present and the future, but the person with AD [Alzheimer's
> disease] will eventually outlive much of his or her brain. The progressive
> destruction of the brain before the destruction of the body is a more
> vexing social, ethical and economic issue than death itself.

Frankly, I was astonished that he did not include 'personal' in his last sentence
as the most important issue; in an otherwise excellent academic review, the
personal view of the Alzheimer's sufferer is little in evidence. I am astonished
because, caring for my wife with advanced dementia, I am aware of her daily
vocal indications of personal psychic disturbance.

Professor Post is a strong advocate of ACDs, and the appointment of sur-
rogate decision makers ('medical treatment decision makers' in Victoria), and
supported Professor Ronald Dworkin, who maintained that an ACD made by a
competent person should not be overridden if they became incompetent, as 'his
former decision remains in force because no new decision by a person capable
of autonomy has annulled it', and strongly opposed futile interventions that prolong dying and prevent natural death.

On this basis, Post also strongly opposes artificial nutrition and hydration.
He observes that 'one walks through a dementia unit and sees a person with
advanced AD staring blankly into space, seemingly unresponsive, and able to
slowly eat only with the intense assistance of an aide for the better part of an
hour'. Here he is clearly describing the laborious process of assisted spoon-
feeding – a form of forced feeding, in my opinion. Despite this observation,
and his opposition to artificial hydration and nutrition and futile treatment, he
makes no comment on assisted spoon-feeding. Curious: perhaps 2000 was too
early to expect him to criticise standard practice, despite recognising its futility
(and perhaps harm).

The sum total of all this experience has led me to describe dementia as 'the
worst disease known to man', a phrase suggested by Apsley Cherry-Garrard's

title – *The Worst Journey in the World* – for his winter journey in the Antarctic in 1911 to collect emperor penguin eggs, during Scott's second expedition. One could easily apply this title to the dementia journey.

It also led me to the conclusion that the only possible legal assistance for someone who had lost mental competence due to dementia was a watertight advance care directive, which I set about developing. It had to be a directive that would allow natural dying in dementia, and prevent the use of life-prolonging treatments, which ultimately were simply prolonging suffering in the advanced, usually vegetative, state.

In 1906, Alois Alzheimer described the pathology in the brain of the condition that bears his name. He described tangles of nerve fibres and plaques of the protein amyloid, together with brain atrophy, the combination producing progressive loss of cognitive function, ultimately resulting in a vegetative state. This is the commonest type of dementia (60 per cent of cases), followed by vascular dementia, where small blood vessel blockages lead to sudden brain cell death with loss of cognitive functions, and often shows episodic progress. Alzheimer's and vascular conditions are often mixed. The cause of Alzheimer's is unknown, although there may be some genetic factors associated with early-onset disease. At least 100 causes or types of dementia are described.

Alzheimer's dementia (AD) is now described in seven stages:

- asymptomatic – diagnosed on a brain scan
- very mild memory loss, which is called mild cognitive impairment – exceedingly common in older people, and may not progress
- mild decline – increasing memory loss, forgetting names and places, losing things, word loss, poor planning and critical thinking
- moderate decline – forgetting the day, month and time; loss of the ability to do simple maths, and attend to financial matters; loss of cooking skills, and cooking may become dangerous – leaving this person alone becomes problematic
- a moderately severe stage, with confusion, problems with dressing, repetition of speech and thought, and problems with personal hygiene – dependence is now severe, and the individual cannot be left alone

- a severe stage – wandering, personality change, behavioural problems, loss of recognition of objects and people, incontinence of bowel and bladder, and lack of interest in food or inability to eat
- finally, a catastrophic vegetative state, where effective contact and engagement with one's surroundings are lost.

These stages are not exact; they blend into one another, and can vary from person to person, depending on the most affected areas of the brain.

However one looks at it, the final stage of immobility, double incontinence, inability to communicate and being spoon-fed closely resembles an infantile state, or Shakespeare's 'last stage of man'. This is not what I want. Do you?

Dementia is a terminal illness with no effective treatment. Henry Brodaty and Glenn Rees of Alzheimer's Australia stated in 2011 that 'the promise of a cure has now been a tantalising "five years away" for more than 15 years [now more than 27 years]. We have neither found a cure for AD nor a way to slow down the disease.' Louise Waite stated in 2015 (*Australian Prescriber*) that 'current therapies for AD do not modify the course of the disease and are not universally beneficial. Clinical trials of drugs targeting amyloid and tau in established AD have been unsuccessful, as it is thought that treating the established disease may be too late.'

Professor Constantine Lyketsos, an eminent authority on dementia and guest speaker for Alzheimer Australia's annual conference in 2009, described the disease with this succinct summary:

Dementia is a clinical syndrome used to describe the symptoms of a large group of conditions that result in a progressive decline [in] cognition. People associate dementia with loss of memory, but there are many other consequences, including decline in reasoning, communication skills and the capacity to organise daily life.

[...] At some time every individual with dementia will experience depression, psychosis, aggression, apathy, or wandering.

Dementia is usually preceded, sometimes over years, by mild memory loss or confusion but without affecting daily life in a major way.

These precursor symptoms are known as mild cognitive impairment or MCI.

[...] In the terminal stage which can last months, sometimes years, the patient is bed bound, non-verbal and totally dependent on others. Dementia accelerates death through debilitation, by making the victim vulnerable to infection, aspiration and damaging falls, or through wasting away.

[...] The carers of people with dementia become isolated from their personal and social networks because they spend almost all their time supervising or caring, with precious few moments alone. Research has repeatedly shown that caring for someone with dementia is unlike any other carer experience.

Dementia care is more physically and emotionally overwhelming and as a consequence, it is more damaging to the carer's health.

Dr E. Campion, in a *New England Journal of Medicine* editorial in 1996 – 'When a mind dies' – stated: 'People dread both the indignities of dementia and becoming a burden on others.' An editorial in *The Lancet* (2008) titled 'This unremembered state' declared, 'Dementia is perhaps the cruellest manifestation of ageing, inexorably melting away all that which makes us individual and human.' A carer's story is relevant here:

My mother-in-law came to live with my wife and me in February 2014, a few weeks before she turned 88. She is now 92. She'd had a heart attack in 2009, and had had four stents inserted. When she arrived, she was stressed, anxious and confused. After coming to us, she was diagnosed with vascular dementia and a CT scan indicated she'd had a stroke at some point in the past. In the second half of 2015 she had a series of TIAs [transient ischaemic attack – when blood cannot get to all parts of the brain for a short time] and in February 2016 she suffered a stroke that left her without speech and paralysed on the right side. She was moved to a residential care home.

Since then her condition has gradually deteriorated. My wife and I visit most days, usually to give her dinner. Most times she is asleep. Her only deliberate behaviour is to eat. Often now she eats without opening her eyes. When she does wake, she shows little awareness of our presence and no recognition.

Sometimes – less often now than before – she becomes agitated, her legs scissoring, her hands plucking at the bedding, her face contorted, tears in her eyes. We are sure that if she could, she would cry out. Several times in the early days, she threw herself out of her bed.

She is on a range of medication: an opioid patch, paracetamol, daily doses of antidepressant and anti-anxiety medication. She has been seen by a pain specialist, a geriatric psychiatrist and a clinical psychologist, as well as being visited by her GP. Her medication has been periodically changed in an attempt to improve her wellbeing. Yet she still becomes agitated and distressed – cerebral irritation, the clinical psychologist told us. When she is agitated, she is given an abdominal subcutaneous injection of midazolam. But this takes up to an hour to calm her; increasingly, the injection is now being given preemptively.

When Margaret went into the nursing home, a palliative care nurse assured us her suffering could be alleviated, but over two years later, this has yet to happen. The nurse ruled out increasing Mary's sedation because of the risk of causing her death. We want to give her the best possible quality of life, the nurse said at one case conference. But she has no quality of life; she just exists – somewhere between life and death.

We look at her when she is agitated and think: surely we (as a society) can do better than this? It is not a humane way to treat the elderly as the end of life approaches.

Thirty years ago, Robert Gray wrote 'The carer's view', published in *The Lancet*:

Despair is the great temptation for families with a member stricken by Alzheimer's. There may be good days and bad days, but the overall prognosis is one of irreversible decline into mental and physical incapacity, with every likelihood of delusions, paranoia and aggression en route. Those who voluntarily or involuntarily find themselves responsible for care will be obliged to devote their lives to tasks at once ungrateful, unrewarding, patience-sapping, and time-consuming.

'Your patient will get worse no matter what you do or how well you do it.' This only serves to emphasise the horror of the malady.

Has anything changed since 1988? Journalist David Campbell expressed his view in 'Dementia takes the choice out of death decisions' (*The Age*, January 2016):

I watched as dementia steadily destroyed my mother's quality of life in the two years before she died. […] I can't forget what I saw and heard when visiting my mother in a high-care nursing home. It was a nightmare, a shelter for the living dead. The manner of dying casts a long shadow over the living.

[…] Don't talk to me about palliative care as if it is some sort of all-powerful miracle procedure that will automatically make life bearable in extreme situations. It didn't work for my mother. All it did was prolong her distress.

How do you fight a ghost – a pitiless, relentless, insidious ghost? Something you can't see because it cripples your capacity to understand what is happening. It's a horrifying thought.

Dr Arthur Harrison, a psychogeriatrician, had this to say in *Australian Medicine* (3 June 1996):

My concern is particularly for the welfare and quality of life of patients suffering from progressive, advanced dementia, and for their relatives and friends. Over many years I have repeatedly heard relatives and nurses express their pleasure and relief when such a patient has died comfortably, and the implication of such statements has been that an earlier comfortable death would have been preferable. A profoundly demented patient, who has lost the ability to recognise members of his/her family, is totally dependent, and incontinent of bowels and bladder is a sorry caricature of a once independent responsible citizen.

Such a citizen was Alfred Deakin 1856–1919), three times prime minister of Australia, who from the age of 48 was battling insomnia and failing memory. Six years before he died of dementia he wrote:

> To live among the scores of books one has forgotten, after a public career that now remains wrapped in clouds [...] No banishment was ever so complete – no collapse could be ghastlier [...] A stranded mariner, in a deep sense a solitary, without a memory or the flow of speech that once ran always free and sometimes shot higher than I can now realise.

Later, physician and gerontologist Greg Sachs stated in the *New England Journal of Medicine* (2009) under the heading 'Dying from dementia':

> Now, some 30 years after my grandmother's death [from AD], end-of-life care for many patients with dementia doesn't look all that different from the treatment she received. Patients in nursing homes who have dementia are at risk of under-treatment of pain and for treatment with burdensome and possibly non-beneficial interventions, including tube feeding. They are also referred to hospice care at rates far lower than for patients dying of cancer.
>
> Yet patients with advanced AD had a median survival of 478 days. Very few patients had 'sentinel events', such as stroke, myocardial infarction, or hip fracture; rather, most patients died from infections, eating problems, aspiration of food into the lungs, and other conditions related to the underlying dementia. Palliative care is warranted in advanced AD because of the frequent occurrence of distressing symptoms of dyspnoea, pain and agitation.

In 2004, Susan Mitchell and colleagues, in a paper titled 'Dying with advanced dementia in the nursing home', recorded that only 1.1 per cent of people admitted to a nursing home with advanced dementia were perceived to have a life expectancy of less than six months; however, 71 per cent died within that period.

In addition, residents with dementia were less likely to have directives limiting care, but were more likely to experience burdensome interventions. They reported distressing conditions common in advanced dementia that included pressure ulcers (14.7 per cent), constipation (13.7 per cent), pain (11.5 per cent), and shortness of breath (8.2 per cent). They concluded that nursing home residents dying with advanced dementia are not perceived as having a terminal condition, and most do not receive optimal palliative care.

Once the late immobile stage develops, lack of movement leads to muscle contractures and fixation of joints – extremely painful when washing, dressing or turning, and where any movements are required. Mrs V demonstrated that in spades. It is commonly unrecognised, but can be diminished by pre-emptive pain administration – if anyone could be bothered in the current circumstances. This requires more thoughtful work from an overworked and unskilled staff, who are not trained to recognise or report such events. Given that more than half of residents in aged care have dementia, it is tragic to learn from the chief executive officer of Alzheimer's Australia, Maree McCabe, that 70 per cent of training for aged-care workers does not contain mandatory or even optional training in dementia.

Michael Bachelard's report in *The Age* (21 September 2017) bears this out. He tells the story of Dawn Weston. She was 83 when she died after two-and-a-half years in a Christian not-for-profit aged-care home, suffering from dementia, during which time she lost 24 kilograms (one-third of her entire body weight) and developed pressure ulcers on her left heel and sacrum – which caused her death. In the year Dawn died, her Christian not-for-profit aged-care provider made a surplus of $14.5 million.

Her daughter Kaye noted that towards the end 'her personality had changed, she used to smile but she wasn't smiling any more', and she was rubbing her left leg and crying. She was not able to speak. It was clear that Dawn was in the late vegetative stage of dementia, but Kaye thought that the home had 'deliberately covered up the seriousness of her injury', and she finally realised that her mother had been in 'horrific pain' from her heel. She complained to the Aged Care Complaints Commissioner (something more relatives should do before their loved one dies), who 'expressed serious concerns about the treatment of her pressure sores' and that the home had taken 'minimal actions' to address Dawn's weight loss. Kaye, a year after her mother died, remains bitterly angry and stressed. She said, 'I'd rather euthanase myself than enter aged care.'

Dawn developed a bedsore, a theoretically preventable complication with optimal care, and which causes significant unrecognised pain in people who cannot communicate their pain except through facial expression. Changes of dressings of bedsores are painful for competent people – equally so for those with dementia, but it is commonly not acted on.

Many reports emphasise that dementia patients in nursing homes suffer unrecognised and unrelieved pain, and the serious lack of palliative-care advice and action. Pain in dementia was discussed in the *Journal of Pain and Symptom Management* in 1999 by Kovach and colleagues. They stated that 'people with dementia have often been excluded from pain studies. There is evidence that people with dementia experience frequent pain, often poorly assessed and under-treated, and that the aetiology for pain descriptions is poorly documented.' In 2011, Ballard (*International Journal of Palliative Nursing*) acknowledged that unrelieved pain could cause agitation, distress and aggression – often treated with antipsychotics.

Good language and cognitive skills are needed for the vast majority of pain-assessment tools, hence the exclusion of dementia patients. A 2018 report of British research (published in *Age and Ageing*) found that more than one-third of hospital-bound dementia patients are suffering in silence because they are unable to communicate their pain. Their condition is often under-diagnosed and under-treated. Researchers found that almost half (49 per cent) of the patients studied were suffering from pain at rest, and delirium developed in 15 per cent.

Sandra Zwakhalen et al. reported in 2006 that pain among nursing home patients is a common and major problem. The prevalence of pain in elderly nursing home residents is 40–80 per cent. Dementia causes serious and unique barriers to pain assessment. Symptoms attributed to dementia may actually be an indication of pain. They summarised that there is evidence that pain assessment is currently inadequate and that elderly people with dementia are being under-treated. A number of assessment tools were analysed.

The Abbey Pain Scale is highly regarded. This scale describes signs of possible pain or serious distress as restlessness, rubbing, vocal 'complaints', facial expression such as grimacing, aggression, altered sleep patterns, sweating, and protection from interference. Its authors stress that relatives' reports of such behaviours should be encouraged, and not ignored. Yet when I and a relative complained of unrelieved pain evidenced by facial grimacing in an end-stage dementia patient, we were told that a nurse who had been trained in palliative care was using the Abbey Pain Scale, and that grimacing was not an indication of pain!

Alzheimer's Australia (NSW) chief executive officer Lewis Kaplan stated (in 2007) that 150,000 Australians were suffering from moderate to severe dementia. He was concerned for people taking on the burden of caring. Of the national dementia toll, only 46,000 people find places in nursing homes, where they make up 60 per cent of the 77,000 residents. 'There are high levels of psychological distress among [family] carers – a lot of depression, they are socially isolated, their quality of life drops, there is financial hardship.' The current focus on nursing home care is demonstrating that many nursing homes are outdated, ill-suited and inadequately staffed to cater for dementia patients.

'When you are diagnosed with dementia, there's always a secondary patient, the carer', said the professor of psychogeriatrics at the University of New South Wales. A 2015 article in *The Age* by health editor Amy Corderoy was poignant: 'One in 10 dementia carers think about killing a loved one: study'. The author quoted 'Sandra', who said, after nearly 15 years of caring for her father at home: 'It's tiring, it's exhausting, it's never-ending. It just got to the point that I was just thinking it would be much easier if it was all over'. A study by Griffith University's Menzies Health Institute, published in *Ageing and Mental Health* (2016), found that almost 20 per cent of carers had verbally or physically abused the person they were caring for, while the same number had wished their family member dead. Another two of the group's 21 participants had actively thought about how they might kill their loved one. Carers are secondary victims of the disease.

Even more concerning was the report from Griffith University (*International Journal of Geriatric Psychiatry*, 2013) which found that an 'alarming' one-quarter of people caring for a family member with dementia have contemplated suicide. The study showed that carers with suicidal ideation reported more behavioural and psychological symptoms in the person with dementia, and one-third of the group had been caring for more than five years.

What can we expect of carers? I am now the carer of my wife, who is in the moderately severe stage of Alzheimer's. It is a full-time occupation, in the sense that I cannot leave her alone. Although I can spend time writing this book, there are constant interruptions for trivial assistance – I am immediately available if she has a need. Fortunately, I am retired and still physically and mentally active. Intelligent conversation with her is gone. My patience and tolerance are constantly tested. I constantly provide her with love and support. She recognises this and is most appreciative. Our personal bond saves her from despair. But could I realistically expect the same level of care for her in an aged-care environment, from a constantly changing team of poorly trained staff who do not know my wife and owe her no emotional allegiance? After all, they are doing a paid job of hard work, are poorly paid for it, and their team is commonly under-staffed for the task. It is probably unrealistic to expect impeccable care in institutions; we should be careful not to blame those at the coal-face if our expectations are not met.

Let us not forget the difficulties faced by professional carers. After a three-year survey, reported in 2004, one chain of nursing homes in Victoria found that 80 per cent of care staff reported that they were assaulted daily by residents (*The Age*, 1 March 2004). The report found that:

> The care of those with dementia is particularly specialised and complex. Some of the triggers for their behaviours can actually be the staff themselves, the way that the staff approach them and the environment we accommodate people in. It doesn't take much for mild agitation to escalate and unless staff are perceptive, they're not necessarily able to put in place preventative measures to stop agitation escalating.

It requires considerable psychological skills to recognise and respond appropriately to such situations. That was 2004 – we have just heard from the royal commission in 2019 that Certificate 3 aged carers do not receive any training in dementia behaviour.

Dementia is now cited as the second-commonest cause of death in Australia. This is astonishing, because dementia as such does not kill people; it is the complications of dementia that kill people. As mentioned above, it is principally infections of the chest (often aspiration pneumonia), or of the blood (septicaemia) from bedsores or kidneys, complications of falls and fractures, and malnutrition (which diminishes the immune system's resistance to infection) due to loss of interest in food or inability to swallow. Very intensive medical intervention and very high level nursing can prolong life in end-stage dementia, by preventing or treating these complications. But these are the natural ways in which people with dementia die; should they be prevented, or should natural dying be allowed? Shouldn't the sufferer be encouraged to have a say through an advance care directive?

Such interventions are now being seriously challenged as futile and unethical. Tube-feeding, introduced in the 1980s because it was considered to be more efficient and save carers' time, has now been largely abandoned in Australia. Its alternative, hand-feeding (spoon-feeding), is, however, common as a consequence. This is very time-consuming, inefficient, and eventually leads to malnutrition, despite any specialist nutritional advice.

In 2013 Alzheimer's Australia commissioned a report by a highly regarded Australian expert in dementia nursing, Professor Jennifer Abbey, titled *Wrestling with Dementia and Death*. Professor Abbey stated:

> When a person begins to refuse food and fluids it is often a sign that the death process has begun, and anorexia [loss of appetite] is very common in people with late-stage dementia. Lack of energy, dysphagia [difficulty in swallowing] or nausea can all lead to lack of desire for nutrition and hydration. The absence of nutrition leads to isotonic dehydration: the loss of salt and water from the body. Whilst potentially distressing for the families and health professionals, the evidence indicates that death by terminal dehydration is not painful and that attendant physical discomfort can be adequately alleviated.
>
> [...] Dysphagia is common in nursing home residents. [...] It is recommended that making an order for '*nil by mouth*' for people with

dementia with suspected dysphagia is the strongest measure that can be taken to prevent choking and pulmonary aspiration. Again, this is hard for families to cope with, but a much more comfortable death will be achieved through dehydration than through death with fluid in the lungs which results in choking. Throughout this period mouth care is the most appropriate comfort measure that can be supplied.

To paraphrase Professor Abbey, refusal of fluids and food is a natural way of dying in dementia, but it is clear that excellent communication is necessary with all the parties involved. I will discuss the argument about spoon-feeding in a later chapter.

William Osler, the doyen of physicians at the turn of the 20th century, stated in 1898 that 'pneumonia may well be called the friend of the aged. Taken off by it in an acute, short, not often painful illness, the old man escapes those "cold gradations of decay".' Any distressing symptoms of the disease were humanely dealt with by the doctors of his day (this would now be called palliation). The advent of antibiotics in the 20th century gave doctors the ability to defeat pneumonia – a wonderful result for most people, but ultimately understood to be a questionable benefit for those with end-stage dementia. The predominant form of pneumonia at that time was due to pneumococcal infection; even before antibiotics, people would either die after four or five days (usually in the elderly), or survive.

Unfortunately for Osler, 20 years later he developed pneumonia following influenza, complicated by pleurisy and pus in the pleural cavity surrounding the lung; he died a lingering and painful death after two months in bed. He said, 'I have been having a devil of a time', and found the only thing 'of any service whatever in checking the cough have been opiates', but apparently even he could not get enough for effective palliation. This was despite the fact that he had 20 years earlier stated that it was a doctor's duty to 'ease death'.

Pneumonia is the ultimate cause of death in 33–71 per cent of nursing home patients. In death from pneumonia, discomfort was an average 2.6 points higher on a 28-point scale than in death from other causes. However, that doesn't have to be so – better palliation would prevent this.

Jenny van der Steen et al. in 2002 studied non-use of antibiotics. They found:

The high discomfort levels and lack of association between decrease in discomfort and symptomatic treatment found in our study poses questions about the effectiveness of treatment initiated for symptom relief. [...] Although breathing difficulties were common, which is not surprising, many patients did not receive treatment to relieve this symptom. Moreover, treatment of symptoms did not seem to lead to an immediate decrease in discomfort. Therefore, symptomatic treatment may not have been adequate in quality or in quantity.

Six years later (in 2009), van der Steen and colleagues found:

Mean survival time of those who died [without intervention] was 4.0 days for pneumonia patients, and 4.9 for patients with food and fluid intake problems. Two week mortality among patients receiving antibiotics was 23.5%, while for those not receiving antibiotics it was 87.1%. Clearly antibiotics prolonged life. Invasive rehydration for intake problems or pneumonia was associated with more discomfort shortly before death.

Erika D'Agata and Susan L. Mitchell criticised this futile and somewhat abusive treatment in 2008. They found that 'Persons with advanced dementia are frequently exposed to antimicrobials especially during the 2 weeks before death', and that, in some nursing homes, 'antimicrobials are the most frequently prescribed pharmaceutical agents'. They continued:

The two purported reasons to administer antimicrobials are life prolongation and symptom control. Limited observational studies have failed to demonstrate that antimicrobial treatment achieves either outcome in this frail population [...] The extensive use of antimicrobials [...] in advanced dementia raises concerns not only with respect to individual treatment burdens near the end of life, but also with respect to the development and spread of antimicrobial resistance in the nursing home setting.

They concluded that the administration of antimicrobials to frail older patients who are near the end of life is also a potentially burdensome intervention.

An editorial related to this article concluded: 'If antibiotics are not required to restore comfort (either because the patient is in no distress or because palliation can be achieved by other means) and cannot be expected to enhance duration or quality of life, might not their use be considered futile?'

My last close association with an end-stage dementia patient was with Susan De Ravin. I visited her in a well-regarded nursing home on several occasions at the request of her son. She was in end-stage dementia, the vegetative state. As Julia Medew wrote in 2014: 'If it were not for some occasional snores, Sue De Ravin could be dead. The thin woman is lying motionless in a chair with her arms crossed over her chest. Her mouth is resting wide open. Inside, all but a couple of teeth are missing.' She was completely mute and immobile. Her day consisted of being hoisted mechanically out of bed in the morning into her wheelchair where she remained all day in a community room. During this time she uttered no word, and was spoon-fed her meals. She was then returned to her room, and again hoisted mechanically back into her bed. It caused her obvious pain on one occasion I observed. I asked her two carers if they were aware that she was in pain, and they acknowledged that they realised that she was. Asked why no action was taken to prevent that pain, they shrugged their shoulders – either it did not occur to them to report it, or no prophylactic pain relief was ordered. Requests by her son for more effective management on my advice brought improvement. As it was, she died soon after.

At the beginning of this chapter I said I was assured by nursing staff in aged care that their residents, passive though they seemed, were not suffering. At this point in my journey with dementia I believe this is utterly false, a fiction without foundation, and constructed to make dementia patients, relatives and the community less concerned in the face of medical impotence. There is no doubt that people with early dementia express great concern and fear at the diagnosis. Alzheimer's Australia (now Dementia Australia) brochures show smiling patients and family members; they are designed to minimise the fear and stigma of the disease and encourage people to seek support and information. Fair enough, I support that, but it encourages the fiction, instead of educating these people about their future and assisting them in preparations such as appointing medical treatment decision makers and creating advance care directives while still competent. When incompetence sets in, it is too late for these important tasks.

In the middle stages of the disease, sufferers may appear calm, and probably have no physical symptoms of the disease. But can we assume, because they make no complaint, that they are at ease? Certainly not – how can I say this? Linda Clare and colleagues in 2008 undertook an interpretative phenomenological analysis of dementia patients in care who could still communicate. They found that 'the subjective psychological experience of people with moderate to severe dementia living in residential care is insufficiently understood', and that:

> The experience of living with dementia in residential care was fundamentally one of experiencing difficult and distressing emotions relating to loss, isolation, uncertainty, fear, and a sense of worthlessness. Participants generally tried to cope by accepting and making the best of things and affirming their past sense of self and identity, but some also expressed frustration and anger.

Moreover, I can say this because my beloved wife of 56 years is in this stage of the disease. She was firmly diagnosed two years ago, but I noted the earliest symptoms at least two years before that. She has an apparently happy demeanour and rarely complains, but I can observe her distress at her loss of executive functions (cooking; making a cup of tea or coffee; remembering the correct place for cups, dishes, cutlery – even where the fridge is). She has become socially reclusive (except with family) because of embarrassment in company regarding her understanding of conversation and making appropriate responses. On occasions when my patience has failed, and I have been unkind to her out of frustration, a gentle exploration uncovers a distress at being ignored or discounted. More than that, as time goes on, there are subtle intimations of purpose and mortality.

Competence may be gone, but an ability to express feeling and emotion has not disappeared, if one is close enough to listen and hear.

Dr Janey wrote of her mother's dementia journey in *The Age* (12 November 2014). She remembered the pain of watching her mother trying to paint in her studio: 'It was tragic, she would just stare vacantly because she had forgotten how to mix paints. [...] On days when she had insight, that was incredibly distressing for her.' My wife too was a brilliant artist: she painted, sculpted in ceramics and stone, created in glass, and finally drew with textured pencils. Her creative imagination was outstanding – now it is gone. Strangely, I think I feel this loss more than she does, such is the vacancy of her mind.

As I write, I am listening to Purcell's 'Dido's Lament' (*Remember me*), which brings tears to my eyes as I remember my partner in her previous wonderful creative life.

Thus far I have been fortunate. Ultimately, as my wife enters the later stages I fear the onset of aggression and psychosis, fear and depression, and ultimately the loss of the little sensible communication she has now. In this late stage, because sufferers cannot complain, or do not complain because of the antipsychotic medication they are on, it has been assumed that there is no suffering. Do not psychosis, anxiety and depression indicate severe suffering in the mind?

In the last stage – akin to a vegetative state, where the face can grimace, and small amounts of food or fluid put in the mouth may be swallowed – the person may groan or cry out, but they utter no words and make no spontaneous movement. This suffering is denied by some, but is evident if you know what to look for. The discomfort scale for late-stage Alzheimer's lists noisy breathing, negative vocalisation, sad facial expression, frightened facial expression (grimacing), frown, tense body language, and fidgeting (restlessness). Positive signs of contentment are content facial expression and relaxed body language.

Professor Jenny Abbey stated in her 2013 report:

Pain is often not recognised in people with dementia. An accurate diagnosis of pain is notoriously difficult for a population where individuals cannot tell you when, whether, where, why or how much they are hurting. [...] The core principle behind good pharmacological pain management is to use analgesics regularly, not just as required. The lowest dose possible that provides pain-free comfort should be prescribed.

Essentially, she is recommending pre-empting pain when there is a potential persistent cause present.

One final story sums up much of this chapter:

My husband died in September after weeks of hell. He was brain damaged in a car accident years earlier and was diagnosed with dementia in 2003 and entered a nursing home five years ago. The first was dirty. He had an old army bed, a worn lino floor, no window, a dirty painted cupboard and no private bathroom for which I was to be charged $1000 a week. He was very distressed. I removed him after two days and found the private owners had deducted $2500 from my bank account three weeks after he left. They said it was 'too late' to refund it. I went to the Ombudsman and had the money refunded two days later.

The second nursing home looked better. I was told that my husband could use the garden, feed the birds, use the cafe and the miniature gym (which he had used in day care). Then, I found that he was locked in and, from the pharmacy bill, I discovered that their GP had given my husband four different antipsychotic drugs to stop him from walking around. They succeeded. After being fully mobile, he was asleep in a circle of about 20 others around the TV from 9am onwards. The side effects included loss of balance, and sure enough he fell and fractured his hip and was hospitalised for two months. The drugs were labelled 'not to be prescribed for elderly patients with dementia because they hasten death'. My complaint to the GP received no response and I was told by the hospital social worker that the nursing home manager was fearful that I would sue them and was 'bad mouthing' me to ensure that other nursing homes wouldn't accept my husband.

He spent the next four years in a home which provided loving care but the dementia unit is locked like a jail and unless people have regular visitors, they never see the sun. Boredom was a huge problem and they sit sleeping in front of the TV or with their heads on the dining room table. Lots of life-skills workers were employed but they tended to work with residents elsewhere. I presume that it was more rewarding. When he could still talk, he would cry and say, 'I just want to die'.

In August, I received a phone call saying that my husband was in great pain. The nurse said when she touched his leg he screamed. I went immediately and realised that he also had pneumonia. A locum arrived 20 hours after being called (by which time I'd gone home). I asked staff to call me when he arrived, but they didn't and I returned to the home at 5 am. I found that staff mentioned the pneumonia to the GP but forgot to mention the painful leg. The next morning staff made my husband shower and change and asked me to leave to avoid hearing the screams. I insisted on the doctor being called again and once again the staff failed to mention the leg. Fortunately, I was present and called him back. He pulled back the sheet and said, 'What's wrong with you three (staff)? This is a classic case of a fractured hip. One leg is longer that the other and his foot is rotated. Get him to hospital'.

My husband had not been able to communicate for several years and was confined to a wheelchair.

The orthopaedic surgeon said that the fracture was so bad that he must have fallen and contrary to regulations, no-one had reported it.

Although I had medical power of attorney and my husband had a legal document saying no treatment if the quality of life was impaired, he had a hip replacement with a 30% chance of surviving four weeks. The alternative was to send him back to the same nursing home in great pain. He was treated for pneumonia, his swallowing was impeded and then the hospital decided to starve him. After three weeks, I drew the line when they wanted to feed him by tube. I was told that if I didn't agree I would have to go for counselling. I pleaded throughout that I didn't want him to suffer any more, but I was told that they have to keep patients alive because relatives might sue. He was then discharged back to the nursing home and died the next day. He was 84.

There were five hospital doctors assuring me that they would 'get him back to where he was', a geriatrician, orthopaedic surgeon, lung specialist, physician and urologist who didn't seem to communicate with each other. 'Where he was' was hell and had been for years.

In the nursing home there were others who were bed bound, asleep most of the time, unable to communicate or eat and staff also said, 'We have to keep them alive because the relatives might sue us if we don't'.

I pray that I never have to go into residential care!

This wife describes one home with appalling conditions and financial deception, and another with undiscussed chemical restraint causing severe complications, a prison-like restriction and regimentation, apparent failure to report a fall, inadequate relief of severe pain, not giving relevant information to an emergency doctor (twice), threats and bullying by hospital staff who were providing inaccurate advice regarding futile treatment. All this in circumstances where palliative pain relief and effective nursing were more appropriate than a hip replacement. Why didn't this happen? Because of fear that 'relatives might sue'. And all this abuse to a man who, despite his dementia, had been able to cry and say 'I just want to die' – a clear indication of a completed life. This poignant story substantiates Professor Abbey's advice to Alzheimer's Australia:

> Instead, the usual end-of-life care for a large number of people with dementia involves the removal from home to emergency hospitalisation, which may include unnecessary medical tests while pain and other symptoms are unrecognised and under-treated. In some cases, medical decisions are made by health professionals with little regard for the person's wishes or those of their family.

I hope that I have provided enough evidence to convince you that physical and psychic pain are common in this stage, but poorly diagnosed and managed. Why is this so? Two basic reasons stand out: first, staff are poorly trained to recognise such pain, and do not have the skills or the time to provide an appropriate psychological response (antipsychotic medication is much simpler); second, there is an underlying fear of complaint of hastening death if pain is adequately relieved, and of failure to communicate the reality of late-stage dementia. Good, sensitive communication can deal with these problems, but it takes time and skill.

When good communication occurs, care improves. When researchers looked more deeply into the reasons for treatment decisions, they discovered stark differences based on what family members knew about dementia. When relatives understood the disease's progressive and terminal nature, only 27 per cent of patients received aggressive care. For family members who did not understand the disease, the figure was 73 per cent. Geriatricians say a large part of the problem is that in the absence of an advance care directive, family members often struggle with guilt and are afraid to stop aggressive treatment, because they do not want to be seen to be abandoning a loved one in mental decline.

Nor can we plumb the depths of the demented mind. I was astounded by the story told by Hazel Hawke's daughter. In the very late stage of Hazel's Alzheimer's, which she bravely (and sensibly, in my opinion) made public, Bob Hawke was persuaded to visit her, and he kindly did. He sang songs to her that they had shared when they were in love. As he left, Hazel was heard to say, 'I still love you, Bob.' On another occasion, an Anglican vicar, who was a patient of mine, told me of one of his flock who was in a nursing home, non-verbal from Alzheimer's. The patient's wife, tragically, was in another nursing home. When she died, the vicar visited the husband, and held his hand as he told him of the loss. He was in no doubt that the apparently insensate man squeezed his hand, not once but twice in response to the news. I have had others tell me of similar experiences where a person with dementia, who had not communicated for weeks, suddenly exhibited recognition or comment.

We cannot assume or presume that there is no deep retained memory or understanding which might not be affected by pain. An analysis of suffering in dementia reveals four areas for consideration. They ebb and flow as the disease progresses. The predominant suffering is existential; there is no illness that better explains the nature of existential suffering. Existential suffering is the suffering of loss, the loss of those things that make existence tolerable or even exhilarating. Central is the loss of independence, our greatest prize as we grow as individuals. Then there is the loss of language, of communication, of social activity. Christopher Hitchens wrote poignantly of his loss of vocal communication and subsequent difficulty in writing. His psychological pain was wretched, but at least he could describe it. It is arrogant and presumptuous to assume that a mute person does not have a similar pain. It would be more compassionate in the circumstances to presume that it might be present.

The loss of memory destroys the remembrance of one's past, of events and relationships, of all those facets of life that make us human. It destroys our day-to-day participation in even the simplest actions, and it destroys our future – our imagination of what might be. For some discerning persons, an understanding of the burden that they are and will create for those they love can be crushing, and is a reason why some people choose, while still competent, to end their journey. Fortunately, perhaps, this loss may disappear as the journey progresses. This suffering in dementia might be described as 'relational' suffering, or 'inverse' suffering: you cannot see it from the outside.

The second loss is of social life: a steady withdrawal from company, even the company of people who are well known, due to embarrassment regarding dress, behaviour and conversation, which can lead to social death. 'Social death' was described by Frances Norwood as 'there is something about a person that can die prior to the death of the body'. It is a gradual accumulation of losses which 'culminates in a perceived disconnection from social life'.

The third element of suffering is in the psychological realm. Fear and anxiety arrive early in this parade, followed by depression, and later psychosis. These are all states of mind that cause psychic pain, which should not be considered in any way less serious than physical pain. These states can be medicated and diminished, but only with the loss or alteration of any remaining personality. The drugs used are not called chemical restraints for no good reason.

Finally, there is the physical suffering, thankfully usually confined to the late stage. Apart from the commonly unrecognised and under-treated pain, the onset of incontinence creates one of mankind's greatest threats to dignity.

Michael Wolff wrote of his mother's journey in *New York Magazine* in 2012:

When my mother's diaper is changed she makes noises of harrowing despair – for a time, before she lost all language, you could if you concentrated make out what she was saying, repeated over and over and over again: 'It's a violation, it's a violation, it's a violation.' [...] That is the thing that you begin to terrifyingly appreciate: Dementia is not absence; it is not an nonstate; it actually could be a condition of more rather than less feeling, one that, with its lack of clarity and logic, must be a kind of constant nightmare.

Is this a physical or an existential suffering? Surely both.

You will hear experts state that people with dementia do not suffer. Don't believe it – it is a gross assumption to say someone is not suffering simply because they have lost the ability to express themselves, unless you sensitively inquire. It is an assumption that may be designed to make *us* feel better, but it condemns the mute person to suffer more.

One more story. Writer Sophie Cunningham described her father's journey with advanced dementia in her book *City of Trees*. When admitted to dementia high care, he was initially 'cheerful', but things quickly unravelled at a 'dizzying' pace. Soon 'he was begging us not to leave him there, to take him away'. Sophie wrote that she learnt new phrases like 'chemical restraint'. She argued with his doctors about the sense of continuing to treat his heart condition, which simply kept him alive in these dire circumstances. She described her 68-year-old father 'snarling in a wheelchair, pulling against the straps and cursing, over and over at the top of his voice. I reached towards him and he hit me. I will never forget. His deep distress. His terrible rage.' When she told him she had to go away for three months, 'he looked at me and started crying'. And experts say that people with advanced dementia don't suffer! Sophie's father could still express his anguish, but when dementia sufferers lose the ability to vocalise, why should we presume that their suffering has disappeared? Such a presumption is arrogant, and lacks understanding and compassion.

Dementia is surely a punishment, not sought and not deserved. Is it any wonder that I call dementia the worst illness known to man? Is it a journey you would seek or wish to prolong?

Life needs a purpose to be fulfilling. We each have a time to die – tragically some, like Hitch, die before their time – but for many today, when we are ready to die does not match our time to die, and suffering commonly occurs in that gap. Nowhere is this more relevant than for dementia. The least we can do in dementia is allow natural dying, and not intervene and thus prolong suffering.

Aged care and dementia are a very significant problem for our community, but it will not be solved by putting the solution into the hands of entrepreneurs.

The worst disease known to man

Dr Helga Kuhse*

When Rodney Syme died in October 2021, he was 86 years old. Were it not for Rodney, we might still not have voluntary assisted dying laws in Australia.

For many years Rodney and I had been fellow fighters for law reform that would allow voluntary assisted dying for seriously ill and suffering patients in Victoria and beyond. We became good friends.

VAD (voluntary assisted dying) laws were passed in Victoria in 2017 and came into effect in 2019. Now, five years later in 2023, the legislation is due for official review. Although the law has allowed hundreds of Victorians to die peacefully and with dignity at a time of their choosing, several legislative shortcomings have also been identified. Here I will concentrate on only one of them: the virtual silence of Victoria's VAD legislation on the suffering, rights and dignity of individuals with dementia.

When Rodney died, he left behind an unfinished manuscript for the present book. In that manuscript several chapters deal with the problems raised by dementia – problems that did not feature prominently in his earlier writings. By now, Rodney had become the carer of his wife, Meg, who was suffering from dementia. This would, no doubt, have heightened his awareness of the magnitude of the many problems relating to dementia: in the manuscript he refers to dementia as 'the worst disease known to man'. Sadly, Rodney died before he had mapped out the legislative and social changes he would like to see.

Whether or not one agrees with Rodney that dementia is the worst disease known to us, I have no doubt that it is 'the elephant' or 'monster' in the VAD legislation. Even though dementia is a common condition and causes enormous heartbreak and suffering, it was ignored in Victoria's pioneering but conservatively drafted legislation. In 2021 about 386,000 Australians were living with dementia. It is the second leading cause of death in Australia and the leading cause of death for women. As a result, large numbers of Australians are

---

* This article contains content from a letter by Helga Kuhse published in *The Age* on 11 May 2023.

effectively ignored by the law and forced to fight 'the monster' of dementia on their own.

This is so because two legal requirements must be fulfilled before VAD can be granted. Firstly, applicants must have a life expectancy of no more than six months for most medical conditions and 12 months for neurological conditions. Secondly, applicants must be competent. These requirements are unlikely to be met by people with dementia. At diagnosis, life expectancy will be more than 12 months; and it is unlikely that an individual with dementia will be competent when life expectancy is 12 months.

Bill, my husband, watched first his grandmother and then his mother lose their memory, their speech, their continence and all the mental characteristics that had made them the persons they had been. Bill was determined to avoid that fate.

When a grandchild first beat Bill in chess – the game that Bill had taught our two grandchildren – he took the standard dementia tests. The result of the second test was positive. Having noticed other task-related difficulties in himself, Bill's reaction was swift and decisive: he wanted to die while he was still competent and able to implement that decision.

Because voluntary assisted dying is not available to dementia sufferers in Australia, Bill decided to seek what he regarded as a dignified end for himself in Switzerland. After reams of paperwork and two interviews with a Swiss psychiatrist, we travelled to Switzerland. This was in October 2022. Bill died in a small town near Basel, three days after our arrival. I held him in my arms, and he died with a smile on his face.

I will always miss Bill, but am consoled by two facts: that we had been able to spend 60 wonderful years together, and that I was able to assist Bill in avoiding what for him would have been 'the worst disease known to man'.

End well, all well? No. Bill died in a foreign country without his family and friends. And he died a death of privilege and luck. He had an early diagnosis of Alzheimer's disease, we were well informed, physically able to travel, with the financial means to do so.

Access to voluntary assisted dying cannot, ethically, and should not legally, depend on luck and privilege. Rather, a self-determined death should be available to all dementia sufferers alike. The review of Victoria's VAD legislation must acknowledge the monster or elephant in the room and devise a workable and safe solution.

This will not be easy, but it can and must be done.

As long as the problem remains unresolved, thousands and thousands of people will be forced to live lives they do not want, and die in pain and distress. And the suffering will increase, due to Australia's aging population. By 2058 the number of Australians living with dementia is predicted to reach some 850,000.

I'm sorry, Mum

Guy Pearce

Dear Mum,[*]

It's been a long time since I've written you a letter. And even longer since you've been able to read one. I can only imagine what it's like for you in there, especially knowing the person you were before. Sometimes I still see the 'you' I grew up with, although I haven't actually seen you in person for over two years now, just photos that Helen from the Alzheimer's Ward sends me. I think of all the times you told me you never wanted to end up a 'bloody vegetable'. How, if it ever came to that, I had your permission to 'knock you on the head'.

Instead, I just let you sit in your nursing home, like a piece of broccoli simmering away on a stove longer than it should. And to think I had the chance to pull the plug once. After you broke your hip in March 2015, just two months after my wife buggered off, and one month after my dog died and I was slightly consumed with grief, the doctor at the hospital in Geelong emerged from the operating theatre to tell me you were struggling with aspiration and it would take some doing for you to fully recover. After explaining a few different procedures and inquiring about your quality of life, he then asked me what I wanted him to do.

Why was he asking me? I'm not a doctor.

In my ignorance, I took it to mean he wanted my permission to do what he could to keep you alive. It wasn't until my newly ex-wife's father (a doctor) explained to me your doctor was subtly hinting at something else: that should it seem a better course of action to just 'let you go', he would, in fact, do nothing other than the usual hip replacement recovery business, and you would likely 'kick the bucket'. That would've been your preferred option. It was certainly one of your favourite expressions.

---

[*] This article was originally included in the book *Dear Mum*, edited by Samuel Johnson, published in 2021. It was then printed in *The Weekend Australian*, 27–28 March 2021, as 'What would you say to your mother?'.

So ... you're still here. But of course – not really. Cruel. A failure on my part. And now I must watch from half a world away as you ever so slowly drift further into the abyss.

It's funny when I think of how short and sharp Dad's death was. A shocking flight accident that killed him instantly. Whereas your demise is, as [songwriter] Fiona Apple would say, 'Slow like honey. Heavy with mood.'

I'm sorry, Mum. I'm sorry your doctor was offering you a way out and I didn't see it. I'm sorry you now must endure more years of oblivion, instead of being reunited with your precious love – my dad, taken from you 44 years ago. I'm just sorry. I often picture that scene from *One Flew Over the Cuckoo's Nest*. You know the one. With the pillow ...

You'll probably outlive me. You're going to be 85 this Christmas. Here's to another 10 years of Alzheimer's. At least I can give you the same present I gave you three years ago. I'll just take it off your shelf and hand it to you again. I know the old you would find that funny. But you're not the old you any more. That you – the smart, sarcastic, stoic woman who taught me to keep my chin up and my head down – only lives on in my memory.

I share stories with Monte about you. I want him to know what kind of lady you were. I think he's getting the idea. He just turned four and has quite the sense of humour. I gather that's yours being passed down. I wonder if he'll understand what the doctor is hinting at when my time comes to get a hip replacement. Being from the Netherlands, he probably will.

I love you Mum. More and more all the time. I'm sorry for making you stay, longer than you should. I'm coming home later this year. I'll be sure to bring a lovely soft new pillow for you. Just to lay your head on.

CHAPTER 7

A completed life

There is a time to be born and a time to die.

—*ECCLESIASTES*

'A completed life' – this is not a phrase you will hear or see in common usage. It first came to me ten years ago, as I was writing *A Good Death* and reading some Dutch articles about Justice Huib Drion, Dr Eugene Sutorius, the Australian saga of Lisette Nigot[*] and the concept of 'tired of life'. Drion was arguing for elderly people, especially those living alone, to have the means to end their lives peacefully. He wrote, more than 30 years ago:

> Enter a […] nursing home with all these old helpless people, sitting
> somewhere in a quiet corner staring into nothingness, often incapable
> to bring food to their mouths, being entirely dependent on carers for all
> their needs, and who of us would think it is a good thing that none of
> these people were given the chance to end their lives earlier?

The alternative phrase to 'tired of life', which I profoundly prefer – 'a completed life' – has subsequently been used by others in print, particularly the Dutch

---

[*] Lisette Nigot was a French academic who lived in Perth. She deliberately ended her own life in 2002, just before her 80th birthday, by taking barbiturates. She was not sick, disabled or depressed, and her death was controversial, becoming the subject of a documentary film *Mademoiselle and the Doctor* by Janine Hosking.

group called Of Free Will. It is not a difficult concept when you put your mind to it.

I go again to the *Oxford English Dictionary*. Why? Because words matter. So often, disagreements occur because of different understandings of a word or phrase. The adjective 'complete' has five connotations, one of which is 'having run its full course, finished'. The verb 'complete' means to finish making or doing something. So a completed life is a finished life, having run its course. One might say that a completed life has lost its meaning. Life has meaning when it has a sense of purpose and has pleasure. Interestingly, another connotation of 'complete' is having all the necessary parts, or entire. So a complete life could mean a life full of purpose and pleasure. That is what most people aspire to when they have a full set of physical and intellectual attributes. One could say, after finishing a beautiful lunch with friends, that the meal was a 'complete experience which was now completed'. Peculiar language, English, but that is to ignore tense: 'completed' is, significantly, in the past tense.

There is no doubt that much of one's purpose in life comes from work, and from professional, social and family life. We are all individuals with our different life paths, experiences and values, and therefore different views on purpose in life. But a common thread is doing good for others and not being a burden on others. And there is no doubt that we seek pleasure, or at least contentment, when we are not busy with purpose. We do this in myriad ways, from the very physical to the highly intellectual. A completed purpose can bring untold pleasure.

In this modern world, mobility is a key to social life and its pleasures. Confinement to an aged-care home, or particularly a single room, is a significant loss of pleasure. With ageing, pleasure may be confined to reading, listening to music and radio, or watching television, and these faculties can be seriously diminished with age. Having moved to the country to look after my wife, I am desperately trying to maintain my 25-year-old connection with my city orchestra. Family is critically important as one ages, but modern families can be widely dispersed, and have many involvements, which makes caring for aged parents very difficult. So it is not surprising that as we age people can migrate from a complete life (full of purpose and pleasure) to a completed life with an absence of purpose and pleasure.

Anthropologist Frances Norwood wrote a penetrating analysis of Dutch people's thoughts on euthanasia. While mostly discussing cancer, she described loss of meaning of, and purpose in, life – involving loss of control, loss of social engagement and loss of spirit as critical losses, leading to end-of-life requests. These same losses occur in the frail aged and in dementia, and requests also came from these groups.

So let me define a completed life as one without pleasure and purpose. It is usually accompanied by physical, intellectual and existential losses. It is usually present when a person is 'ready to die': they have come to terms with their mortality and would be content if they went to sleep and did not wake up. I believe it is a common state in people threatened with aged-care incarceration, and even more common in those in aged care, if we took the trouble to look for it. Jack (in chapter 1) realised that he had a completed life, when I asked him the question.

Time can go so slowly as one gets old and without a structured life – even worse when one is alone. As one's physical abilities diminish, reliance on senses increases, but sight and hearing can also decline. What may then be left? By the time many people enter aged care, a completed life is either already present or rapidly approaching.

The classical Roman rhetorician Cicero wrote:

Now there is no fixed point at which old age must end, and we may properly go on living as long as we can maintain and carry out our obligations. But life comes to its best end, when with mind unimpaired and senses intact, nature herself breaks up the fabric to which she gave form and order. It follows that old age must not grasp greedily after those last few years of life, nor must they walk out on them without cause.

Professor Kenneth Hillman wrote in *The Conversation*, in an article titled 'How the care conveyor belt tortures people back to life', that 'I am an intensive-care physician and I often see people who appear to have rationally considered that death is preferable to life.'

I began thinking about the completed life after I met Bronwyn (whom I discussed in my 2006 book *Time to Die*). I called on her in her home over many months, met and talked with her son (and carer), and had many discussions with her and her very close friend – who provided this picture of Bron's life:

The day Bronwyn died was pretty terrible for her. She had evaluated it thoroughly and decided she would have to wait through the whole day until about 10 o'clock at night after the last of the many, many carers of the day had put her to bed, before she had the privacy she needed to take her life. There was not enough space between carers' visits to be certain that the medication would have had time to be effective before someone arrived and called for an ambulance to resuscitate her.

The night Bronwyn died was all she could have wished for. She spent separate time with each of her children in her softly lit bedroom and then they told me it was time for me to come. I brought in the medication. One child took it from the bag, another opened the bottle and the third put the straw in and handed it back to me. I asked her if she was sure this was the day – that she didn't have to die today – that she could change her mind – and she said she didn't want any more days. She drank the medication, gagging a bit on its bitterness, and followed it with a glass of a liqueur she'd chosen. We drank with her. She curled down and her children stood where they could see her face and I stood behind her and stroked her and loved her.

Her daughter said in amazement, 'She's just gone to sleep', and that's just what she did. She slept and then she died. And she had no more pain.

I've never met anyone who loved life and people more than Bronwyn. I've never met anyone who wanted to die more than Bronwyn.

She was a clever, funny, caring woman who had lots of serious physical problems; heart problems, impaired lung function and diabetes, for example. She'd had a fall from a wheelchair that had broken her back. She needed an indwelling (permanent) catheter. Above all she had chronic, progressive and extreme muscle weakening and wasting that was finally diagnosed as IBM – Integrated Body Myositis – for which there is no treatment to slow it and no cure.

Most of Bronwyn's huge, loyal and active circle of friends never knew the extent of her problems and pain because she refused to discuss them and distracted people with her wicked sense of humour and her enormous capacity for caring for others.

Because her body was so badly affected and there was no more home help available (she already needed three people just to shower and dress her every morning, let alone the cleaners, shoppers, cooks, toileters, ...) her real and not very distant fate was to be put into a Nursing Home. She was classified as 'High Care' which meant she'd be housed with the comatosed and the crying. She was well aware of this. We'd checked out so many places. She was filled with absolute horror at the depressing and fearful prospect but, as we arrived at yet another Home and she saw a workman balancing an enormous and unwieldy plank on his shoulder, she was able to rally and call out, 'Hoy, wait a minute and I'll give you a hand.'

She was in constant, often acute, pain. Basically she was able to do less and less over time and needed more and more help to manage, and managing hurt – a lot. The pain was hard to deal with but what was equally important was her loss of a sense of dignity, privacy and power to choose what she wanted to do. That's easy to read but not so easy to understand, so here are a few examples.

As Bron's muscles failed she sometimes lost control of her bowels. One of the few times she cried was when she told me that some things just weren't meant to be. It was her adult son who'd had to clean her up after one such accident. Imagine yourself there.

If she was away from home and had an accident there was no cleaning up possible until she returned. Her next medical intervention would have been a colostomy bag – no fun for anyone but doubly difficult if you're nearly completely paralysed and yet another instance of her lack of control.

For years Bronwyn was aware she'd want to take her own life. Finding the means to do this became much more urgent as the move to the Nursing Home was becoming inevitable. The disease was never going to kill her – just turn her into a bright, alert mind trapped in an ever disintegrating, pain riddled body. As well, in a Nursing Home she would be so carefully supervised that she would be allowed no opportunities.

So the problem was how to go about it. This was the really hard bit.

Bronwyn went to her sympathetic doctor and explained. He was astonished and totally shocked and then said he couldn't help her because 'he was a Christian.' He did, however, take her seriously. He argued against methods such as the wheelchair under the train (she agreed; it wouldn't be fair to traumatise the driver) or driving the chair into something solid, (she might only end up with a broken leg) and finally suggested that she go to experts in the field. He also stated in writing that he didn't believe she was depressed.

She did some research and the answer was clear. Pentobarbital. There only remained the teeny problem of how to get it.

This was truly the most horrible period. The Nursing Home increasingly loomed. Her ability to swallow was becoming more compromised and she'd been told her ability to breathe independently was being lost. She was despairing and felt especially angry with herself that, earlier in the year when she was in a life threatening situation in Intensive Care, she was so afraid of the pain that she hadn't refused treatment.

Enter Rodney Syme. With the solution. Bless him.

Bronwyn became a different woman. Life didn't suddenly become easy or pain free but now she had control. It was more than having a pain-free end of life solution; it was giving her the gift of choice.

Bronwyn had the Pentobarb for two months before she died. Knowing it was there enabled her to focus differently. She still woke every morning to the almost unbearable pain of needing to be dressed but now she felt able to endure a little longer. It allowed her to deal with things important to her – all the bills were paid, the filing was up to date and the books were tidied. It gave her the will power to say no to routine specialist visits and proposed interventions she'd often felt trapped into. It gave her relief from feeling she had to guard her suffering from her friends. It gave her impetus to send more 'I love you' cards to her grandchildren.

It gave her peace of mind. And then it gave peace to her body.

Bronwyn did not have a terminal illness, she was not dying, but she had no purpose and little pleasure in her life. She was completely competent. She had a very strong sense of burden in respect of her son. I did not need any persuasion that she had a completed life.

The reflections of classical Roman rhetorician Seneca are worth considering here:

> For mere living is not a good, but living well. Accordingly, a wise man will live as long as he ought, not as long as he can [...] He always reflects on the quality, not the quantity, of his life. He does not regard it as a great loss, for no man can lose very much when only a driblet remains. It is not a question of dying earlier or later, but of dying well or ill. And dying well means escaping the danger of living ill.

Oliver Sacks wrote a beautiful essay ('Everything in its place') on Sir Humphrey Davy (1778–1829), the pre-eminent chemist of the late 18th to early 19th century – effectively the founder of modern chemistry, who made amazing discoveries from a very early age. He was profoundly unhappy in the last decade of his life, having entered a prestigious but loveless marriage, and become president of the Royal Society (an aristocratic society which he could not change and led to his being despised), resulting in depressing administrative duties. All this dried up his intellectual scope.

In 1828 he had a paralytic stroke, which still left him intellectually capable. He wrote: 'My health was gone, my ambition satisfied, I was no longer excited by the desire for distinction: what I regarded most tenderly was in the grave.' He died within a year of a fatal stroke. His comments suggest that he had a completed life and was ready to die, but had to wait a year for 'a natural death'. What a tragedy for someone of his intellect.

The Netherlands has been publicly debating this issue. In February 2010 an opinion poll showed that 85 per cent of the population could imagine that old people who do not have a life-threatening illness can consider their life completed. Almost 70 per cent of the population is of the opinion that an elderly person who considers their life completed should be able to have access to help from a doctor to terminate their life.

The Royal Dutch Medical Association in 2011 recognised that where a person has an 'accumulation of geriatric afflictions, including loss of function', possibly resulting in significant suffering – a 'completed life' is the appropriate description, rather than 'tired of life'. They determined that the death wishes of elderly persons with age-related ailments can indeed fall under the euthanasia law; their condition is that it must be a matter of unbearable and hopeless suffering with a medical basis. This is in marked contradistinction to the advocacy group Of Free Will, who simply argues that being over 70 is sufficient, and that no medical assessment was necessary. The Royal Dutch Medical Association was making a clear distinction between age alone and the presence of suffering from severe age-related degeneration. Psychiatric illness may also be involved, but is a separate issue.

New figures from 2012 show that more and more Swiss seniors are taking advantage of assisted suicide, even when they do not suffer from any terminal diseases. One in every five Swiss-French speakers and one in every three Swiss-German speakers opting for assisted suicide are not suffering from a life-threatening illness, reported the Swiss press. This section of the elderly is coming forward in ever-increasing numbers, citing 'weariness of life' together with a bad bill of health as the main reason for the decision. Although not terminal, many suffer from debilitating health, with incurable problems such as blindness, incontinence, and mobility difficulties greatly reducing the quality of life.

My most challenging experience of completed life was Beverley Broadbent. I first met Beverley in 2010. She was seeking advice to help a dear friend who was dying in the Alfred Hospital and whose clear wishes were being ignored (abused). As I got to know her, I realised that this was typical of Beverley – her whole life had been devoted to humanitarian causes. She had worked on public and social health. She was heavily involved in environmental issues, and stood for election as a Green in both state and federal elections. She was passionately concerned about fairness and helping the disadvantaged. In retirement she spent many hours helping young migrants to improve their English. I found it hard to recall a more public-spirited individual. She had many interests, theatre and music, and many friends – she was not lonely. She was a completely rounded individual.

As our communication developed, it became clear that Beverley wanted control over the end of her life, and did not want to die in hospital in circumstances like her friend. At this point she, although 80, had no terminal illness, in fact no significant suffering, apart from the usual ailments associated with people of her age. But over the next two years subtle yet significant changes developed which affected her quality of life. She had already had a hip replacement, bilateral cataracts, a carpal tunnel syndrome, and suffered ophthalmic migraines. She developed disabling nocturnal cramps, increasing and disabling arthritis, a peripheral neuropathy which caused falls, a disturbing loss of balance, and was aware of an increasing loss of geographical awareness when driving in previously familiar areas – an early sign of dementia. She had a lump in her breast which she was choosing to ignore. She was losing her ability to teach her students – in fact, I was present when she said goodbye to her last charge.

She felt she was no longer able to continue the benevolent work for society that had given her life purpose. I recall being very moved by this conversation. If someone can provide such assistance and compassion to others, why cannot others give her the same civilised respect?

It was clear that Beverley had the early warnings of the Six Horsemen of the Ageing Apocalypse; she might have appeared to many to be a fit 83-year-old, but she knew there were troubles in store, and decided to pre-empt them. We had a very long conversation. It was clear that she was contemplating ending her own life, and she had medication. I offered her my advice and support into the future, as I tried to persuade her to be patient.

Beverley was highly intelligent, and she could see the writing on the wall, although it was not writ large. She realised that the ageing process was 'robbing her of her physical and mental fitness'. When I last met her and advised patience, it was clear, as was said of Margaret Thatcher, that 'this lady's not for turning'. Beverley was of utterly sound mind, not depressed, still enjoying a somewhat diminished life, and determinedly independent. She had made up her mind and wanted to make a statement as she left.

I interviewed Beverley in December 2013. Among many questions, I asked her these:

RS: Do you want to live another 17 years?

BB: No, I certainly don't, but my grandmother did. But I don't. Quality of life – I don't want to go demented and I don't want to end up in a nursing home. And it's so close to it – when I fall badly, I could well have to go to a nursing home, as I haven't got relatives to get me out.

RS: What is it about a nursing home that is anathema to you? Have you had experience of them?

BB: Oh yes – I have looked after aunts, one a very strong woman who ran her own business said to me, 'Beverley, you've got to get me out of here, it's terrible, they simply don't care'. I couldn't believe it, because they all seemed so nice, but one day I heard someone calling from a toilet for a whole three quarters of an hour I was there. She was trapped, absolutely. There was no way she had a choice to think of, as I have.

RS: What would you think of the statement that you now had a completed life?

BB: Yes, I think that would be a very good statement, a very good statement. I haven't done everything I wanted to, but I've stopped my ambition. It is becoming difficult to achieve the same sort of things as in the past, and the main thing I am nervous [about is] that the two things that worry me are going to happen. My frustration, that reduces me to tears actually, is that I've been very organised all my life, I've always known where everything is, and now I lose things all the time, I don't know where to look for them, and I spend hours looking for them. The other day I spent an hour looking for something that actually wasn't there. This actually makes me very angry and frustrated. I have a worry that my wishes will not be carried out. Nursing homes – they're pressured to follow their routines, so you are not in control any more. I've always been in control. You'd be stuck there every day with not much stimulation and why?

It was crucially clear to me after our three-year dialogue that Beverly was fully informed and of sound mind – two critical components of assisted dying for a completed life.

Beverley was accompanied at the end by a nursing friend who sat with her, and they shared love as Beverley went serenely to sleep and died about 30 minutes later. Her friend said: 'She did not suffer a lonely or painful death, but rather a calm and beautiful end.'

I arranged an interview with the wonderful journalist Julia Medew, to be published after Beverley died. Beverley said that if physician-assisted suicide were legal, she might have pushed on, but her fear of deteriorating to the point where she would be unable to end her life made her want to go sooner rather than too late. She said that she 'was ready to die, and believed that many elderly people wanted to die when their life was complete'. Beverley's story was published on the front page of *The Age* on 2 April 2013; it created the vigorous debate that Beverley wanted. Many moving articles and letters were published. My response in a column published in *The Age* attempted to sum it all up:

Beverley Broadbent would be thrilled at the discussion that has followed her story in *The Age* – it was just what she intended. She would have laughed at the psychiatrist who made an obscure diagnosis without even speaking to her. She would have questioned the notion that doctors are healers as being only partly true, and not applying to the degenerative associations of old age, strokes and dementias, and the terminal illnesses that ultimately claim us all. She would have quietly cried as she read Judith Taylor's tragic story of a 26-year-old son who mistakenly and irrationally ended his life using information from Exit International. She would have argued vehemently that such information should come

through a careful, sympathetic medical dialogue. This is what protected
Fay Manoni's depressed mother-in-law.

She would have been particularly pleased with the larger stories
of David Campbell, Geoffrey King and Warwick McFadyen. David
Campbell's mother died in a nursing home in degrading circumstances
without a choice. That is exactly what Beverley (and many other writers)
desperately wanted to avoid. Geoffrey King's beautiful piece described
how he believed his Christian faith would sustain him through the harrowing decline due to motor neurone disease. He believed in redemptive
suffering. What was most impressive was his empathy and lack of con-
demnation of Beverley's decision. As he wrote 'I do not want to impose
my views on those who do not share that faith'. Warwick McFadyen's
moving story of his father's inexorable and miserable journey to death
due to cancer reveals an indomitable spirit and will to live, presumably
for different reasons to Geoffrey King. His story illustrates how strong
is the will to live – even in countries that allow voluntary assisted dying,
only a few per cent of dying persons are helped in this way.

What these stories, and Beverley's, illustrate is that we are unique
individuals, and that we are all capable of making different choices at
the end of life. Most people will not know now what choice they might
or might not make at the end. They may have a strong inclination, but
until they face the end, they cannot be sure. Two things I do know for
certain is that almost everybody wants to make their own choice, and
that the ability to make that choice, to have control, has a profound palliative value. It eliminates the deep, crushing, hidden psychological and
existential suffering that accompanies all journeys to the end. Geoffrey
King understands this, but believes his faith will help him cope – I sincerely hope that it does. Many people will make a similar journey to
Warwick's dad, not because of an indomitable will, but because of the
lack of another option.

None of the choices described is either right or wrong, good or
bad. They are the different responses to different circumstances and of

different people – people who are unique because of their genes, child-hood, education, religion, culture and life experiences. They are valid expressions of our autonomy as individuals, our inherent right to make our own decisions about those things that affect us personally – and nothing is more personal than dying. Autonomy is now the predomi-nant ethic in Western civilization and philosophy, but unfortunately it is denied full expression in Victoria at the end of life. Our law mandates that we must go on to the bitter end, to a 'natural death', not hastened by medical assistance. Of course, we can refuse medical treatment, but this option does not always exist, and the path to death is then not always easy. Most citizens are unaware that the Medical Treatment Act states that 'it is desirable that dying persons should receive maximum relief of pain and suffering' – and that includes doctors.

The current prohibition on doctors providing assistance in dying on request has the consequences associated with all prohibitions. First, it does not work – many doctors provide assistance, risking their freedom and their reputations. However, this assistance is hidden and the drugs used are not ideal, and the outcomes not always what is anticipated. It is a highly arbitrary practice, more available to the educated and well connected. Second, it leads to tragic consequences such as the recent Klinkermann prosecution for attempted 'mercy killing', an all too com-mon event that occurs because suffering people cannot engage in open conversation with their doctors about these problems. Third, and this was dear to Beverley's heart, it condemns many old, frail people to pun-ishment and persecution simply because they are old. Too often, without consent but by default they end their lives in David Campbell's 'vision of hell'. Finally, it leads to a mass of suffering of patients despite the best palliative care, which, although it rarely fails to help, often fails to provide what is wanted. It also results in prolonged grief and disturbed memories on the part of families, as has been eloquently described in *The Age*.

Some years later, I was contacted by a man called Kenneth. After several months of phone conversations and personal meetings, culminating in a meeting with two of his children, I received this letter from Kenneth, entitled 'A personal reflection', which says it all:

It is early September 2014 – I am a 91 year old man with two debilitating medical problems. First I contracted MRSA [methicillin-resistant *Staphylococcus aureus* – an infection that is resistant to many antibiotics] in hospital when I had my third left hip replacement prosthesis in 2006 and was in hospital for 10 weeks whilst the infection became controlled. The only measure of control (not cure) is the taking of three strong antibiotics three times a day for life. Whilst this has worked for over eight years now it has taken its toll in the steady progressive loss of agility and general feeling of well-being.

The second debilitating problem is chronic arthritis, particularly in the knees, and back pain. This was aggravated by the hip replacement leaving me with a fore-shortened left leg and the right knee with very little cartilage remaining. A knee reconstruction is ruled out because of the MRSA.

Neither of the above conditions is life threatening so whilst I have serious restrictions I could live for several more years, but with what quality of life, and how dependent would I become on others for my care? I value my independence very highly and the thought of life in a nursing home with its limitations and restrictions appalls me.

Added to this I developed a rectal sinus in December 2013, which is draining infection from an unknown site quite possibly linked to the MRSA infection. This is manageable but requires a change of dressing every four hours, which imposes certain limitations on my activities. I had a similar sinus problem in January 2012 which lasted for five months before suddenly drying up, but during that time I seriously considered my options.

Eight weeks ago I was unfortunately involved in a car accident which left me with a fractured sternum and other lesser injuries. This has set me back very considerably but I am back home again now and enjoying a somewhat more restricted independent living.

But let me reflect a little on my life and how I regard the remainder of my time. I consider myself very fortunate in having had an interesting and rewarding career in medical physics at a leading cancer hospital and believe I have made a significant contribution to the discipline. I had a very happy marriage of 43 years until my wife died in 2002, having three children in stable marriages with grandchildren, so I have much [for which] to be thankful, and in many ways much to live for still. Two of my children have large enough homes to accommodate me if I so wished, and with the agreement of their spouses have generously offered to do so. However there are many considerations to be thought through. I am sure I would be made very welcome and any loss of independence on my part would not be difficult to manage, but I would still feel I would be imposing some constraints on their family life. Furthermore, it would be very inconsiderate of me to bring into their home my MRSA and suppurating sinus infections however well I might be managing them.

At 91, I have no further ambitions to fulfil and I plan to make the most of my remaining weeks in quality time with my children and their families, and with friends, and then hope to retire graciously from the scene on my own terms and with dignity.

Kenneth's daughter subsequently wrote to me:

Dad passed away on Sunday. He was surrounded by his three children, all holding his hands. He had spent the morning on his own, by choice. We then arrived after lunchtime, knowing in advance how the day would pan out. It seemed unusual to be arriving at dad's, knowing this day would be his last. It was with some reluctance that I made this journey.

The last several months have been an amazing journey for me, and I am sure [for] my brother and sister. It has opened my eyes to the whole complexity of the dying on one's own terms. It is an issue with so many layers and personal view points. As discussions were spoken and personal views put forward, it became acutely apparent that dad wasn't asking our permission but for our support and blessing. In some ways, knowing his unwavering views made things easier. He was the one in the driver's seat. Such a major decision was his and his alone.

I chose to use my remaining time with dad by spending as much quality time with him as possible. In some ways, knowing you have finite time left with someone is a gift. You make it count.

I will never forget the look in dad's eyes when you chose to assist him with medication. It was a look of relief and gratitude, almost humble. I am not sure if you recognized this look, not knowing my father well, but I wanted you to know his appreciation. Seeing dad's reaction, D—— and I were also thankful for this, knowing it was dad's ideal outcome. We really had no expectations of how this meeting would go.

He had been thinking about this for years, initially he was going to carry out his wishes without involving his children. I am not sure what led him to change his mind but he was definitely pleased that he did. He was also pleasantly surprised to find we were all so supportive towards his decision. He had initially been fearful that we would not forgive him for choosing his own death. The subsequent discussions surrounding this topic were so personal and bonding that this time was quite special. I will treasure it always. So his final day was like any other day, normal conversations, laughs, food, photos, but with an eminent ending. It definitely was what I would consider dying with dignity.

Kenneth's death could be described as bitter-sweet – bitter for his family in the loss of their father, but sweet in the memories they will carry into the future. Such memories, and the communication that preceded his death, are powerful in diminishing grief, and abolishing any guilt that may otherwise have existed. Kenneth changed his mind about involving his children in his decision at my strong suggestion. The discussions that follow this step can open the door to 'letting go' and to being able to celebrate the precious time that is left. Remember Christopher Hitchens in chapter 2: I would be astonished if such an eloquent communicator as he did not ultimately find a space to 'let go'.

If there is one thing I hope people will remember from this book, it is the critical role of effective, honest and completely open communication in finding a dignified and 'good' death: communication with family, friends and treating health professionals. The earlier this occurs, once an unalterable disease state is diagnosed, the better.

In April 2018, Professor John You of McMaster University in Canada reported that a national, multi-year study involving seriously ill Canadians revealed that, even though 28 per cent of the participants stated a preference for 'comfort care' (meaning no curative treatments), this preference was documented in the charts of only 4 per cent. Professor You cited a 2014 Ipsos poll finding that only 26 per cent of primary care physicians are comfortable having end-of-life discussions. I doubt that Australia would do any better.

The importance of communication, however subtle, is vital. Gerontologist Elaine Brody wrote in 2010:

> Many years ago, in a study of older persons' day-to-day health concerns, we debriefed interviewers and asked them, 'What is the main piece or advice you can give health professionals?' The interviewers, over and over again, said, 'Listen to what older people are really saying ... not only to the words but to cries, whispers and silences. Really listen so that they know their concerns and feelings are being recognized.'

Compare Kenneth's journey with his family with that of Keith. Keith took his family on an extended overseas holiday, leaving his very independent mother, in her late seventies, at home alone, her husband having died in hospice with dementia after a series of strokes. While he was away, his mother was diagnosed with a bad breast cancer, but kept it to herself. She was already suffering from severe swelling in one leg, which restricted her favourite activities.

On arriving home, Keith could not contact his mother and rang his brother, who said, 'Keith, I'm sorry, a few days ago, Mum killed herself. She left a letter for you.' She had asked Keith's brother to visit her in the morning (after sharing a beer with him and her neighbour the night before), which he did, only to find her 'dead in her chair, a tumbler of drained whisky (Glenmorangie – she always had great taste) beside to assist her with the sleeping pills she had collected, her head in a plastic bag'. Keith recalled:

> I felt so miserable and choked I think I was in a depressed haze for four months. I felt incredibly guilty about not knowing more of her conditions, not making her come and stay closer to me. I went over my last conversation with her, a rushed Christmas chat with a mobile phone passed from hand to hand on an icy Washington street. 'The lack of a last farewell has hurt me to the core in a way I really can't explain. [...] I think of my Mum every day. Sometimes I see her in my dreams. I wish I could have said goodbye.

Keith's experience highlights the importance of communication and of being able to say goodbye. It is echoed by the deaths of Pat and Peter Shaw together in 2016 in what was euphemistically described as a 'suicide pact'. Julia Medew wrote the Shaws' story on 15 January 2016 under the heading 'The big sleep'. Their end is a classic description of completed life, and I paraphrase the article here.

Peter and Pat Shaw were both highly intelligent, independent human beings, both scientists, lovers of nature, and adventurers. They had three daughters – two PhDs and one concert violinist, who being raised in this free-thinking humanist environment shared their views. Peter and Pat had long held views on having control of their own lives, and planning one day to end their own lives. They made it clear to their daughters that 'they wanted to avoid hospitals, nursing homes, palliative care units – any institution that would threaten their independence in old age'. Peter wrote a letter to *The Age* in 2007 in which he declared 'our reason for suicide may be anticipation of pain and incompetence, but quite likely just a sense of a life accomplished and coming to a conclusion'. By late 2015 Peter said 'My head swims. [...] When I am reading, I can't follow a difficult argument. [...] My condition is getting worse bit by bit, slowly week by week. On top of all this, my eyesight and hearing are no good. [...] I am not afraid of dying but I am dead scared of incompetence'. Meanwhile Pat was also troubled by her old age. 'Arthritis was corroding her joints and she was getting dizzy [...] and was finding it increasingly difficult to get out of bed and out of chairs'.

They set a date for their departure – one daughter, arriving from overseas, was shocked at how frail they looked.

On the day in question, the Shaws spent the morning with their family in the backyard native garden. At noon, the daughters left after embracing their parents and left without tears, but out of fear of being present when their parents died.

Pat did not want to die alone, so she took her lethal drug in her bed, after which Peter walked to his shed where he, alone, died, reclining in his chair. He left a note stating 'I have had a good life, and prolonging it will not make it better.' Pat also left a note, which included this statement: 'Having seen my two sisters die in nursing homes, I have no wish to go that way.'

Julia Medew wrote:

Today the Shaw sisters are still coming to terms with the loss of both parents. [...] But they respect their choice and feel strongly that suicide can be rational. All three say their parents should not have had to risk prosecution to die together at the time of their choosing. Nor should they have had to be alone for the legal protection of their family.

I was dismayed by these statements, and wrote to *The Age* as follows:

It is high time the community was rid of the fear of prosecution if they are present when loved ones end their lives as Peter and Pat Shaw did. Victorian criminal law states it is an offence to 'aid and abet suicide'. This means one has to do something, to be practically involved. Just being present to say goodbye is not a crime. No one has ever been prosecuted for simply being present. Following a two-year investigation into the death of Nancy Crick, at which 21 people were present, the Queensland Police Commissioner stated that 'being present when someone takes their own life does not constitute an offence'.

It is true that, if the death is reported to the coroner, the police will interview anyone known to be present, but this is a formality to provide the coroner with information, and not for the purpose of prosecution. The contrary ill-informed view is widespread in the community, which is sad, because it condemns many people to die alone. Adjunct Professor Elizabeth Dabars (secretary of the Australian Nursing and Midwifery Federation in South Australia) agrees: 'It is sad to think that people with terminal illnesses may isolate themselves and die alone in order to spare their family and their health care team from prosecution. The ANMF supports the right of individuals to end their lives with dignity, as long as the required voluntary euthanasia criteria have been met' (Parliament House rally, 11 September 2013C).

This problem could easily be corrected if the Office of Public Prosecutions issued a statement to clarify the matter. The response from the Office of Public Prosecutions? I am afraid, an utterly useless iteration of the currently vague state of the law. The Office suggested that people with concerns have the option of 'obtaining their own independent legal advice', no doubt at significant cost and no greater certainty (2 February 2016).

Julia Medew subsequently reported that it was estimated that the story was read by more than a million Australians; thousands made the effort to comment on Facebook, many sharing their own, often harrowing, stories. Doctors and social workers who worked in aged care said they were saddened by the lack of choice around death in Australia.

An example of how simply a completed life can end is Bruce and Hazel's story. Hazel, living interstate, wrote to me:

You know it's time when the last thing you think of before sleep is 'I hope I pass away in my sleep'. When you wake in the morning and think 'Another miserable day ahead', with mobility decreasing a little more each day. The future looks bleak with nursing home a possibility and lymphoma lurking in the background. Quality of life has gone [...] I think that says it all.

131

Hazel did not lack a devoted husband. He rang me on a number of occasions, and I spoke with his wife; he visited me in Melbourne twice, to find relief for his wife. She alerted him that she was ready to die. He recalled:

> The day was a strange day. I sensed some foreboding. At 5 pm she murmured 'My dear, it's time tonight'. Extraordinary — I felt no fear. We watched a DVD, then listened to some of our favourite music. 11 pm to bed — I will treasure this moment for the rest of my life. Hazel faded promptly away in my arms — completely at rest. In the morning she looked so peaceful and tranquil. Thank you for making the closing years so happy following 64 years of marriage.

Is there a difference between a completed life and 'tired of life'? Neither phrase has an accepted definition, and an opinion depends on how one views language. I see no very clear distinction, except at the margins. In my experience, the majority of people with whom I engage have considerable physical illness, some terminal — although they are not necessarily close to death — others with no terminal illness and no clear end point. They commonly also have significant psychological and existential suffering, the sum of which leads them to a considered decision.

'Tired of life' suggests a predominant psychological element, but there is no doubt that physical ailments may lead to that psychological state. Certainly those occasions where the term 'tired of life' is used are rare, and the emphasis on the distress is due to a state of mind rather than a state of illness. One needs to be extremely careful in these circumstances that treatable mental illness does not lie behind the matter, but it need not necessarily be so. It seems to me that Lisette Nigot was a clear case of 'tired of life'. However, in my experience, such situations are so uncommon that they need to be considered with extreme caution.

To this point, you have been reading my views, and those of a few people (actually a few of many) who have contacted me with their end-of-life stories. Unlike other chapters, where I have presented a considerable amount of Australian and world facts and opinion, there is very little research on the views of old people on death and dying. A literature review by Ingalill Hallberg in 2004 found only 33 publications, and very few studies on the very old. Overall, they found a lack of studies dealing with older people's view of death and dying. They did identify older people's readiness to talk about death and dying, anxiety about death, being a burden and dependency, the fine line between natural sadness and depression, and worry about the end-of-life phase. Tim Sharp and colleagues in 2013 found only 15 papers on their topic, 'Do the elderly have a voice?'. They focused on conversations about end-of-life care with frail and older people who had no overriding diagnosis. They estimated that this group accounts for around 40 per cent of all deaths, and is often associated with multiple co-morbidities and a degree of cognitive impairment. They found prognostication in this group to be very difficult, and, for those with the frailty of old age, the dying trajectory is more unpredictable than the clearer trajectory of malignancy. These difficulties make it unlikely that this group will be helped by Victoria's Voluntary Assisted Dying Act, which requires a definitive prognosis. Essentially, they found that old and frail people did not have an adequate voice – which is why I am writing this book.

The Dutch health minister stated in 2016, in regard to a proposed law for assisted dying for a 'completed life':

> It is needed to address the needs of older people who do not have the possibility to continue life in a meaningful way, who are struggling with the loss of independence and reduced mobility, and who have a sense of loneliness, partly because of the loss of loved ones, and who are burdened by general fatigue, deterioration and loss of personal dignity.

After 25 years of counselling, 15 years of end-of-life workshops, numerous public talks with questions, extensive reading of books and newspapers with public responses via letters, I am convinced that there are many people in our community with completed lives, or who are approaching completed lives. Stories like those of Bron, Kenneth, Keith, the Shaws and Bruce and Hazel are just the tip of the iceberg. I have many more in my files. Those who speak out or write are those with the courage, the knowledge and the passion to try to change how things are done. They helped to achieve the passage of the Voluntary Assisted

Dying Act. But most of those with completed lives will not qualify under that same law. I encourage them to keep shouting until the volume they make forces further change that includes them. The Australia-wide royal commission into aged care will provide an opportunity to maintain pressure – do not let it drop off the public agenda after a few weeks of discussion, as happens with so many important issues.

It is notable that Bron, Kenneth, Keith, the Shaws and Hazel all had completed lives but were not yet in aged care; they were all desperate to avoid that outcome. The evidence of the Victorian coroner to the state Parliamentary Committee of Inquiry into End-of-Life Choices (2015) showed that about two or three Victorians suffering from chronic unrelievable or terminal illnesses were ending their lives every week, in violent circumstances. It is conceivable that some of these people may have had completed lives. We do not hear of those who are already incarcerated in aged care, except for some recent research from Briony Murphy (see chapter 9). People with a completed life who are now in aged care are effectively trapped until they die 'naturally', long after they might have chosen to do so if they'd had the option.

As I write these words, I think of Jack from chapter 1, who had a completed life but was not yet ready to die. I hope that when the Victorian Voluntary Assisted Dying Review Board reviews that legislation after four years, it will have accumulated enough evidence of suffering in completed life to recommend important changes to the Victorian Parliament.

The consideration of a completed life encompasses the quality of one's life. Two factors are of critical importance in contributing to the quality of life. They are the importance of caring for oneself (independence), and the importance of helping others (a sense of usefulness and purpose). Without these, there is a profound sense of being a burden. No amount of caring and patronising by others will alter this psychological distress. Patronising argument may appear to bury it, but it does not; the patronised person may appear to give up, but the pain remains.

People with terminal cancer or a progressive neurological disease may reach a point of completed life, but their voice is heard and recognised in our society. In Victoria they have access to the Voluntary Assisted Dying Act (and such people in the other states and territories will almost certainly have similar benefits soon), and also to palliative care. But what of those with a severe but not progressive neurological condition, such as a severe stroke? My aunt had a profound stroke, and was completely paralysed unilaterally, totally dependent, and could not speak. She had survived her stroke and her prognosis was totally uncertain: she might survive like this for some years. Every time my cousin visited her, she drew her mobile hand across her throat, indicating her wish to die. I repeat this story because it is so important. A completed life? Yes. But a choice to end it? No – unless she refused fluids and food. A good choice? No (and she was not aware of it anyway).

One can go further with the analysis of my aunt's situation. She certainly had a completed life, and she had decided it was time to die. But more than that, she was *ready* to die. Her decision to die was not just vaguely formed, or slowly developing, present but not compelling. She was ready to die *now*, and every day of life awaiting her 'natural' death was agonising for her. Her daughter 'heard' her, and agonised with her, but no-one else did. She deserved to be heard, as do many in similar situations to hers.

How does one assess whether someone has a completed life – what objective criteria are there to measure? The answer is: none. How do you determine that someone has a completed life? The answer is simple: ask them. Jack, and Beverly Broadbent, knew exactly what I was intimating, even though they (and most people) had not previously considered their lives in that context. It is a question I constantly ask people who seek end-of-life counselling, but only after a long, in-depth dialogue, often on a number of occasions over time. Their attitude and understanding often change over time and further thought. A completed life is a reality, and needs to become part of our end-of-life discussions.

My experience with someone whose life was completed

Dr Nick Carr

65-year-old male, 86 kg, bike versus ground, lacerated elbow and knee, query scaph-oid fracture.

As I lay on the cold, mossy boards, this was how I fantasised that the notes would be taken by the emergency department doctor. Less than 0.3 of a second between enjoying the watery winter sun reflected on the Yarra river and lying on the ground, tangled and dazed. Enough time to put out a hand in defence, not enough time to know what had happened.

I should have known better. I'm an experienced cyclist, there had been a series of wet days. The boards on the bike path at Southbank had become mossy and greasy, with all the grip of black ice. But I was in a hurry, and just the slight-est of turns was enough.

Fortunately, I'm also well behaved. My head hit the deck protected by a good helmet, and although it was jarring, I knew there was no head injury. The torn clothes, the bloodied knee and elbow were obviously just superficial. The wrist, I wasn't quite so sure.

A guy sweeping leaves at the front of a desolate hotel asked if I was okay. There was no-one else around: this was 2021, in the middle of whichever lockdown it was at the time. I assured him I was fine, and he showed no further interest.

I checked my wrist and thought I could probably cope. There wasn't a lot of choice. Someone nearby was waiting for me to arrive. I had been summoned there urgently that morning.

She needed me there so that she could die.

I heaved myself back on the bike and limped the last two kilometres to the tower block.

The family were relieved to see me; the patient, whom I'll call Moira, even more so. She had been in unbearable pain from her disseminated cancer. Palliative care had been wonderful to her, but she hated how the powerful drugs made her distressed and disorientated. Her voluntary assisted dying medications had been delivered that morning, and she was desperate to take them.

Now that I was there, the sense of relief was palpable. She promptly mixed the medication and drank. Despite the foul, bitter taste, she relaxed and smiled, knowing she finally had her last wish fulfilled. Her end was exactly as she had wanted: swift and very peaceful.

Only once that was done did one of the family members, a doctor himself, turn to me and say, 'My God, what happened to you?' Quite rightly their focus had been entirely on their mum, but now they gazed at this dishevelled creature with torn trousers and shirt, bloodstains on both.

By this time I realised the wrist wasn't that bad (it's just that I'm a wimp, convinced that every bump means a broken bone or two), so a swift clean-up, a bandage, and I was back on the bike heading for work.

Moira was fortunate. Although she had a horrible malignancy, with brain secondaries, she retained her mental capacities right through to the end, so was able to make the decision to take the medications. People with dementia may not be so lucky. (Lucky sounds an odd word to use in this context, but I suspect any reader of this book will know what I mean.)

I was taught this lesson by Beverley. Beverley – her real name, because she went very public with her story in 2012 – had been a patient of mine for a long time. She was a fabulous, feisty and independent woman who loved the theatre. One of her great pleasures in life was to treat her friends to an outing to the latest show.

Many years before she died, Beverley brought in an ancient bottle of pills with the request for me to prescribe some fresh ones. The label was completely worn and illegible, so I had no idea what they were.

Beverley knew: 'They're barbiturates.'

'What on earth do you need those for?'

'So that I can kill myself if the need arises.'

I was, to say the least, taken aback. I told Beverley that I had no idea what sort of doses she would need to use, or whether this was even a reasonable thing for me to consider.

'Don't you worry about that, dear. You just give me the prescription, I'll sort out everything else. And it's not as if I plan to use them, it's just an insurance policy. In case.'

What Beverley meant, was in case she developed anything that incapacitated her and made life not worth living. And the main thing she had in mind was dementia. She had seen her close friend devastated by this hideous disease and was determined not to undergo the same experience herself.

Beverley never had children, and lived alone. But I was not concerned about suicidality. She had never suffered mood disorder and was entirely rational in her request (if not a little confronting). She was anything but lonely, with a tight circle of great friends. She was enjoying life to the full. I wrote the prescription and thought no more about it for a long time.

Around ten years after the barbiturate conversation, Beverley started getting noticeably older and more frail. Most importantly, she knew that her memory was beginning to fail her. She told me that it would not be long before she made the decision to end her life. Before she did so, she had several things that needed to be done: get rid of all the stuff that she had so that others didn't have to sort it out, write her life story, and – most importantly – make sure there was someone to look after her little dog after she died.

One January morning, Beverley came to see me for a long appointment. She thanked me for looking after her all those years and handed me a bound booklet, which was her completed life story. She told me of her plans, how she planned to do it, and when.

I asked her, 'You've thought about this for so long, how do you know that this is the time?'

Beverley smiled her wonderful, wise, enigmatic smile: 'You know how my friends and I love the theatre? Well, I saw that there's a new show coming on in Sydney which I really wanted to see. But then I realised, I've seen enough shows. That's how I knew.'

Beverley was such a brave woman. She made the decision to close her life before the final curtain was closed on her. Dr Rodney Syme used to talk about how we don't have to stay until the end of the last act. It's *our* show; we should have the choice to leave when we want to.

Someone like Beverley was able to make that choice, but in the end only – it turned out – because she had had help from Rodney himself.

Beverley didn't develop dementia. She made sure of that. But the way she did it required great courage and the good fortune to have been able to contact Rodney.

Beverley went very public about her experience, and the whole story was published in *The Age* newspaper after her death. It was stories like hers that helped the momentum towards voluntary assisted dying becoming a reality in Victoria in 2019.

But, paradoxically, the legislation would not have helped Beverley. She did not have a terminal illness, so would not have qualified. And by the time she might have developed a terminal illness that would qualify, there was a very good chance that her cognitive decline would have meant that she was no longer eligible.

It is a tragic irony that someone like Beverley, who believed so passionately in the right of older people to make up their own minds about their time on this planet, would have been denied that choice once the legislation went through. I fervently believe that we need to honour Beverley's memory by making sure that in future people in her position are not denied that choice.

And next time I'm pedalling off in a hurry to help someone who does have that choice, I'll make sure I'm more careful when I turn the corner.

Everything went quiet

Dr Cathy Henkel

Finding peace and magnificence in death.

Her last breath was effortless. It was a silent sigh and then she was still. Released and free. Like the gentle rustling of a swan's feathers in a light breeze, I felt a surge of something enormous filling the room. It was magnificent. And then everything went quiet.

The last day of my mother's life is etched exquisitely into my memory. Those final hours with her were made more vivid and profound because we knew what was about to happen. She had an appointment with death. And we'd been preparing for it for months.

⤙▭ ▭⤚

The church bells across the square wake me up. Those first few moments as I emerge from deep sleep, and some weird crazy dreams, are blurry and disorientating. Where the hell am I? Oh yes, Switzerland. We're in a hotel in Basel. Sam, my daughter, is still asleep in the bed next to me. It's just starting to get light. I can hear a tram scratching on the tracks. Holy crap! It's today! The day my Mum is going to die.

I edge shakily out of bed and look out the window. The Christmas markets below are waking up too. Stall shutters are being lifted, a man with a trolley is unpacking boxes, people swathed in colourful scarves and coats are waiting for a tram. There's a kind of silvery mist in the air, and it looks deliciously cold. A smart young woman hurries down the cobbled street below sipping coffee. The sound of Christmas carols wafts up to the window. It's the 19th of December. The day we have been planning, anticipating and dreading in equal measure is here. I need coffee.

I head out to the bakery, and marvel at what an ordinary day this is for everyone else. No-one can imagine that I am ordering my mother's last-ever coffee. It's inconceivable that by this evening, she'll be gone. It doesn't feel real, and yet I know it is. It's taken over a year of planning, and so much of what the three of us – Mum, Sam and I – have been doing and thinking about has been aimed at this day. I remind myself, as I have every day for months, that this is what my mother, Laura, wants: to die here, in this town, today, on her own terms, with Sam and me by her side. She's not sick, she doesn't want to get sick, she doesn't want any suffering. She wants a dignified death and she's ready. Oh, and also, she wants us to film the whole thing!

When I get to Mum's room, Sam is already there, setting up the camera. Mum is sitting on the bed, putting on some lip balm using a small mirror.

'I bring hot coffee and a bag of pastries.'

Mum's face lights up like a beacon. 'Ah, you angel. Just what I want.'

As we sip our coffee, Mum looks pointedly at Sam: 'Is the camera ready? There's something I'd like to say. I've been practising it in the mirror this morning.'

⊰⊱

The concept of filming everything had been Mum's idea from the start. She'd been surrounded by filmmakers all her adult life, and understood the power and potential of film for impact and change. My Dad was a filmmaker in South Africa, where I grew up, one of the finest editors in the country and the director of several features and documentaries. I followed in his footsteps, and Sam followed in mine.

When my mother was 59 and living in Johannesburg, she experienced a horrific attack and sexual assault in her home. She identified the perpetrator from a school photograph, but the man was never charged, due to police collusion with the family of the young, white man who committed the crime.

After the attack, I brought my mother to Australia. Her facial and body wounds healed over time, but her mental and emotional recovery was stunted by the police corruption and her fury that the perpetrator had faced no consequences. So, when I asked her if she'd like me to go back to South Africa, find and confront the man, and see if I could get some justice for her, she said yes, without hesitation. And when I suggested I make a film about it, she was equally enthusiastic.

My journey back to Johannesburg is documented in my film *The Man Who Stole My Mother's Face*. I found and confronted the perpetrator and secured the justice my mother so badly needed. When the film was released, Laura came out of isolation and took numerous standing ovations at film festivals and women's events. She became a vocal advocate on the effects of victim-blaming and led several 'reclaim the night' marches. The film gave her a sense of power and pride. So, it's not really surprising that, when she decided she wanted to end her life on her own terms, she would ask the two professional filmmakers in her family, her daughter and granddaughter, to make a film about it. She told us she felt 'almost obliged' to use the power of film to highlight end-of-life choices for the elderly and to show what a good and dignified death looks like. She wanted to start a conversation and leave behind a proud and meaningful legacy.

Sam and I were hesitant at first, but agreed to bring out the cameras early on to humour her, and perhaps make a small home movie. But as she became more serious about the venture, and started looking into the clinics in Switzerland, we realised she was serious, and we had to either fully support her or walk away.

Sam has cleaned the lens and buttoned on. 'Okay, I'm rolling. Whenever you're ready.'

We've done this so many times over the past 18 months that it all feels quite normal now.

'Wait a minute, I need to comb my hair.' And just like that, Mum launches into her final piece to the camera. 'My name is Laura. Today is 19th December 2019 and I'm in Switzerland. I'm here to end my life in the most wonderful, peaceful way by just going to sleep with my loved ones around me. This is my own choice.'

We have breakfast in the hotel lobby like any other day. Mum has boiled eggs and toast. I am enthralled by how casual she is about everything. The waitress comes over: 'Will you be doing anything special today?'

We all laugh, and she looks puzzled.

'Just heading out to the Christmas markets and maybe a bit of sightseeing.' I feel obliged to give her a civil answer. The truth will be too weird.

The clinic is about 40 minutes' drive from Basel city. Philip Nitschke and his partner, Fiona, arrive to pick us up. They've driven over from their home in Amsterdam to support Mum in her last days and help us with anything we might need. Philip is the author of a book Mum bought early on in her quest for information, *The Peaceful Pill*. He and Fiona are very experienced in assisting people with end-of-life choices and information about assisted dying. They are also good friends with Rudi, who runs the clinic, and know what's in store. Their calm demeanour is deeply reassuring. I feel like I am walking into a snowstorm, and have no idea what to expect from the day. I am so glad they are here.

On the drive to the clinic, Mum sits in the front with Philip and chatters away cheerfully, peppering him with questions about the why and wherefore of everything. She's always had an enquiring mind, and often drives me to distraction with her endless questions. 'What type of plant or bird is that? What's the history of that building? Why is that called that …?' I seldom have the answers, but that doesn't stop her asking. Luckily, Philip has a wealth of knowledge, and he enjoys her curiosity. In the back, Sam and I stare out the car window and are silent. Fiona sits in the middle and respects our privacy. A train rolls along beside us, and I remember Sam's comment just before we left Australia.

'I'm still not sure if I agree with what she's doing. It just feels like there is a freight train going, and who am I to try and stop it?'

⭢▬◉ ◉▬⭠

Five years earlier, I'd moved to the opposite side of Australia from Mum. I'd secured a full-time position at Edith Cowan University in Perth and was excited to begin a new chapter in my life. Mum had an apartment in Ballina, northern New South Wales, and had no interest in moving. She put down deep roots wherever she was, and the thought of severing them filled her with horror. Even when Sam moved to Perth, she still refused to budge. So, we talked on the phone regularly, and I visited her every holidays.

Then one day she called me up and said, 'Can you come over and bring a camera. I have something I want to say.'

As usual, I did what my mum asked.

When I arrived, and set up the camera in her living room, she checked herself in the mirror and asked: 'How do I look? Do I need to comb my hair?' She already had an audience in mind. I look back at this moment as the beginning of the momentous journey I was about to undertake. And I had no idea.

Speaking clearly and without emotion, she told me that she'd come to the point in her life where she'd had enough, life wasn't interesting or fun any more, and her aches and pains were only going to get worse. She feared getting dementia or having a stroke. Her mother had had dementia and cried for years that she'd wanted to die, and the distress of witnessing this had always haunted Mum. She wanted to go quickly and painlessly before that happened.

She showed me a stash of sleeping pills she'd been hoarding in a drawer, and a plastic bag. She was ready to take her own life and wanted me to help her. This really is an outrageous thing to ask of anyone, especially a daughter. I was horrified, terrified and a bit angry. She wanted to do it right there and then, on this visit. I told her that I couldn't do that, she needed to give me more time, and I needed to tell Sam.

I came away confused and distressed, and when I told Sam, she burst into tears. Sam's relationship with her grandmother had been complicated by a trip to Europe a couple of years earlier. Mum had a bucket-list wish to cruise the Rhine and Danube rivers from Amsterdam to Vienna, the home of classical music. And she wanted Sam to go with her. But on their second day in Amsterdam, Sam was pushing Mum on her walker when she hit a stone and Mum fell off, hitting her head on the concrete path. She was rushed to hospital but luckily had only a mild concussion. But back on the cruise, she developed pneumonia, which quickly became life threatening. When the ship docked in Vienna, Mum was taken to hospital and the dream trip became a nightmare for both her and Sam. So when she heard that her grandmother wanted to end her life, Sam was wracked with both grief and guilt, thinking that somehow she was responsible. Mum assured her several times that it wasn't her fault, but Sam carried that guilt with her all the way to Switzerland.

A few months after Mum first announced her intentions to me and the camera in Ballina, something happened that shifted her focus from that apartment to a clinic in Switzerland. David Goodall, a 104-year-old man from Perth, had decided he'd had enough and wanted to die. With the help of Philip Nitschke, he travelled to Switzerland, where he was able to end his life peacefully at a special-purpose clinic, using the barbiturate Nembutal. David's story was the subject of an in-depth report on the ABC, and when Mum saw that, she called me up and said she was going to write to Philip and ask for his help to get her approved by the same clinic in Switzerland. She also told me she'd saved up enough money from her pension to pay for Sam and me to go with her. We were astonished and extremely relieved that we were no longer being asked to help her with something unimaginable and illegal. But we still had our doubts and weren't sure the clinic would accept her.

Mum embarked single-mindedly on the long and arduous process of gaining approval from the clinic. This was not easy, especially for an octogenarian not proficient with computers or the internet. She had to locate, digitise and send numerous documents, fill out forms, and wait for answers that often arrived in German. It took more than six months, but finally she was approved, and the date was announced: 19 December. This is when the freight train took off, and Sam and I found ourselves scrambling aboard.

->—◯ ◯—<-

After a meandering trip through the mountains, we arrive at the clinic at around 11 am, and the clinic director, Rudi, comes out to meet us. He is a kind, quiet man who looks a bit like the classic image of Father Christmas. He immediately puts us all at ease. Also there is Dr Christian, the anaesthetist who will be administering the drug. They have set up the space beautifully, including a Christmas tree filled with lights. There are tea, coffee, champagne and snacks. The overall effect is welcoming and calm, but inside me there is a storm brewing, and I can feel myself slipping into a daze. I have no precedent for this day, no map or compass. I remember the stash of pills and the plastic bag in Mum's apartment, and I'm washed with relief that we're in the hands of kind and caring professionals here and it's all legal.

We've hired a film crew from Vienna to capture everything, so that Sam and I can be present with Mum rather than thinking about camera shots, angles and focus. Sam has taken the lead on managing the crew, for which I am extremely grateful and relieved. My coping mechanism is to focus entirely on what Mum needs, and ignore everything else.

There's some final paperwork to fill out, and we check the room where the procedure will take place. It's a simple, uncluttered room with a large bed in the middle and an intravenous drip to the side. Mum hesitates before moving into the room. Her only concern is whether they can hold off putting the intravenous line into her arm as long as possible.

'I've had this procedure many times before in hospital, and they always have trouble finding my veins,' she tells Christian.

He laughs this off, assuring her he will find the vein quickly and painlessly.

'Good,' she says. 'I don't want any pain or suffering.'

The night before, at Laura's last supper, with Philip and Fiona, we'd asked her what mood she was after for the occasion.

'Fun. Humour. Do not weep for me when I am dead.' Then she turned to Sam: 'Is that going to be hard?'

Sam struggled with this. 'I don't want to cry, but I just think … fun and laughter. We can only do our best.'

Then Laura made the really peculiar statement, 'I'm not going to cry. But it won't worry me all that much if you want to cry. But you don't have to cry to impress me.'

No wonder my emotions are in the spin-dryer. Mum wants laughter not tears, and I am frantically trying to conceal any distress or sadness. I shift further out of my body and just focus on Mum and Sam.

In the room with the bed, Mum removes her jumper and shoes and then hands me her glasses. 'Bye, bye glasses,' she says cheerily. Mum has been an avid reader her whole life and loved her books more than anything in this world. Essential to this love of reading were her reading glasses, and heaven help us if ever they were mislaid or damaged. And here she is, parting with them without a tinge of sadness. It strikes me again in this moment: she is so ready to go. She has let go of everything that matters to her. I suddenly see her in a way I've never experienced before. She's in a state of peace and equanimity that comes from letting go of all attachments. In Buddhist teachings, wisdom, joy and happiness arise from truly letting go. My mother has become a wise and peaceful sage, and I am in awe of her.

She doesn't follow any religion; in fact, she has always been very disparaging of the notion of religion. But she has read every scripture and studied all the great spiritual teachings. She would know that this willing detachment is aligned with Buddhist teachings. But she did not subscribe to the notion of an afterlife or reincarnation. 'When I die, that's it. I'll be gone. Ashes to ashes, dust to dust,' she would tell me.

Mum didn't give me any spiritual or religious guidance other than 'go out and seek answers for yourself'. I've done this, and explored many spiritual teachings and practices, including Buddhism, which I found most compatible and aligned with my experiences in life. When I was 33, my first husband was killed instantly in a car accident, a major life event that changed everything. It was the events that occurred in the days and weeks afterwards that convinced me there is an afterlife and that those in spirit can contact the living.

Late one afternoon, talking to Mum on the phone as I walked around my lake in Perth, I saw two black swans preening in the orange glow of sunset. Impulsively, I said, 'If you get out there and discover I'm right and you're wrong, will you come back as a swan?'

She thought for a minute, and then chuckled. 'Okay. I will.' I was pleased that she agreed to humour me, but, after she died, both Sam and I experienced some truly surprising and magical moments featuring swans, which neither of us could explain.

But at this moment, sitting beside her as she readied herself for death, believing that this was the end, that there was no next chapter, I was filled with enormous admiration and respect. How was she able to let it all go so completely, without the safety net or umbilical cord of an afterlife or returning in another form? To me, this made what she was about to do more courageous and sublime than anything I'd ever witnessed.

In the days leading up to this moment, and especially the past four days in Switzerland, Mum had never wavered. She knew what she was doing and was resolute and proud of herself that she'd pulled it off. She also remained joyful and intent on having fun. Yesterday, her last full day on earth, we'd played Monopoly. She was delightful company, we ate Swiss chocolate and strawberries and laughed until our stomachs ached. And she was magnanimous in Monopoly defeat. It was as if she didn't have a care in the world.

At dinner that night, Mum regaled us with stories of her life, including the eight times she had almost died. 'This time I will succeed,' she announced proudly.

Fiona turned to Sam: 'Have you ever seen a dead person before?'

'No,' Sam replied. 'Tomorrow will be my first.'

I knew that to be true. But I also realised in that moment, that in all my 60-plus years, I've never seen a dead person either. This will be a first for both of us.

Rudi has set up sound speakers in the room, and Sam flicks open her phone.

'DJ Sam,' she says, and Mozart's Piano Concerto No. 21 fills the room. Mum has always loved classical music. Her father was a classical composer and the conductor of the South African Symphony Orchestra, and her childhood was filled with the music of the masters. So Mozart was the obvious choice for this momentous moment. I open the champagne.

'This is decadent,' Laura says with a cheeky smile.

As we sip champagne, Mum gifts me her gratitude. 'Thank you so much, Cathy. You have been an absolute joy in my life. You as a child loved me very much, and I loved you immensely. If you hadn't come along, I probably would have been gone long ago, because without you, life was not worth living.'

My relationship with my mother has always been complicated, and I don't think there's been a lot of gratitude expressed. I'm struck with how kind and gracious she is being in this moment, telling me all the things she appreciates and loves about me. This has the powerful effect of negating all the bad stuff, all the difficult years, all the battles and struggles. Here we are, together in this moment, and she is gifting me her love and gratitude. I kiss her gently on the cheek and lay my head beside hers. We are at peace with each other.

The intravenous line goes in with minimal pain, and Mum's grateful to Christian for that. My sense that we're all in a trance-like dream goes up a notch as Philip and Fiona step in to say their final goodbyes. So do the film crew: two remarkable young men who have been quietly and respectfully recording everything without fuss or attention. Watching them say goodbye to this woman they've just met and are about to watch die brings tears to my eyes. Everything about this moment is so surreal.

'What is the time?' she asks.

'It's half past two.'

'Probably time to go,' she says with quiet serenity.

We call Christian back in, and he pours the Nembutal into the drip. He hands mum the blue lever with a little wheel that stands between her and death.

Rudi has to film her while Christian asks her some fundamental questions for the police. 'Can you tell me your given names and your date of birth, please?'

'My name is Laura Katherine Henkel, I was born on 1st November 1929.'

'And can you tell me why you are here today?

'I am here to die.'

'Okay. I've put an IV line on the left side, and I have explained to you the mechanism. Can you tell me what will happen if you push the little wheel up?'

'Well, I will die.'

'Okay, if this is really your wish, you can now push the little wheel.'

'Aright,' she says, then turns to us. 'I love you so much. And please, get your following and do what you can to get this conversation happening. The world needs you.'

And with that, she pushes the little wheel. It takes about three seconds. 'Done.'

It's 55 seconds until she stops breathing. In that time, Sam and I tell her again several times that we love her. What else is there to say at such a moment? We've said and done all we can in the months and days leading to this moment. Now it's just love. And for Mum, it's also about the film: 'This is a good, good cause, and you're going to make a good, good film, and cause a tsunami.' And with that baffling prediction, she breathes out deeply one last time, and is still. There is no struggle, no discomfort, no suffering. It's exactly what she wanted. She just breathes out and falls asleep.

I am filled with the most intense awe, love and respect for her in that moment. This is the first time I've watched someone die, and she has shown me that it can be painless, effortless and so intensely peaceful. And then everything goes quiet.

It's as if the soundtrack to my life is turned right down. The quiet lasts for the next three days. I sit quietly, trembling slightly, as the aftermath unfolds. Sam is sobbing and I comfort her as best I can. There are more forms to fill out, the police arrive and quietly and respectfully inspect the scene, the video and the paperwork. A representative of the coroner comes and spends considerable time in the room with Mum, while Sam and I snuggle together on the couch. Two men from the cremation service bring in a coffin and gently place her in it, dressed now in a white nightdress. As they drive away, I quietly murmur

'Bye, Mum.' She is being well cared for now, with the respect she deserves.

In Switzerland, a cremation cannot take place until three days after death. This is to allow for a death certificate to be issued. Sam and I move into a little bed-and-breakfast house on the outskirts of Basel to wait. It's cold but not quite snowing, and everything outside is so quiet – but it's even quieter in my head. I realise my mother's voice has been in my head my whole life. Now she's quiet and at rest, and everything about this moment feels right and serene. I am filled with the most intense peace I have ever felt, and perhaps ever will. Sam heads out to get a tattoo in honour of her grandmother. We all have our own ways of coping.

⊷▆◉ ◉▆⊷

A few weeks after the cremation, Sam takes some of Laura's ashes to scatter in the Danube in Vienna. As she is doing this, a white swan swims serenely up to the jetty and watches the ashes being scattered, and then swims alongside the jetty with Sam for quite a time. It is a striking and unusual encounter, and very comforting and meaningful for Sam, who is still struggling to come to terms with what has happened.

Back at the Herdsman Lake, near where I live, I regularly see small groups of black swans. But when I return from Europe, I visit the lake one afternoon and am astonished to find a gathering of more than 50 swans. They stay there for three days: enough time for me to call my cinematographer friend to come and film them for the documentary. The day after the filming, they are gone.

I've been asked many times to describe the effect of my mother's death. The right words are hard to find. There was something surreal and serenely beautiful about it. I feel very privileged to have been able to farewell a parent in this way. People ask if I miss her. Of course, I miss her physical presence sometimes, but we have such beautiful memories, many captured in the film. And missing someone means we're still hanging on. I'm not. We said and did everything we wanted to before she died. We'd reviewed our life together, made our peace, celebrated and grieved. With her final breath, I was able to fully let her go.

Many people wrote on our social media pages or spoke the words 'sorry for your loss'. I understand that this phrase is intended to convey kindness and compassion, but it jars with me. I do not see my mother's death as a loss. We knew when and how she was going to die, we were prepared for it, there was no suffering. And, since her death, I continue to discover ways in which her death is enriching my life. It's a gift that just keeps on giving.

Her bold and defiant approach to dying has opened me to new possibilities about how we frame death and whether we can have more control over when and how we say farewell to the world. Perhaps one reason we avoid the topic of our own death is because we fear it's going to be merciless, traumatic or painful. The fear may come from not knowing how we will die and expecting we will have no control. My Mum showed me a different kind of death. She has changed the way I feel about death and has given me a new framework for my own end-of-life choices. I'm forever grateful to her for this.

CHAPTER 8

Voluntary refusal of fluids and food

Careful readers may have noticed the strange construction of the title of this chapter. It is not a printing error, it is deliberate. For more than 20 years, serious medical writers and bioethicists have discussed 'voluntary cessation of food and fluids' (VCFF) or 'voluntary refusal of food and fluids' (VRFF), or 'voluntary stopping eating and drinking' (VSED). These terms are predominantly those used in American literature. These arguments have been made in response to the ethical need to hasten dying to relieve intolerable suffering in certain circumstances, at times when voluntary euthanasia and so-called medically assisted suicide were not legally available, the only quasi-legal assistance was terminal sedation in palliative care, and you had to be very close to death to earn that privilege.

I have followed these arguments closely, and have for more than 20 years fallen into the trap of using the common expression without deep thought – I have continued to write and speak of 'voluntary refusal of food and fluids'. In 2014, academic lawyers Ben White and Lindy Willmott, writing in conjunction with eminent bioethicist Julian Savulescu, published an elegant paper in the *Journal of Law and Medicine*. It was titled 'Voluntary palliated starvation: A lawful and ethical way to die?' Their legal and ethical arguments are impeccable, but, after I re-read their essay while preparing this book, it struck me that their title did not best describe the process.

Words and how we use them are important. In the course of my lectures, workshops and counselling, my use of 'voluntary refusal of food and fluids' would seem to place the emphasis on food rather than fluids – it took much tedious discussion to explain that I was talking about dehydration, not starvation, which is why I think that White and colleagues' title places the process the wrong way around. I have no doubt they fell into the title because of precedent.

People have been dying of starvation in large numbers for centuries, and still do so today. They do so not by will, but by circumstance – a lack of food and nutrition – and it is a slow and macabre process, of which most of us see only short glimpses on the television news. These poor folk still eat any scrap of food they can find, and continue to drink. As a result they die miserably, by inches. They hope by some miracle to survive.

Another category of death by starvation is by a deliberate process undertaken by some religious mystics, or political hunger-strikers. The former are making a personal statement, the latter a powerful political one. They both stop eating, but continue drinking. This is the critical point: because they continue drinking, they die of starvation – lack of food, and thus of calories. They waste away and die of inanition (exhaustion caused by lack of nourishment). Typically, such a process for an initially healthy person takes around 50 days. Surprisingly, after an initial few days, hunger disappears, as ketones flood the body from the breakdown of reserves of fat and protein. Fatigue is the principal symptom, and eventually coma ensues. What this requires is enormous willpower.

This is not the process that White had in mind, nor any other writer on end of life. They are actually talking of dehydration – a very different process. In contrast to starvation, a normally hydrated person ingesting absolutely no fluid will die in 10–12 days; if they are already very ill, weak and dying, they may die in 5–7 days, or, if receiving some palliative sedatives and/or opioids, even earlier. This is a critical distinction from starvation.

Food is included in the exclusion of intake because some foods have significant fluid content, particularly fruit and some vegetables. Those who cook will realise that the addition of stock or water to dishes can be significant, and grains such as rice, pasta and couscous absorb much of the fluid they are boiled in. Continuing to eat might add 100–400 ml per day to intake and prolong dying, which is why it should be ceased. An average human requires a minimum of 700 ml of urine output to maintain body stasis, which requires a minimum fluid intake of about one litre. Taking no fluids at all rapidly reduces urine output, causes retention of dangerous waste products (including drugs) and a relatively quick death.

Readers may be recoiling at the idea of not drinking at all – they will die of thirst. Certainly not a nice thought, but put this firmly into your mind: have you ever been thirsty? The reason for thirst is a dry mouth; moisten the mouth and thirst abates. That is one reason why we have saliva, which dries up when we dehydrate, but it is relatively easy to keep the mouth moist without ingesting any fluid.

It is a very common practice to restrict fluids in the end stage of palliative care, when patients are being sedated to unconsciousness. Palliative-care nurses are expert at meticulous mouth care to prevent thirst. Such restriction of fluid is entirely ethical, even though it may contribute to the hastening of death, since, as people die, their kidneys fail, and the concentration of medications such as opioids increases; continuing fluids may cause fluid retention and moist lungs, inducing coughing, choking and breathlessness. With excellent mouth care there need not be any sensation of thirst. After 2–3 days, some lethargy and confusion may develop, leading to coma after 4–6 days, which deepens until death.

A 1987 report by a palliative care doctor (Stephen S. Cox) titled 'Is dehydration painful?' stated:

> It was our strong conclusion that it [terminal dehydration] did not cause pain or suffering [...] Proper attention to nursing measures, particularly oral hygiene, is sufficient to provide comfort (exclusive of pain associated with specific diseases, such as that of cancer). Oral alimentation should not be denied, but simply made available as the individual requests or tolerates it. Forcing oral feeding or fluids actively increases patient distress and can lead to painful choking and aspiration.

This experience speaks to the appropriateness of withholding artificial feeding/hydration in the gradual process of 'natural death' (Cox is alluding to persistent vegetative state and advanced dementia): 'It is my strong conviction that an individual demented to the state of needing artificial alimentation is beyond appreciable suffering.' Clearly, I and others would not agree.

Professor J. L. Bernat and colleagues wrote in 'Patient refusal of hydration and nutrition' (1993) that:

> There is no disagreement that physicians are legally required to respect the competent patient's rational refusal of therapy, and they are morally and legally allowed to provide appropriate treatment for pain and suffering involved.
>
> A pact should be made with the patient that the physician will do his or her best to minimize suffering during the dying process and will remain available to comfort the patient by physical presence as well as skillful treatment of symptoms including pain, dyspnoea and dryness of the mouth.
>
> Effective mouth care can relieve most of the unpleasant symptoms of thirst and mouth dryness. Physicians should be willing to prescribe narcotics and benzodiazepines in doses sufficient to relieve pain and other unpleasant symptoms.

A description of such a death was published by Professor David Eddy in 1994, titled 'A conversation with my mother'. At age 85, she had overcome cataracts with lens implants, poor hearing with aids, a broken hip with surgery, and depression with drugs. Then she had gallbladder surgery, and the house of cards began to fall. Ultimately a severe rectal prolapse led to further surgery, but with the complication of total faecal incontinence. She went rapidly downhill, developed pneumonia for which she refused antibiotics, hoping to die, but recovered. She had long 'dreaded the thought of being in a nursing home, unable to take care of herself, her body, her mind and interests progressively declining until she was little more than a blank stare, waiting for death to mercifully take her away'. She suddenly thought, 'Can I stop eating?'. Advised by her local doctor and physician son that it was better to stop drinking, she did so with palliative support. Her son describes her elation and smiles with visitors as she did so over four days. After that she became drowsy and died peacefully on the sixth day. Professor Eddy wrote that 'this was not a sad death, it was a happy death'. It should be noted that this was a carefully planned and discussed process, overseen by an experienced physician, prepared to use palliative medications.

Sandra Jacobs, writing in the *New England Journal of Medicine* (2003), quoted Harvard palliative care physician Andrew Billings in Boston, who said that, for patients who have received a thorough evaluation, are not deeply depressed, and are already receiving hospice care, 'I believe wholeheartedly that it's an easy procedure. But not enough is known about what it's like for patients and families, so there must be good support in case things don't go well.' His greatest concern is that people will embark on this course without good palliative care.

Psychiatrist Linda Ganzini, studying assisted dying in Oregon hospices, was 'stunned' by the reports from hospice nurses in Oregon that nearly twice as many patients in hospice had chosen VRFF (voluntary refusal of food and fluids) to hasten death as had chosen PAS (physician-assisted suicide). 'The nurses' descriptions of the deaths resulting from VRFF suggested that voluntary dehydration is a surprisingly peaceful way to die.' The primary complaint, dry mouth, can be treated with ice chips or swabbing. Once again, this is a report of a carefully discussed process, with full palliative assistance.

Dr Tom Preston of Seattle, Washington, wrote: 'I have watched this ending dozens of times, and when done optimally, with a patient who is not well hydrated or nourished to begin with, it usually is over in 3–5 days or less.' He stated that if someone had already lost weight due to a chronic ailment, and is emaciated, the process may take only a few days, but if well nourished it will take a week or longer; complete cessation is essential, and supplemental medical therapy is necessary (good palliative medications as needed) – and, I would add, good home nursing in support.

Psychiatrist Dr Stan Terman, director of Caring Advocates, with direct clinical experience with a couple of dozen patients, and many more via clinical colleagues, confirms Dr Preston's views. Dr Louise Printz wrote in 1992: 'Physicians should continue to provide palliative care to patients who seek voluntary death by terminal dehydration [...] they have moreover, after a few days, the responsibility to provide palliative care to patients who have resolutely chosen voluntary death.'

With regard to any suffering from lack of food, it is completely established that when fat is burned after two days of starving, ketones are formed, which have an analgesic effect, and hunger dissipates; further, after a few days, natural endorphins are produced, which relieve pain.

There is no doubt that refusing fluids and food is a completely legal decision for a competent person. Justice Morris's decision (Victorian Supreme Court) in the case of 'BWV' in 2002 clarified the right to refuse tube-feeding (artificial nutrition and hydration), determining that it was medical treatment. Chief Justice Martin (Western Australian Supreme Court) affirmed the decision of high quadriplegic Christian Rossiter to refuse further tube-feeding in 2009. Rossiter was competent, unlike BWV. Chief Justice Martin determined that Rossiter had the same right as any other dying patient to palliative treatment to relieve any suffering caused by his refusal. This decision was confirmed in 2010 by Justice Kourakis (Supreme Court of South Australia), who made a further significant judgement. He concluded that since refusing life-sustaining treatment is not suicide, then refusing life-sustaining food and fluid should not be considered suicide. This decision removes any concern that providing palliation is 'aiding or abetting' suicide.

There is no argument that treating or caring institutions must, in these circumstances, offer or provide fluids and food, but they cannot administer such. This is a subtle difference, based on the fact that to 'provide' simply means to make available, but not to take action in delivery.

The Netherlands, of course, has a far greater experience and careful clinical study of end-of-life matters. It is not therefore surprising that the Royal Dutch Medical Association and the Dutch Nurses' Association issued, in 2014, a very detailed and well researched document on this subject. They chose to title this *Caring for People who Consciously Choose Not to Eat or Drink So As to Hasten the End of Life*. Their reason for creating this report was the realisation that this was already taking place in the Netherlands to a significant degree (estimated at between 0.4 and 2.1 per cent of all deaths in the Netherlands), and they were concerned that Dutch physicians were 'insufficiently trained to prepare and offer guidance to such patients'. (Most Australian physicians, let alone care-home staff, would have absolutely no knowledge, training or experience with this matter.) The Dutch patients were predominantly older, competent people who had been refused euthanasia by their doctor, largely on grounds of a lack of terminal illness, and/or were considered to have insufficient suffering. For the doctors, there was fear of legal consequences, or objection on moral grounds.

In the Netherlands, the Dutch Association for a Voluntary End of Life (NVVE) describes this option as the self-chosen death of the elderly. In that country, every patient has the right to refuse treatment, even when this refusal leads to death. Doctors must respect a treatment prohibition by the patient. In 2005, some 21,300 persons (15.6 per cent of deaths) died as a result of abstinence from life-prolonging treatment.

For old or sick people, stopping eating and drinking can be an acceptable and natural way to die. For an acceptable outcome, empathetic involvement of nurses, doctors and family is essential. How long it takes before death depends very much on the condition of the person. Sometimes it occurs after about six days, often after one or two weeks, but it can also take longer. To stop eating and drinking is difficult, but not an impossible way to die. The better the condition of the person, the harder it is. Of the next of kin, 75 per cent hold it in a dignified way. The estimated annual number of such terminations of life in the Netherlands is 2,800 (2.1 per cent of deaths).

The Royal Dutch Medical Association document is utterly comprehensive and extraordinarily valuable and should be adopted by Australian medical, nursing and aged-care organisations. I have included much of its advice in my Protocol for Voluntary Refusal of Fluid and Food (in Appendix A).

There should be societal acceptance that physicians have a moral duty to respect the rational wishes of competent, chronically ill patients who wish to die by voluntary refusal of fluids and food, or other valid refusals of therapy. Currently in Australia, however, most doctors will be ill-informed in this matter, and may insist on a psychiatric assessment of competence. Regrettably, if that is what is needed, I would advise people to submit, abusive though such a referral may be. It is the outcome that matters.

So much for decisions by competent people. People who have lost capacity for decision-making clearly cannot explicitly refuse fluids and food; nor can they refuse tube-feeding if a tube is in place – they have lost the ability to make their own considered decisions. However, the Victorian Parliament in 1987 created the legal ability for a person, while competent, to create an agent (then called an enduring power of attorney for medical treatment) who could make refusal-of-treatment decisions for their appointee if they became incompetent. 'BWV' was not competent and had not appointed an agent, but Justice Morris relied on the very strong evidence of all her family that she would no longer want tube-feeding to continue.

Subsequently, in 2016, the Victorian Parliament passed the *Medical Treatment Planning and Decisions Act*, which allowed people while competent to create a legally binding advance care directive for refusal of treatment. This was consistent with the 2009 decision by Chief Justice McDougal (New South Wales Supreme Court) that a carefully prepared and succinct advance care directive must be respected by the medical profession.

It is almost universal that people with dementia will develop eating problems, which become more complicated as their dementia progresses. Certainly in the later stage, but sometimes earlier, dementia sufferers lose interest in food. They have to be encouraged to eat, but they eat less and less, and eventually stop feeding themselves. It is as though they have lost an understanding of the meaning and importance of food. They then need someone to feed them with a spoon (assisted spoon-feeding). For a while, when the food is placed near the mouth, under the nose, the mouth voluntarily opens with verbal encouragement, and the food is taken and swallowed, with enjoyment.

As time goes on, this process takes more time, encouragement and co-operation, while swallowing diminishes. Eventually there is no response to offered food, and the 'snout reflex' is relied upon. This is a primitive neurological reflex, found in babies and infants. If one taps the person's lips with a spoon carrying food, their mouth will open reflexively (not voluntarily) – this allows the food to be placed in their mouth, and there it sits. Some chewing and swallowing do occur, but much of the food dribbles out of the mouth.

This feeding process is extremely time-consuming and inefficient. It is not surprising that wasting occurs in late dementia, with the associated problems of weight loss, bedsores, diminished immune resistance, and infections. It is for these reasons that tube-feeding became exceedingly popular in the USA in the late 20th century. In 1991, more than 75,000 PEG tubes were placed under the Medicare system alone. This procedure was also recommended because of an additional problem: some dementia patients lose the ability to swallow, and may inhale food, leading to pneumonia. However, research showed that tube-feeding did not improve survival or presumed quality of life.

American groups have filmed this feeding process and other aspects of late dementia. Showing the film to older people without dementia, to inform them about what might lie ahead, has a very significant influence on their decisions about life-prolonging treatment in late dementia.

There is a serious ethical problem with assisted spoon-feeding, in that at some point – certainly when the snout reflex is relied on – it can be argued that this becomes forced feeding. In virtually all these instances, the person's dementia is very advanced; they are in or close to a vegetative state, and the effect of this feeding is simply to prolong life and prolong suffering – life that has lost all semblance of humanity, except that there is a body that breathes and a heart that beats, and clearly no improvement is possible. What is more, Professor Jennifer Abbey states that forced feeding can lead to choking and aspiration pneumonia.

Chief Justice Rehnquist of the US Supreme Court stated in 1997: 'It seems odd that your bodily integrity is violated by sticking a needle in your arm, but not by sticking a spoon in your mouth. I mean [...] how would you force-feed these people in a way that would not violate their bodily integrity?'

The Australian Medical Association issued a statement in 2013 on forced feeding that categorically rejected the practice on ethical grounds. Although the statement's focus was on the forced feeding of forcibly detained refugees, in ethical principle it applies equally to detained people with dementia who refuse feeding via a valid advance care directive. Australian Medical Association president Steve Hambleton said that 'a fundamental role of medical practitioners was to relieve distress, and prisoners and detainees needed to be treated with respect and dignity, and to be accorded the same right to humane treatment as the rest of the community'.

Many people who work in aged care, especially those with a Catholic ethical background, oppose the withdrawal of spoon-feeding in any circumstances, arguing that there is a fundamental 'duty of care' to provide nutrition and hydration in all circumstances, irrespective of an advance care directive. Many other homes have similar concerns, but from a legal perspective.

Of relevance is the report of the Institute of Medical Ethics Working Party on the Ethics of Prolonging Life and Assisting Death ('Withdrawal of life support from patients in a persistent vegetative state', *The Lancet*, 1991), which stated:

> We agree that good oral hygiene can be maintained by appropriate nursing care after food and fluids are withdrawn. Finally, giving food and water to the sick has symbolic significance as a mark of continuing care and an expression of humanity. But the symbolic significance of an act cannot be divorced from its purpose and context. In vegetative patients the normal purpose of maintaining life and easing the ravages of hunger and thirst do not apply, and feeding does not provide benefit.

In the BWV Supreme Court hearing, the Catholic Church argued that sanctity-of-life doctrine required continued tube-feeding. Justice Morris cited Lord Goff (from the famous Bland case in the UK in 1992), who wrote that 'the principle of the sanctity of life must yield to the principle of self-determination'; the Morris decision implied that autonomy trumped sanctity of life.

This was in relation to whether tube-feeding was medical treatment. The question as to whether assisted spoon-feeding can be refused by an incompetent person via an advance directive has not been decided in a court. It seems logical to me that, if a competent person can refuse tube- or spoon-feeding, indeed legally refuse any fluid or food in order to die, and be provided with support and palliation when dying, then a person who is incompetent with dementia, but who was certified as competent when they appointed a medical treatment decision maker and created a circumstance-specific advance care directive (ACD), would have the same rights. I have the opinion of an eminent Queen's Counsel that this would be so. After all, creating a medical treatment decision maker has the effect of transferring autonomy to another trusted person if competence is lost, and an ACD has statutory legal power in Victoria. People in other jurisdictions should take advice.

A significant decision occurred in New Zealand in 2010. A woman, who had suffered a brain haemorrhage 20 years before, had been living in a Wellington care home for ten years as her movement and speech deteriorated. In 2010 she decided she no longer wanted to live and stopped eating (and presumably drinking). Her husband wanted her admitted to hospital, and force-fed. However, three psychiatric experts found her lucid, and that she should not be force-fed. An expert in mental health law said that forcing food on her would be regarded as assault. If it would be assault to force-feed a competent person, then it would surely be an assault to force-feed an incompetent person who had created a relevant advance care directive that refused administration of fluids and food.

Professor Jennifer Abbey's 2013 report states:

> If a person with dementia tries to refuse nutrition or hydration they are presumed not to have capacity – and often have a person sit in front of them putting a spoon in their mouth saying things like *'just a spoonful'* or *'try it for me'*. If there is a clear advance directive from the person with dementia and the family feel that the pushing food away, or spitting it out, is the desire of the person with dementia, then it is not the right of nursing staff to insist that the person be fed.

I agree, but note that this was written in 2013, before the *Medical Treatment Planning and Decisions Act 2016* (Vic) giving statutory value to an ACD was passed. Unless the ACD makes provision for it, the family cannot override a clear directive.

The Australian Commission on Safety and Quality in Health Care stated in 2011 that 'dying patients should be supported to receive oral food and fluids for as long as they wish'. By implication, one could come to the conclusion that they can also refuse oral food and fluids if they wish.

A study from the Netherlands titled 'Discomfort in nursing home patients with severe dementia in whom artificial nutrition and hydration is forgone' (2005) is helpful in understanding this problem: 'Patients already had a range of symptoms including apathy, fever, restlessness, dyspnoea, pressure ulcers, pain and constipation.' Items used to assess discomfort after ceasing fluids were 'noisy breathing, negative vocalization, sad facial expression, frightened facial expression, frown, tense body language, fidgeting, content facial expression and relaxed body language.' Approximately 30 per cent were on analgesics, and 40 per cent on sedative medications at the time of decision. These levels did not essentially change. Patients continued to be offered fluids by mouth. Their consciousness declined with time, as did their levels of suffering, although there were higher levels of discomfort in the first two days. 'Patients who are asleep have much lower levels of discomfort.' Survival was proportional to the level of hydration.

The authors stated: 'It is remarkable that analgesic medication (including opioids) and psychotropic medication, usually given to improve the comfort of patients, had no significant longitudinal effect on discomfort.' Surely this reflects inadequate dosage of appropriate medications; there are few symptoms relating to refusal of treatment that cannot be adequately relieved by palliative medication.

Almost all of the medical comment on this subject quoted above comes from the USA or the Netherlands. There is an ominous and regrettable silence on this subject in Australian medicine. According to the eminent head of clinical ethics and health law at the University of Newcastle, Professor Peter Saul, Australian doctors have an appalling knowledge of medical law, and thus of patient rights at the end of life. There is commonly an obstructionist attitude in nursing homes, which is why I speak about it.

The possibility of ending one's life in these circumstances is horrifying to many people. However, thanks to the legal power of advance care directives, you can create a directive that categorically requests palliation if one refuses assisted spoon-feeding, and defines the circumstances when this direction is to operate. You can, if you wish, give your agent (in Victoria, your medical treatment decision maker) some limited discretion in the decision.

Some personal experiences of dying by refusal of fluid and food in Victoria are relevant here.

Bunty, aged 90, was in a nursing home, dying slowly from lung cancer. She had a medical background, and wanted to bring her slow demise to an end, but was trapped. She elected, after discussion, to stop drinking and eating, and eventually died after 21 days. As advised, she discussed her decision with her doctor and nursing home administration, who, in 2017, had not had any previous experience with such a decision.

Despite this, Bunty was subjected to three cognitive assessments, the last on day nine from a young geriatrician (who had no experience with the process) and who did his best to persuade her not to proceed. However, she was delighted to pass the depression tests with flying colours! Bunty noted a positive: as her dehydration progressed, her sputum diminished and she no longer vomited when she coughed. She remained mostly coherent and was 'amused by her hallucination' (her daughter's observation). Due to consistent mouth care and daily applications of moisturizer, she was in excellent condition when she died. She received excellent and supportive care from the low-level carers, in contrast to the confused attitude of management.

Voluntary refusal of fluid and food is not an ideal end-of-life process: it takes time, it takes determination and courage, and some may feel angry that society makes them take this path. It can be emotionally distressing for some people and their families. Keith Andrews (director of medical and research services at the Royal Hospital for Neuro-disability in London) wrote in 1996 that 'the present attitude of ending the patient's life by withdrawal of nutrition and fluids is highly unsatisfactory, if not inhumane, and the option of euthanasia would be by far a more satisfactory solution'.

The key, as in all end-of-life events, is good communication, and good preparation, so that all can be confident in the outcome.

So, what is the place of voluntary refusal of fluids and food at this time?

The paper by Ben White and Lindy Willmott quoted at the start of this chapter asks this question: 'Is there a means to achieve this same outcome [assisted dying], a comfortable death desired by a competent adult at a time of their choosing which is justifiable according to current medical ethics and within the law?' This careful analysis clearly finds a legal basis for VRFF by a competent adult, a legal requirement to provide palliation as for any other dying person, and a judicial opinion that VRFF is not suicide. The addition of palliation to VRFF does not give rise to criminality.

The 2017 Victorian Voluntary Assisted Dying Act allows competent, suffering persons with less than six months to live to obtain assistance from a doctor to die (after a complicated process). However, many frail aged persons, who are competent and have intolerable suffering – a completed life – will not fall within these guidelines, and if they are in an aged-care home, they will be effectively trapped from taking any action to bring their life to a peaceful end, except for the legal ability to refuse fluids and food. Similarly, people with dementia who have lost competence fall outside the VAD Act – sad, but true, in our 'civilised' society.

So, until our laws are revised, two groups of people may have a need to at least consider and explore the concept of refusal of fluids and food. These are competent people who do not qualify under the VAD Act, or who are in jurisdictions that do not yet have a similar law allowing some choice at the end of life; they include people who have been diagnosed with early dementia, but who are still competent. Groups of such people could comprise:

1. terminally ill cancer patients whose prognosis is thought to be more than six months, or who are having extreme difficulty in obtaining two supportive medical opinions
2. people with severe organ failure of heart, lungs, liver or kidney, who, while they may have a terminal illness, have an unpredictable prognosis
3. people with severe unrelievable suffering from a disease that is not considered terminal
4. frail elderly people who do not have a specific terminal diagnosis, are nevertheless within unpredictable sight of the end, and have a completed life.

This last group may be either faced with imminent admission to aged care, or already trapped in aged care.

The eminent philosophical GP columnist for the *British Medical Journal*, Iona Heath, observed in 2010:

Death in extreme old age is often timely. When the ageing body begins to fail, diseases are like Shakespeare's sorrows: 'they come not single spies, but in battalions.' All clinicians caring for older people have the experience of treating one disease process, only for another to take its place; and the more diseases that coexist, the greater the hazards of overtreatment and polypharmacy, and the more challenges of daily life become a struggle. When one cause of death is curtailed, others must inevitably come forward to fill the gap. Everyone is obliged to die from something. If we close off all the alternative strategies, more and more older people will face the prospect of dementia.

Words of experience from a GP knowledgeable in treating the older person.

Sad though it is that these people may have to consider VRFF, they should be aware that it is a legal option and, if properly managed, can be accomplished with minimal distress. The key words here are 'if properly managed'. This is not a process to attempt without careful discussion with the family doctor, and aged-care management (if appropriate). Good medical and nursing care are essential if a good outcome is to occur, and having a supportive family is a huge benefit. An unaccompanied end by this means is hard work.

The High Court of Australia made it quite clear in its decision Rogers v Whitaker (1992) that a person consenting to medical treatment must be fully informed about that procedure, to the extent of providing information that a reasonable person would consider significant if they were made aware of the risk. It established a 'duty of disclosure', a higher standard than that of 'informed consent'. It would be reasonable to believe that a similar standard of disclosure would apply to the refusal of treatment.

In Victoria, the *Medical Treatment Act 1988* provided a statute right to refuse medical treatment, but not palliative care. Palliative care is defined as:

a. the provision of reasonable medical procedures for the relief of pain, suffering and discomfort; or
b. the reasonable provision of food and water.

This description does not explain whose judgement determines what is 'reasonable'.

It has been determined that the artificial provision of food and fluid (by intravenous or tube delivery) is medical treatment, and can be refused by a competent person, or by an agent (medical enduring power of attorney), even though such refusal of treatment will result in a hastened death (Morris J in *Gardner; re BWV 2003*). It is also clear that when such refusal of artificial food and fluids is enacted, any suffering must be palliated by carers. The preamble to the Medical Treatment Act states that it is 'desirable that dying patients receive maximum relief of pain and suffering'.

There is no doubt that a rational, competent, capable person has a right to cease eating and drinking – to refuse food and drink with the intention to die. Their autonomy must be respected, and they cannot be force-fed.

Advance care directives have statutory recognition in many states. Such statutory recognition does now exist in Victoria, following the passage of the Medical Treatment Planning and Decisions Act 2016. The common-law status of such a document was recently validated in the Supreme Court of New South Wales.

Persons who develop dementia will commonly ultimately die of inanition and starvation, due to their ultimate complete lack of interest in food (a loss of understanding of its essential nature for the maintenance of life) or a loss of the ability to swallow. PEG-feeding was first introduced in the USA in 1979. By 2005, 51 per cent of patients with dementia had such tubes in place when they died. It was considered essential medical treatment for the preservation of life. Following the decision of Morris J (see above), such feeding is now very uncommon in Australia.

In the absence of tube-feeding to maintain life, hand-spoon-feeding by a carer is almost universal as an alternative. It is the alternative to a recognised medical treatment, and although it is not traditional to describe it as such, it could be considered as treatment in these circumstances. Without it, the person will die. It is generally considered to be a moral obligation to provide such oral-assisted spoon-feeding, and part of palliative care. However, the Medical Treatment Act 1988 definition of palliative care includes 'the reasonable provision of food and fluids'. Apart from the question of who makes the consideration of what is 'reasonable', the interpretation of 'provision' is significant. If I place food and fluid before and within reach of a person, with an explanation of its significance and encouragement to partake, then I have *provided* food and fluid. Once I begin to actively feed that person, then I have begun to *administer* that food and fluid. Further, in dementia there is a progression from a person who seems willing to ingest food and fluid to one for whom swallowing is virtually lost, and the feeding can take on a 'forced' character.

A person who is competent without dementia, or a person who is competent in the early stage of dementia, may create an advance care directive regarding the refusal of treatment during the course of that disease. There must be full disclosure about the course of the disease, and the consequences of refusing various treatment options during the course of the disease, for such a directive to be valid. If it has been properly constructed, and applies to the circumstance in question, then it must be respected.

Such a directive can clearly refuse artificial (tube) feeding in order to prevent prolongation of life in an incompetent state (or in fact for any, or no, reason). Hand-spoon-feeding is the medical alternative to tube-feeding. I would argue that such spoon-feeding should be capable of being refused via an advance care directive, properly constructed by a capable person. They could refuse such feeding if they were competent. They should have the same right if requested via a valid advance care directive, even more so if supported by a medical agent (medical treatment decision maker).

It is obvious that good communication, and the creation of a concise advance care directive when competent, are essential for your protection from prolonged suffering in dementia. Yet the great irony is that the voluntary refusal of fluids and food is legal for the frail aged and some with dementia, but gentler and more dignified means are not available.

CHAPTER 9

Ending one's own life, or suicide?

oluntary assisted dying, or state-sanctioned suicide?
'That a person can know when to die and can die at will, intentionally, with full awareness of what he is doing, is a concept so alien to our culture that one scarcely mentions it without an apology.' So wrote Robert S. de Ropp in *The Master Game* in 1968. Of course, he was talking about suicide. I, more than 50 years later, make no apology.

Suicide. SUICIDE! The word conjures up violent thoughts, possibly unwanted memories for some. Tragic, silent, unexpected violence, in the context of depression, disordered thought, maybe transient severe distress due to emotional – or perceived social or financial – disaster. Tragic, because of the loss of a life that might easily have been saved with timely and appropriate help. Tragic, because of the profound sense of grief, and often guilt, that is left behind. Tragic, because of the stigma which is associated with the word and all those left to suffer.

The detailed final report of Professor Brian Owler's Ministerial Advisory Panel to the Victorian Government on Voluntary Assisted Dying contained some very important statements on language. It clearly explained why the proposed Bill was to be described as a Voluntary Assisted Dying Bill, and that the language of 'assisted suicide' was totally inappropriate. The recently introduced Western Australian Bill is even more specific on this point. Suicide is not recognised as the cause of death. But this has not stopped opponents of such legislation describing the proposed law as assisted suicide, even state-sanctioned suicide, and – more extraordinarily – as 'killing'. The reason for the use of such language is simple: the tragic occurrence of suicide in our community carries an enormous and unfortunate stigma, one that resonates in a very negative way in the community, and may lead politicians and the public to fear a change in the law. The English language has only one word for ending one's own life: 'suicide'. The *Oxford English Dictionary* defines suicide as 'the action of killing oneself deliberately'. An alternative way of expressing such an action would be 'ending one's own life deliberately' (which is much preferred to 'taking one's own life deliberately', which retains a pejorative ring). They both mean the same thing, but the first wording is harsh, pejorative and stigmatic.

Historically, suicide has been seen as a sin by the Catholic Church, and as a crime by temporal law until the 1960s. The Catholic attitude to suicide dates from the writings of St Augustine (died 430 CE), and has become embedded in Catholic dogma ever since. It is a mortal sin, one of the worst that can be committed. This severe dogma has deeply affected civil thought and practice, until the advent of a psychiatric approach to the problem in the late 19th century.

The Catholic Church has fought tooth and nail against assisted-dying laws. It has predominantly fought the battle through the mouths and pens of committed Catholic doctors and bioethicists. It has rarely spoken openly of the Church's moral objections, hiding behind specious arguments based on fear, uncertainty and doubt. However, with the imminent introduction of the Victorian law, it exposed its real position. Four eminent Victorian Catholic bishops stated: 'We cannot co-operate with the facilitation of suicide, even when it seems motivated by empathy and kindness.' So the Catholic Church's opposition to voluntary assisted dying, as well as its position on a number of other civil laws such as abortion, certain aspects of withdrawal or refusal of treatment, and patient-controlled palliative care, are unlikely to change in many decades, if ever. The Church would rather condone the gradual induction of dying people into a deep coma, without the provision of fluids and food, and denying them the opportunity to say a close and personal goodbye.

Aiding and abetting, or inciting, suicide (the interpretation of this is unclear in law) is still regarded as committing a crime. Since the 1960s, suicide is no longer a crime. Society still uses the phrase 'committing suicide', which suggests criminality (as in committing murder, torture or rape), which is not correct and adds to the unfortunate stigma associated with suicide.

The Voluntary Assisted Dying law will allow a doctor, on request from a competent patient, in the strict circumstances of unacceptable suffering in the context of a terminal illness, to provide medication to that patient, which they must self-administer, so they may end their own life (in order to end their suffering), if the person finally comes to that decision. The doctor cannot 'kill' the person; the suffering person has complete control.*

In the late 19th century, suicide came to be recognised as a consequence of an unsound mind (principally associated with depression or psychosis) which should be treated, not punished. Criteria for diagnosing depression have been developed by psychiatrists (*Diagnostic and Statistical Manual of Mental Disorders* IV), which are nevertheless subjective and acknowledged as difficult to apply to terminally ill patients, simply because some of the symptoms of depression may also be the intrinsic symptoms of dying persons. Even the two most critical symptoms for the diagnosis of depression, anhedonia (a lack of any pleasure in one's life) and 'suicidality' (the thought of ending one's own life) are questionable when people are terminally ill. Is the idea of ending one's own suffering life days, weeks or even months early when one is already dying so bizarre as to demand a diagnosis of severe depression?

The diagnosis of depression in an end-of-life situation is not easy. However, the very experienced Canadian psychiatrist Harvey Chochinov found the answer to the question 'Are you feeling depressed?' to be as accurate as more elaborate assessments. Experienced psychiatrists see a clear distinction between the psychology of such end-of-life decisions and the psychopathology of suicide as it is generally understood. A loss of quality of life and meaning in life, associated with intolerable and unrelievable suffering, are not uncommon experiences at the end of life; they may reasonably and rationally lead to a decision to consider ending one's own life.

---

* Publisher's note: the *Voluntary Assisted Dying Act 2017* (Vic) also allows for practitioner administration in limited circumstances: if the patient is physically incapable of self-administration or digestion of the voluntary assisted dying substance, by special arrangement a doctor may assist by injection.

Eighty-six per cent of British psychiatrists stated that such an action (described as suicide) may be rational, and 38 per cent thought assistance should be legal.

The characteristics of suicide in the general sense are quite distinct from those of a person requesting assisted dying. On the one hand there is a disturbed mental (not physical) state associated with depression or psychosis; false and erroneous views about the future; a total lack of discussion with family and friends about the impending, usually violent, solitary event, where a goodbye to others is impossible; and an overwhelming sense of grief, shame and failure is left behind. Contrast this with voluntary assisted dying, where a terminally ill person makes a clear and considered decision, from a factual and realistic view of the future, which is discussed with two doctors and family; an understanding is reached, where the support of family is possible; and a shared goodbye is an integral part of the process. The death that follows is shared, peaceful, calm and dignified, and the grief that is left is minimised.

Associate Professor of Psychology at Florida State University, Joseph Franklin, responding in 2018 to the totally unexpected suicide of two eminent Americans, indicated that it was virtually impossible to predict suicide. He stated:

As a scientist who has focused on this question for the past decade, I should have a pretty good idea of who is or isn't going to die by suicide. But the sad truth is, I don't. [...] The fact that suicide is so hard to predict unfortunately took about 50 years for most scientists to appreciate. [...] About 2 percent of severely depressed people eventually die by suicide, which is only slightly higher than the 1.6 percent of people from the general United States population who eventually die by suicide.

These comments make it abundantly clear that suicide, as seen by an experienced academic, is unpredictable, in complete contrast to the contemplated, considered and openly discussed end of life after dialogue with doctor and family. Chalk and cheese: not to be confused, nor to be described or remotely considered under the same name.

Above all, the key question is whether a depressed mood is affecting the person's competence to make rational decisions. There is sound evidence that competence can be retained in this situation. If a person has the ability to reason, can understand relevant information, has a realistic world view, is acting in accordance with their fundamental interests, and wishes to avoid harm to others, then their decision can be assessed as rational and considered. The critical point is that the suffering person has control over the end of their life, and they will determine if, when, and where their life will end, and who will be present to say goodbye.

Should such a death be categorised as committing suicide in the sense of a crime or a sin – or described as ending one's own life to end intolerable suffering? The Victorian parliamentary inquiry and the government bill, wished to consider it in the latter terms, whereas religious zealots would try to convince you of the former. The government wishes to improve and expand palliative care, and this legislation will increase the scope and choices available to people in palliative care, will help to end suffering, and will open up opportunities for deeper dialogue between doctors and their patients.

A win-win situation, I would have thought.

Oregon's *Death with Dignity* law was passed in 1994, and reaffirmed in 1997. After a number of failed citizen-initiated referenda in western states in the USA for legalisation of voluntary euthanasia (lethal injection), Oregon considered the question from a different perspective: patient-controlled end of life. The doctor would provide the medication and the patient would administer it (or not). This was initially described as 'physician-assisted suicide'. The law was passed in 1994, held up in district courts and finally in the US Supreme Court, until the Oregon people emphatically reaffirmed the decision in 1997 and it became affirmed law, as the *Death with Dignity Act*.

Opponents of the Oregon law constantly referred to this medical aid in dying as suicide, assisted suicide, or self-killing (as do some unenlightened journalists and commentators), and were intent on using the phrase 'physician-assisted suicide'. This was because the word 'suicide' carried a stigma of sin and crime, and made the act less acceptable to the public, even though it was far safer from abuse than euthanasia (a lethal injection in the same circumstances). Oregonians were disturbed by this stigma, and the wording of the legislation was changed to 'aid in dying'.

For many years I have been disturbed by the use of the word suicide, as in the phrase 'physician-assisted suicide', when there are discussions about end of life. I first discussed this in *A Good Death*, and later presented a paper on rational suicide at a conference on suicide prevention in Sydney in 2008. This phrase, 'rational suicide', was used in the initial Dutch Remmelink Report of 1991 into end-of-life practice (Van der Maas et al., 1991). Timothy Quill did not use the phrase in his seminal article of 1991 regarding the death of Diane, but did so in 1992 ('Care of the hopelessly ill', *New England Journal of Medicine*, 1992).

Yet a little careful analysis quickly reveals the difference between the common understanding of 'suicide' and voluntary assisted dying. The legislation in Victoria, passed in 2017, which allows a doctor to prescribe medication that the person may self-administer to end their life, uses the wording 'voluntary assisted dying'.

The only reason for combining 'rational' and 'suicide' in the same phrase is to draw attention to the fact that not all people ending their lives deliberately are mentally ill. Some are rational, competent and do not actually want to die; they are considering dying only in order to be relieved of intolerable and otherwise unrelievable suffering. Sydney psychologist Sarah Edelman told the story of Aina, suffering grievously from an untreatable neuro-degenerative disorder. After Aina disclosed her 'suicidal' thoughts, she was referred to a psychiatric assessment team in hospital, who found her to be of sound mind, and appraising her circumstances realistically. Sadly, I have seen brutal interventions involving arbitrary sectioning on far too many occasions. It remains a great fear in suffering people's minds if they talk frankly with their doctor.

The following story graphically explains that difference.

I recently had a discussion with a woman who had the extraordinary experience of having her 17-year-old son, and her 87-year-old father 16 years later, end their own lives deliberately. The two events are starkly different.

Her young second son – handsome, extremely popular and a celebrated sportsman – jumped to his death from a cliff onto the rocks below. A violent, unpredictable act, and he died at the scene despite emergency services intervention. For his mother, his death was unexpected and devastating: no explanation, no chance to say goodbye, although she and her husband witnessed the futile efforts at resuscitation. Her grief and guilt were profound and led to depression. Due to the love and support of her husband and other children, medical help, and her own inner strength, she has, after 16 years, healed to a large extent, but will never forget.

Fifteen years later, her 87-year-old father was diagnosed with advanced prostate cancer, which caused severe and unrelenting bone pain. Long a believer in having control at the end of his life, he had obtained a quantity of medication, but a dose at the margin of certainty. He took to his own bed, said goodbye to his family, swallowed his medication, went to sleep over ten minutes, and died two hours later. His daughter was with him, but found it stressful, being uncertain that the dose was sufficient, and anxious about the outcome. She wished that a doctor could have prescribed the appropriate medication, and been present for reassurance and comfort.

Nevertheless, her father did die at a time of his choosing, peacefully and with dignity, after saying goodbye to his family. He ended his own life deliberately – but what a contrast with the death of his grandson. The mother could say goodbye to her son only *after* his violent death. Should two such different ends both be described as 'suicide'? I strongly believe they should be distinguished. The Victorian Voluntary Assisted Dying Act, which allows a terminally ill person to end their own life deliberately with the assistance of a doctor, does not use the word 'suicide' at any point. It goes so far as to indicate that the death certificate cites death as due to the underlying illness.

A Montana psychologist, Victor Lieberman, wrote:

Previously mislabelled as 'physician assisted suicide', the choice of a dying patient to act, with medical assistance, upon their own readiness for a peaceful death is more accurately referred to as 'aid in dying' [which is exactly the phrase ultimately accepted by the Oregon legislature] [...] It is more truly understood as one way to accept death as the completion of life. [...] Among the terminally ill, however, a life-ending act can be more properly considered life-completing. I disagree with the assumption that all such acts must be prevented. Such an attitude treats all readiness for death as mistaken, or it insists that all active expressions of readiness (beyond waiting for death) signal a lack of mental competency. [...] I am also convinced that, with sufficient communication and mutual understanding, such an event does not have to produce the complicated forms of grief we typically see in deaths that are suicides.

A Victorian psychiatrist wrote:

From my experience in psychiatry and from my life experience, my understanding is that the mental state of those contemplating suicide and those wanting to play an active role in choosing their time to die, are very different. [...] Suicide comes from hopelessness and despair. Acceptance of the inevitability of death may lead to a desire to have some choice about the timing of one's end of life.

So clear was the distinction to this psychiatrist, that she found the term 'rational suicide' to be an oxymoron – in psychiatric terms, suicide in association with mental illness could not be rational – hence the moronic association.

Jonathon Glover, in his 1977 book *Causing Death and Saving Lives*, observes:

Our estimates of the quality of our lives are especially vulnerable to temporary changes of mood, so that the only reasonable way to reach a serious evaluation is to consider the question over a fairly long stretch of time. Even this has limitations because of the difficulty of giving weight to estimates made at different times and in different moods, but anything less is hopelessly inadequate.

He also urges consideration of possible harm to others. I completely agree with his evaluation; it is essentially one of careful and prolonged communication about a very serious matter. The great French writer and philosopher Albert Camus wrote, 'There is only one serious philosophical problem, and that is suicide. Judging whether life is or is not worth living amounts to answering the fundamental question of philosophy.' Yet it is clear he is discussing a healthy person, not someone who is approaching death and has intolerable suffering. Camus is not considering the 'completed life' context of this book. Nor, specifically, is Glover.

Glover does recognise that there are 'many different kinds of suicidal act'. He recognises that the person who tries to kill (Glover's word) himself in a state of severe but temporary depression differs from the act of someone who, after prolonged deliberation, decides to kill himself rather than face any more of his incurable illness. He also recognises altruistic suicide, as a civil or political protest (perhaps a hunger strike), and 'heroic' gambling suicides – as in war, or in terrorism (depending from which side you look). To my mind, to include all these very different acts, with different reasons and meanings, under the same banner makes no sense. Moreover, it is harmful, because it is derogatory to rational human beings who are approaching the end of their completed lives and who consider this option carefully with their family. After all, the Parliament of Victoria, like most parliaments today, is unfortunately not always a place of rational and considered debate on social issues. However, even so, it did accept that suicide was not an appropriate word to use in the Voluntary Assistant Dying Act.

The Times of London reported that the verdict of 'suicide' would be scrapped under sweeping plans to overhaul coroners' powers and death certification procedures. The term, which has been in use for more than three centuries, would be replaced by the more neutral phrase 'death by own actions'. The change was designed to take away the stigma attached to a person taking their own life. Unfortunately, this expected change did not occur.

Attitudes to this question are changing, as seen in recent parliamentary and court decisions. The Victorian Parliament passed the *Medical Treatment Act* in 1987, which allowed a competent person to deliberately refuse medical treatment, knowing that to do so would be to die. This could be a deliberate decision to end one's life, and if that decision meant they would die, their doctor was exhorted to 'provide maximum relief of pain and suffering'. Deliberately choosing to die – suicide? No! Not according to this law. In 2010, Justice Kourakis of the South Australian Supreme Court declared (in relation to a 74-year-old competent woman confined to a nursing home) that 'I find that the refusal of sustenance and medication is not suicide within the common law meaning of that term', and that doctors and nurses must provide palliative assistance to relieve any suffering associated with such a course of events.

Judge Rowan Darke (New South Wales Supreme Court) subsequently dealt with a request from a 28-year-old man who had been dependent on a mechanical ventilator since the age of seven. His request was to have his ventilator switched off. Darke dismissed the concerns of some hospital staff about aiding and abetting suicide. 'The legal concept of suicide, being the intentional taking of one's own life, is not engaged in a case where medical assistance is refused, even in the knowledge of certain death.'

In 2015 an alert was issued over the supposedly 'inappropriate' use of opioid patches in aged care, as a result of a cohort study of 60 residential facilities and 600 patients (mean age 87 years). Such large studies have value, but may lack discrimination and nuance; for example, was there discussion with the resident or the treating doctor on the cause and level of pain, or the attitude of the resident to the acceptance of risk in order to be completely free of pain? Much of this 'inappropriate' use of opioid patches may have come about after careful discussion between the resident and the doctor, and been an entirely ethical trade-off of risks (hastening death) and benefit (complete relief of pain).

Here we confront a dichotomy in medical practice: the wishes and values of the 'patient', and the safety of practice and protection of the profession and the care homes. The authors of the above report would no doubt argue that safe practice ('best practice') from the medical point of view is to avoid opioid patches, or to slowly titrate the dose up from weaker medications. If such an approach is in conflict with the best interests of the resident, whose interests should prevail? Bioethicist Daniel Sokol has no doubt; he stated in 2008 that dying patients know best what is in their best interests. He asserted that 'overall best interests may legitimately differ from medical best interests, and the two should not be confused'.

Yet there is an intransigence in medical attitudes. Many doctors and nursing home administrators refer people to psychiatry on the mere suggestion of wanting to cease fluids and food, or of wanting assistance in dying, despite having no prior concern about competence, or despite having other medical opinions confirming competence. This, of course, is a protective response, but can do extreme harm to the 'patient'. Eminent Catholic psychiatrist Professor David Kissane, Melbourne-based and heavily involved in palliative care, has stated that he has never encountered any patient who had grounds for euthanasia. He has developed his own 'demoralisation syndrome' to explain requests for assisted dying.

Professor Bill Silvester, a champion of advance care planning, made this statement to the *Herald Sun* (25 May 2015): 'Often older people attempt to take their own life, it has been planned for many months in the face of grief, loneliness and suffering – usually a combination of ill-health and having lost a life-long partner.' He went on to describe how a man, who had lost his wife in an institution after suffering dementia for many years, and himself suffering from respiratory disease (he could barely walk ten metres without stopping, and could not drive or shop), tried to end his own life. He was still living alone, valuing his independence. He had saved up some tablets, and, after shaving and dressing in his best clothes, lay on his bed and took them. Two to three days later he was found unconscious, taken to hospital, resuscitated, intubated and placed on kidney dialysis, and he recovered. After six weeks in hospital, he indicated that he still wanted to end his life, and as a result was forcibly committed for psychiatric care. A month after discharge from hospital, he was found hanging in his room.

Is this a story of a great medical success, or a great medical failure? To me it is a monumental failure, but it illustrates a rational decision to end a completed life, which failed because of a gross lack of communication, an abuse of psychiatric process, and a medical profession acting reflexively to protect itself rather than acting in the best interests of the individual. Surely this man and his medical problems were well known to his treating doctor(s) – why hadn't he completed an advance care directive, refusing any resuscitation? Why wasn't he receiving palliative care – or if he was, why wasn't there communication between his GP, palliative carer and the hospital? Nowadays, I hope that a man in this circumstance would have a MyHealth record available. I accept that perfection in medical management is not easy, but it should be vastly better than this history indicates. These errors would have cost hundreds of thousand dollars in futile treatment, but this fades into insignificance when compared with the psychological cost of the abuse of this man's chosen journey to the end of his life.

Professor Patrick McGorry, eminent psychiatrist and Australian of the Year 2012, wrote emotively (*The Sydney Morning Herald*, 10 September 2012) about the toll of suicide on the young. He wrote of 'the link between mental ill health and suicide', of suicide as 'a silent killer whose footprints are actively concealed by a frightened and often judgmental society'; and that 'the culture of shame and secrecy also cripples the ability of bereaved families and friends to recover from their brutal loss', advocating for 'stigma-free expert care available in a youth-friendly environment'. All of these comments I endorse unhesitatingly, but he said nothing about old-age 'suicide'. Time and space probably prevented this, but the focus on youth ignores the fact that men over 85 end their lives at a one-third higher rate than men aged 35–44, and much higher than for younger men and all women.

This did not deter Dr Roderick McKay, director of psychiatry and mental health at the New South Wales Institute of Psychiatry, from saying that the focus on euthanasia led too many to dismiss the role of psychiatric and social problems among the elderly, problems with a solution. He said, 'I've yet to meet a family member who says after a suicide (of an old person) "well that's a relief".' Of course he hasn't, because he's confusing suicide with voluntary assisted dying.

Research by psychiatrist Henry O'Connell and colleagues in 2004 confirmed – not surprisingly – that elderly people have a higher risk of suicide than any other group worldwide. They also recognised that 'Physical health and disability seem to be associated independently of depression with the "wish to die"', and also noted that 'Two other retrospective case-control studies found the burden of physical illness and current serious physical illness (such as visual impairment, neurological disorders and malignant disease), to be significantly associated with completed suicide in elderly people.' The tenor of this paper was that, despite low levels of success in treatment of depression (52 per cent in the general population), suicidal tendencies in the elderly should be detected and treated – even, it seemed, though the cause was not necessarily depression.

It is alleged that it sends a 'mixed message' to acknowledge that not all people ending their own lives have mental illness, and that in the older age group many are rational. So we continue to have a medical message of preventing 'suicide' at all costs, without adequate consideration of the possibility of an underlying completed life.

And so we have the manic prevention of 'suicide' in aged-care homes. Suicide is to be prevented at all cost (at least legal cost). To end one's own life in a nursing home is an extraordinarily difficult task. As described in chapter 4, entering aged care is to enter a prison system, an entrapped environment. The lack of privacy means that the opportunity for a peaceful and dignified death is absent, certainly one accompanied by family to say goodbye. An aged-care worker stated:

> I worked in aged care for over 10 years and many times I have seen people who would die if they had the choice. Once you get into any kind of institutionalized care you lose your freedom of choice. I know of instances where elderly people have attempted suicide in care, and of course it's almost impossible for them because they are monitored regularly.

Nevertheless, suicides apparently do occur in care, as reported by Briony Murphy, Professor Joe Ibrahim and colleagues of Monash University in 2018 (*International Journal of Geriatric Psychiatry*). They collated 141 nursing home deaths by suicide in a 13-year period from 2000; this is an incidence of a little over ten per year in a risk population of more than 170,000, occurring at a rate of 0.02 deaths per 100,000 resident bed days. More than one-third had made a previous unsuccessful suicide attempt, 72 per cent prior to – and commonly close to – their admission, but 28 per cent had made a prior attempt while in care. The commonest methods were hanging, jumping from a height, or asphyxiation using a plastic bag; one can imagine the level of suffering needed to induce such violent acts. To emphasise the difficulty in nursing homes, one-quarter of these suicides occurred outside the nursing home, while the resident was on leave.

The research revealed that 69 per cent of the aged-care residents attempting suicide were male; 66 per cent already had a diagnosis of depression; 50 per cent had resided in care for less than 12 months; major life stressors identified were health deterioration (79 per cent), isolation and loneliness (42 per cent), and maladjustment to life in care (30 per cent). These figures are not surprising; it is already known that males are more likely to suicide than females (even though men are much in the minority in care), that the vast majority of residents have deteriorating health (often in multiple domains), and that depression is very common in residents. I cannot find any reliable research on the incidence of isolation and loneliness, or maladjustment to care, although it is acknowledged to occur. Research reveals a dearth of data. The current declining circumstances in aged care would suggest that the situation is not likely to improve, except through more restrictions on liberty and privacy.

Murphy (Jain) and Ibrahim devoted the May 2018 issue of the *Residential Aged Care Communiqué* to this subject, noting in the introduction that 'despite its existence, it is one that is seldom talked about'. They 'debated long and hard about whether we should cover this topic', but decided to do so because 'if we do not confront the reality of what happens, then how will we know what to change to improve the circumstances?' I congratulate them on coming to this conclusion.

The *Communiqué* gives coronial details of two suicides in residential care, to encourage discussion. One, of a 95-year-old man, occurred in Canada. He had ten co-morbidities; after two-and-a-half years in residential care he developed severe pain from a compression fracture at the L1 vertebra, followed by urinary retention. His daughter complained about his necessary pain relief, that it was sedating him and causing nausea and decreased appetite. She ordered that the pain relief be ceased, whereupon the pain became so severe he was screaming and stated that 'he just wanted to die'. He was placed on suicide watch, which should have involved 15-minute observations, yet he was found dead one hour later with a plastic bag over his head.

Although the information accompanying this case report is minimal, comment is invited, so I will comment. The medical surprise question – Is this person likely to die within 12 months? – is, clearly, answered in the affirmative. His house of cards is collapsing, and he wishes, not unreasonably in my opinion, to die. Traditional medicine decides he must be kept alive, at all costs, by instituting a 'suicide watch'. I could not talk to him, and cannot assess his competence, but would not be surprised if he had a completed life. His wish to die did not appear to be due to mental illness, but rather to acute-to-chronic physical circumstances. What is also evident is that even the most stringent surveillance could not prevent his death, and one can assume that, if he had been found before he had died, he would have been resuscitated. I find it hard to imagine a more extraordinary case report through which to extol the virtues of suicide prevention in residential care!

The second report is also bizarre – so complex it is difficult to summarise. A 72-year-old non-English-speaking woman who had been at home in the care of family had ten chronic co-morbidities, spinal pain for 13 years (unrelieved by three spinal operations, indeed reported as worse after the third in 2010) and, despite a history of depression and a suicide attempt, assessed as suitable for low-care respite when her family decided on a two-month overseas holiday. Red flags are fluttering everywhere, and it is no surprise that she was reclusive while in care, and after 12 days ended her life by hanging. While clearly more could – and should – have been done, this simply illustrates the enormously difficult task that the aged-care system faces to prevent determined individuals, when driven by enough suffering, from ending their lives. Even if the warnings had been noted and acted upon, it is impossible to keep someone in aged care under constant surveillance; all they need is five minutes alone and huge determination. You may succeed in prevention if you make someone even more of a prisoner than they already are!

A University of Western Australia study of 38,000 community-based older men, followed for up to 16 years, found that the strongest association with completed suicide was the number of bodily health systems affected by disease (Horsemen of the Ageing Apocalypse?): those with more than five had an eleven-fold risk of suicide. The authors wrote that 'the fraction of suicides attributable to having five or more health systems affected by disease was 79 per cent while this figure for any mood disorder (bipolar or depression) was 17 per cent'. Not deterred by failing to find that depression (the previous focus of suicide prevention) was the important cause, the authors apparently recommended focusing on these 'multiple morbidities' for suicide prevention. What about discussing the possibility of a completed life and a dignified chosen death, rather than a tragic solitary one? Maybe they could recognise that life is finite, that not all disease can be cured, and that not all patients want to live forever – that some have a completed life, and that is what their suicide, or attempted suicide, is expressing. We might discover this if we did not assume the diagnosis of mental disorder, incarcerate them in an institution for their crime and sin, and ignore their humanity.

Professors Holmes and Ibrahim, in the November 2018 issue of the *Communiqué*, discussed case in Oakden, South Australia, where a man in residential care with dementia, also receiving palliative care for lung disease, was attacked and killed by another resident. The coroner delivered a finding after ten years! No matter how much we feel like criticising residential care, it is necessary, and only fair, to recognise the extreme difficulty in providing total protection to all residents and staff from injury, or suicide, given the difficult and vulnerable people who are their residents.

It appalls me, but does not surprise me, that doctors in the 21st century behave in this way towards this vulnerable population. The profession has lost its way in technical and therapeutic solutions to disease, and has a mania for treating at any cost (cost to the patient and family, not to the doctor), irrespective of the revealed view of the 'patient'. I would make essential reading for all medical students Eric Cassell's classic article in the *Annals of Internal Medicine* (1999) titled 'Diagnosing suffering: A perspective'. Perhaps everyone should read it; it might improve their next consultation with their doctor, if they apply its wisdom.

It is my view that the word 'suicide' should be expunged from the dictionary. It is a cruel word, cloaked in shame and guilt, used in an egregious, pejorative and stigmatic way. It carries associations with sin, guilt and crime which are underserved in any circumstances. It should be banished, not just for rational, considered and openly discussed end-of-life actions by people with intolerable suffering, but for all circumstances where people 'end their own lives'. A difficult task, but it has become a very harmful and misunderstood word.

Adding to the stigma is the appellation 'committing' suicide. The word 'commit' is associated with the worst crimes such as murder, rape and torture, but also associated with 'sins' such as incest or bigamy, and includes suicide. As common law evolved from canon (church) law, these 'sins' carried over into common law with all the stigma that had enshrouded them under the church.

Words come and go; it is time suicide went.

It also appalls me that modern psychiatry determines to treat every attempt by a person to end their life as due to mental illness and to be prevented at all costs, without any consideration of the age or unalterable physical circumstances of that person. Forgive me if I am harsh; I am sure there are many psychiatrists (I have talked with some) who are in disagreement with the public face of their specialty, and who recognise the limitations of their treatment – but where are their voices?

A problem? There need not be. If doctors and care homes took the trouble to be fully informed about their charges' wishes, or more importantly directions, to make such knowledge widely known to staff, and to be taking the trouble to assess and track the competency of their charges, an enormous amount of harm, trouble and cost would be avoided.

I predict that such 'deaths by own actions' in older people will continue to rise until society recognises the reality of a completed life, and has the compassion and grace to allow assistance for these thoughtful people to end their own lives in peace, security and dignity, sharing a loving goodbye with their family. When that happens, both admissions to aged care institutions and such deaths will fall significantly.

Words: consider sexual intercourse, a word that encompasses three distinctly different contexts, *viz.*, rape, a one-night stand, and an act of love in a committed marriage. We are capable of legally and emotionally separating these actions. Why can we not distinguish between different acts that deliberately end life?

CHAPTER 10

Solutions

I have been expected to live my life in a responsible manner. Why should my death be any different?

Aged care in Australia has developed in a haphazard manner through the 20th century to its present disorganised state. It is disorganised in the sense of a lack of overall control, variable facilities, numerous providers, poor management and assessment of care, poor training of staff, and no specified staffing levels. Now it is challenged by allegations of poor care and abuse, as evidenced by the royal commission into aged care.

People using aged care are predominantly terminally ill to varying degrees: those who are universally recognised, such as those with cancer or organ failure, or those who – unfortunately – are not so recognised, such as the frail aged who are dependent, and those with dementia. There is in addition a smaller number with severe chronic disability.

This book is focused on the frail aged and those with dementia for the simple reasons that they have a very weak position in our society and their voices are rarely heard. They do not have a platform. As Nicholas Christakis stated in 2008: 'We do not see marches of terminally ill people demanding recognition of their rights to more resources and more attention.'

This book is based on several fundamental premises.

In 2009, in an address to the Sydney University Law School, I enunciated six medical givens relating to end-of-life suffering in a general sense. They were:

- first, that dying can be associated with intolerable suffering, which can rise to a crescendo as death approaches
- second, that some suffering at the end of life will end only with death

- third, that doctors have a duty to relieve suffering
- fourth, that palliative care cannot relieve all pain and suffering
- fifth, that some persons do make rational and persistent requests for hastening of death
- and sixth, that doctors have a duty to respect the autonomy of a fully informed competent person.

My inescapable conclusion from these six givens was that, if a competent person made a persistent request for relief of intolerable and unrelievable suffering, I would have a medical obligation to provide them with humane assistance to die with dignity. The twin factors of necessity to relieve suffering and undisputed informed consent to assistance are paramount in coming to this decision

In 2019 I have come to another set of fundamental premises relating to aged and dementia care. The first is that while a person remains in their own home they retain a level of independence, even if they require increasing levels of assistance to remain there. This is, of course, best provided by immediate family for as long as possible. Every effort should be made to provide aged care and assistance for the frail aged and those dying in their own home, so they can remain in their own home, without excessive stress on the family carer(s).

The second is that the vast majority of people who enter residential aged care have lost their ability to care for themselves (their independence), and they will either die in aged care or be shunted to hospital or hospice to die. However, this majority does not want either outcome. They do not want these environments as the place where they will die.

The third premise is that the vast majority of people who enter residential aged care have not made a personal choice to be there, but have become residents due to someone else's decision. Due to their circumstances of fragility, old age, and loss of personal power, an aged parent is often at the mercy of their children. These children are also often in a compromised position, already having their own children to look after, limited accommodation to take their loved one to their home, and a necessary job that limits their ability to provide assistance, quite apart from problems of distance. The guilt some of those children experience is extreme when they find that they have no alternative but to admit their parent, against their expressed wish, to aged care. Finally, there is the stress, and often undue haste, to find a – one hopes – satisfactory placement. What is more, the aged person commonly loses the attachment to their long-term general practitioner.

My fourth premise is that the majority of personal suffering in aged care is of a nature that cannot be adequately palliated. This suffering must currently be borne stoically while waiting for death, without adequate recognition of impending death or adequate attention to appropriate palliation.

My fifth premise is that every doctor should aim to assist every person to go as far with their life as possible, but to recognise that a person's competent autonomous decision is paramount, whether it is a contemporaneous decision, or one made previously by an advance care directive.

My sixth premise is that no person should be so distressed as to make a request for an early end to their life solely because of poor or inadequate aged-care support.

My seventh premise is that a competent person, threatened by aged-care admission, or already in aged care, who considers they have a completed life, should be able to make a choice for voluntary assisted dying as an alternative.

Comparisons show that this set of givens for end of life and those for aged care are similar, but with some differences. Aged care is complicated by two very different groups of residents: those with competence and those without (usually cognitive failure due to dementia) – so I will defer discussion of dementia for the moment. First, the major similarities are that people with suffering in aged care may have unrelievable and intolerable suffering, which palliative care cannot resolve. Palliative care cannot alter a genuinely completed life – it cannot change the degenerations of age nor the sense of imprisonment in aged care that many have, and the deep wish not to be there.

The second major similarity is the importance of autonomy. Most doctors are coming to accept the principle of autonomy at the very end of life for a person dying from cancer, but some have trouble accepting it in the slower trajectory to end life in aged care. While virtually all residents in aged care are terminally ill, their trajectory to the end is often unpredictable, so that their requests for assistance are commonly brushed aside, not only by their doctors but also by their families. This unpredictability is commonly because their suffering may be predominantly psychological and existential, in addition to physical. This may be somewhat more subtle than many people understand, and it is often not expressed clearly, particularly when it relates to their environment, and their sense of entrapment.

Families will often give great support to a parent who is dying badly with cancer, but they have much more difficulty in supporting the dying wish of a parent in aged care when they have had an important role in that incarceration. Moreover, they can be loaded with guilt and grief, and sometimes with moral considerations that have become irrelevant to the sufferer.

There are few things I detest more than the view that frail old people are not capable of making considered decisions about the end of their life, or that they should be forced into an unwanted, sometimes uncaring and hostile, environment for the rest of their life, against their wishes. Their crime? Simply to be old and frail, and – naturally – they cannot understand the 'sentence'.

There is one very significant difference between these two sets of givens (or premises), and it relates to my sixth premise for aged care: that no-one should seek assisted dying because of poor or inadequate aged care. The same principle applies to any dying person, but is more critical for the frail aged because their care is so obviously less satisfactory than for those dying of more visible causes such as cancer. Palliation is far more readily available for the latter than for the frail aged. Everything should be done to improve aged care to avoid this lack of adequate palliation.

The similarity between these two groups raises an obvious question. If people dying from cancer or motor neurone disease or heart failure can request an assisted death, why should not the same privilege be extended to people dying from the frailty of old age?

Let us assume for a moment that an uncaring and hostile environment is a significant cause of the frail aged person's unrest, and look at what could be done to improve matters.

The aged-care industry has five major contributors to effective outcomes. They are the relatively unskilled low-level carers, the professional-level nurses, the treating medical practitioners, the overall home managers and providers of care, and the government which controls and funds the care.

Some obvious problems exist. If you want to detect unsatisfactory or dangerous levels of care in aged care, why would you create a system where visits for assessment are announced in advance? If you want to eliminate abuse, why do you not mandate reporting of such incidents, and impose serious penalties for failing to do so? Further, in order to detect and pursue such claims of abuse, should you not establish an ombudsman with powers and adequate resources for investigation and the ability to recommend prosecution?

In this book I take a stick to those caring for the frail aged and those with dementia, and principally with the aged-care 'industry'. That last word says it all. It is unacceptable that the federal government, which funds and administers aged care, has allowed, for its convenience, private industry – entrepreneurs – to effectively take over and to continue to expand its influence in a relatively uncontrolled manner in what is an increasingly vital public health domain. The result is, inevitably, profit over care, as Annie Butler, federal secretary of the Australian Nursing and Midwifery Federation, told the royal commission has been the case since 1997, when the current Act came into force. The Federation raised concerns about the funding, and of the creation of a fractious industry in which hundreds of companies operated with varying levels of skill, professionalism and interest. 'We've adopted business models rather than genuine social models of care. There are some providers out there really trying to do a good thing but it is very much a minority. Too often economic outcomes are the driver and not care outcomes.'

I am critical of the 'industry', but not specifically of those who attend to the residents on a daily basis. They are under-skilled, overworked and underpaid, and although there may be some instances of egregious abuse by residential carers, much so-called abuse is fundamentally due to lack of training, lack of staff and lack of time to attend to needs quickly. Or to do a better job in an environment where acute observation, time to communicate and even touch empathetically – to show understanding of distress – are essential. The recent utterances by industry leaders smack of 'what's the problem', 'we're doing a good job', 'staffing levels are good' and 'give us more money'.

This was graphically demonstrated in April 2019 when allegations of sexual abuse of an elderly woman resulted in a quite reasonable call for aged-care workers to be registered, like other health-care workers. The representative of the industry immediately rejected the concept as too expensive. Once again, profit trumped care. It is obvious that if people want better quality and safety in aged care this will require regulation, particularly of resident–staff ratios, and the registration of workers. Equally obviously, this will require increased investment by either the industry or government, or increased fees from residents or their families.

The appropriate size of care homes is rarely discussed. With any business (aged care is a business, and a competitive one at that), economies of scale lead to increased 'efficiency'. I was informed that an aged-care institution of 60 beds in provincial Victoria, which I regularly visited, had to close because it was not financially viable at that size. This is very sad, because the smaller the institution, the more personal the care and potentially quicker the response to problems. The move to establish small-capacity care homes is most welcome, but it will come at a cost, and such homes will not be suitable for those with more advanced cognitive impairment.

The federal government has passed the provision of what is now an essential public-health asset into the hands of private enterprise, and now finds itself between a rock and a hard place. The system is falling apart, and the industry has the whip hand. If it does not accept change it can threaten to walk away, with a potential financial loss, but leaving the government with a huge problem. Who really lies between the rock and the hard place? Residents in aged care.

Similarly, the imposition of careful scrutiny and hard fines for lack of adequate care could lead to financial difficulty, possible closure, and the sudden displacement of residents – another hard rock.

Much criticism has been made of the standard of training and level of care provided by carers in aged-care homes. In 2006, Paul Cann, director of policy at Help the Aged, reported in *The Guardian* newspaper on a study of 800 health practitioners, which found that:

Older people dying from a non-cancer illness receive a poorer standard of care than those with cancer, according to two-thirds of doctors and nurses who work regularly with older people. [...] Older people who are dying often face additional conditions including pain and discomfort, sensory deprivation, arthritis and depression. Two in three medical practitioners working with older people [...] said these complaints were often overlooked. [...] Too many of us believe dying is what 'they' do, and do not think about it happening to us. So the change must start with attitudes, and continue with training. Half of medical practitioners working with older people have never received specific training to help them deal with people as they die. Well over half said they would benefit from such training.

People who are dying of cancer in aged care are dying slowly, too slowly to remain at home or die in hospice. They still have all the problems of dying people, but are in the worst environment to receive effective palliation. They need a specialised section in aged care to provide them with excellent care.

To provide good care requires a sufficient number of well-trained staff. Three levels of care are essential: medical, nursing including palliative-care nursing, and residential carers who require a minimum of Certificate 2 training.

I am critical of the medical profession, represented ostensibly by the AMA (Australian Medical Association), which, despite reports of inadequate relief of pain and of high levels of depression – facts that have been known for years – have not responded in an effective manner. If any response has been there, it has not been evident. Situations like that of Freda Briggs' husband would not occur if the hospital system gave more respect to patients' wishes, agents' directions, and advance care directives. Freda's husband's hip fracture was a terminal event; his pain could have been effectively palliated with frequent strong analgesia rather than futile major surgery. One suspects that her doctors were victims of 'commission bias', or the need to do something – in this case, what surgeons always do for a fractured hip irrespective of the overall circumstances. Couple this with fear of prosecution, and you have a tragic outcome. A palliative-care assessment in situ rather than a knee-jerk referral to hospital could have led to a more humane and acceptable outcome (quite apart from any question of cost).

The AMA has lifted its game recently and in a submission in 2016 listed a group of obstacles to the provision of good medical care in the aged-care sector. The AMA stated that it was appropriate to adopt specific accreditation standards for medical services in residential aged-care homes, including rules on staffing levels for registered nurses. It identified poor access to properly equipped treatment rooms, a lack of information technology, a strong financial disincentive for doctors to visit aged-care facilities, and a dip in the employment of registered nurses. The AMA further stated, 'the absence of specific nurse-to-patient ratios in the accreditation standards has allowed the shift in the proportions. This has placed additional pressure on nursing and medical practitioners and has most likely led to an increased transfer to hospitals.' Finally, 'Impediments to patient care in residential facilities show that the medical practitioners are not considered integral to the residential aged-care workforce.'

But the AMA is a significant part of the problem, with its intransigent opposition to voluntary assisted dying, even though it represents less than 30 per cent of the medical profession, and its position on this particular matter is supported by barely half its members. The AMA's position ignores the view of geriatrician and ethicist Professor Raymond Tallis, who stated: 'Doctors give hope beyond any practical help they may offer. But there comes a point when giving hope is a rather cruel thing to do. I think one of the difficulties of being a doctor is to decide the point where being cheerful and hopeful should give way to being realistic.' The conflict between hope and realism: the essence of the dying debate. The renowned palliative physician Timothy Quill, when asked in 2016 whether doctors should do no harm, replied:

> It would be difficult for me to construe addressing the suffering of a terminally ill patient in some way as a harm. It's really an obligation. The question is, how can we respond to those kinds of suffering? We are involved in helping people die all the time. Why do we do that? Because we take care of people who are dying. Part of our job, in my opinion, is helping people die better. Again, I say that in a direct way because it irks me when we say that doctors shouldn't help people to die.

There is one area where the medical profession cannot escape severe criticism, or lay fault at someone else's door, and that is in the realm of patient and family communication.

A Royal Australasian College of Physicians working party (chaired by Professor Bill Silvester) reported that terminal patients were being kept alive with unwanted and unnecessary life-prolonging treatment because doctors do not know what their final wishes are. Silvester said:

> There are a lot of things happening in hospitals that really should not be happening if we were all doing a better job of talking to patients about what they want and getting it put on the electronic alert system so if somebody suddenly deteriorates people don't go doing things to people they never actually wanted done.

The problem is a worldwide one. Marisa Mason, chief executive of Britain's National Confidential Enquiry into Patient Outcome and Death said (as quoted in *Independent UK*, 2009): 'There were problems in all areas of care but end of life care stood out as a case where things went wrong. There was poor communication with the patients, with the relatives and between the doctors.' This poor communication blighted the person's final days. About 300,000 patients died in British hospitals annually, but although about 'half were not expected to survive when they were admitted, doctors failed to make the judgment that they were approaching the end of their life which would have enabled medical staff to provide appropriate care.'

Aged care contains some of the sickest and most vulnerable people in our community. I accept the profession's complaint that effective communication with people in aged care is not encouraged by the miserable remuneration for such visits. This requires more than a two- or three-minute visit to aged-care residents by their doctor. It takes considerable time to have these sensitive discussions with their patient and their family, but there are benefits to all: doctors then know what treatment is wanted, families can be prepared for the inevitable future, residential carers know which people need more detailed care, and unnecessary hospital referrals would be avoided. It also allows for realistic expectations about prognosis, and effective treatment to be discussed, avoiding many of the complaints arising from misunderstanding. But such an approach needs to remunerate doctors appropriately for the significantly increased time involved. Many of these discussions may need to take place by phone; they usually take a lot of time, and there needs to be compensation for this if it is to occur. However, in my opinion, there would be significant savings in such an approach by avoiding unnecessary, unwanted and costly treatment.

In addition, every person in aged care should have a regular medical prognostic assessment – an assessment of how long they are likely to survive – and this assessment should be discussed with the person and their family (unless there is an objection). This too should be made clear to staff, so that appropriate referral to palliative care, rather than transfer to hospital, proceeds smoothly and without surprise and rancour on the part of families, who commonly seem to have little concept of just how sick their loved one is, and have unreasonable expectations about their prognosis.

Much, if not most, of the best medical training comes through mentorship. If young GPs do not have mentors to teach them by example how to deal with the specific problems faced by the frail aged in a nursing home, then medical care in those institutions will not improve. The doctor is, or should be, the director of the care, but if he or she is deficient, don't expect the rest of the ship to sail well. Having made that point, it should not be assumed that the doctor is the *only* person to make decisions about end-of-life care. Eighty-four per cent of health-care workers in one survey did not support that view, concluding that 'choices must be available for older people known to be dying so they can have the kind of death they would prefer'. Good communication is the way to achieve that, with the dying person's view predominant.

Why is pain so poorly recognised and poorly treated? To recognise a resident's pain requires taking the time to sit and observe, particularly if the resident cannot speak. In aged care, the person who spends most time with the resident is the carer with the lowest level of skills. Without adequate training, they will not recognise pain or report it to the nurse, and if the nurse does not have time to sit and observe residents, pain goes unrecognised, because it is usually the nurse who brings it to the attention of the doctor. Remember Freda Briggs' story.

Nicholas Christakis wrote a piece in the *British Medical Journal* in 2008, titled 'Too quietly into the night':

> The fact is that the everyday reality of death in the US – and elsewhere in the developed, let alone developing, world – is abysmal.
>
> Our best estimate is that 40% to 70% of Americans die in pain. A large majority of these have other symptoms, such as shortness of breath, nausea, or depression, that are often even more distressing to patients than pain. More than 80% of Americans die in institutions. And roughly 25% to 55% of Americans place a significant burden on family caregivers in the course of their death.
>
> [...] Yet one of the most compelling explanations for this sorry state of affairs is that those in our society who are dying constitute a particularly disempowered, even if numerous, group. It may be fashionable in medicine to think about 'vulnerable populations', but it is hard to imagine a more vulnerable population than the dying, nor one that is more neglected or more invisible.

Although Christakis is writing principally about American medicine, and more than ten years ago, there is little or no reason to believe the situation in Australia is much different.

Professors Ben White and Lindy Willmott of the Queensland University of Technology (Centre for Health Law) observed in 2016 that 'accurate knowledge of the law, and compliance with it, has become critical to good medical practice, while an absence of knowledge puts both doctor and patients at risk'.

Intensivist Peter Saul was quoted in *The Age* (4 May 2013) as saying that:

> I think people even within the health system have really no idea of the legislative background. The general public have no idea at all. Even the people meant to administer this - who are us, the doctors – if I sent a questionnaire to 100 doctors in NSW asking what the law is about end-of-life, there'd be zero per cent who had any idea.

Perhaps a little exaggerated, but he makes a strong point. Nevertheless, Saul is quite right that this lack of knowledge engenders significant fear among doctors treating people at the end of life, and also among nursing-home staff and administrators.

C. S. Cleeland stated in 1998 that 'the optimal treatment of pain and adverse effects of analgesics requires aggressive use of controlled substances, potentially raising fear of regulatory scrutiny or the disapproval of colleagues'. Nothing much in this area has changed in 20 years, yet it should be understood that this fear leads to under-prescribing and under-administration of palliative medications.

Another intensivist effectively confirmed Professor Saul:

> I tried to explain all the complications affecting the patient and the reasons why [withdrawal of treatment should be considered] but there was absolutely no progression from this discussion. So when in the middle of the night the patient deteriorated further, I chose to treat him. Despite my wishes, despite my perspective, despite my professional opinion, because I felt that any decision to the contrary might expose me to all sorts of legal and emotional dangers that I do not wish to face.

As an intensivist he was the last port of call for intervention and was placed in an invidious position to attempt effective communication. It should have occurred at least days or weeks before, not at the last minute, so he caved in to his fear and provided unnecessary treatment. Those treating this patient before him had ignored Dr Robert Cushman, chief executive officer of the Champlain Local Health Integration network (*Ottawa Citizen*, 31 October 2007) who stated: 'It's the ethical responsibility of doctors to encourage discussion regardless of the painful moral, ethical, and political questions that arise.'

The medical profession makes much noise about *Primum non nocere* (First, do no harm), but often succumbs to the less well known *Primum contego sui* (First, protect oneself).

In Australia, the National Health and Hospital Reform Commission reported that doctors are wary of discontinuing treatment, because of possible legal action by families, and that nursing homes send elderly patients to hospital rather than have a death on the premises. The Commission urged the health minister in 2009 to require, as part of the accreditation process, every aged-care resident to sign an advance care plan. In the absence of such documents, and not uncommonly even when they are present, nursing homes and GPs usually call an ambulance so that they can't be blamed for the impending death. The Commission considered that people should be able to die where they want – such as in their own bed – while receiving good palliative care.

I feel sorry for the previous minister for aged care, Ken Wyatt, who I think is a very decent bloke, but who was shackled with a monumental task. He did acknowledge in 2018 that 'research shows that around half of us will be incapable of making our own medical decisions as we approach the end of our lives', and that 'despite this, less than 15% of Australians have recorded an Advance Care Plan'.

We are now entering the area where my remarks apply to all in aged care, but even more to those residents who are incompetent (suffering cognitive impairment).

Professor J. L. Bernat (*Ethical Issues in Neurology*, 2002) stressed that 'physicians have the ethical duty to encourage their competent patients to execute advance directives and the legal duty to follow those directives when choosing a medical treatment plan'. Every person in aged care should have an ACD. Its presence should be flagged on the front of that person's medical record, and brought to the attention of any out-of-hours doctor. And if that person does go to hospital, their ACD should go with them – and there it should be noted, recorded and acted on, and with legal consequences if it is not.

There has been a lack of support and development of advance care directives for this vulnerable population. A strong system of promotion of advance care directives for older people, particularly through seniors' health checks by GPs, would allow these people to avoid unnecessary and unwanted medical interventions by refusal of treatment, but it would require effective and aggressive palliation of any consequent symptoms. Instead of a doctor saying 'You will suffer dreadful pain if you don't have this treatment', he or she could say: 'If you refuse treatment, I can still keep you comfortable and free of pain until you die.' This is always possible if the doctor is providing aggressive sedation and pain relief for a terminal circumstance and the intention is to relieve suffering.

There is a serious lack of vigorous support for increased provision for palliative care for people in aged care. My recommendation is that all aged-care institutions should have a dedicated palliative-care section where such patients would be managed. All such institutions should have nursing staff who have palliative-care training, and a direct connection to a specialist palliative-care centre for advice and assessments if necessary. GPs attending aged-care institutions should also have an interest and training in basic palliative care. I am advocating that effective palliative care should be available to people dying in aged care without the necessity for transfer to advanced hospital care or inpatient palliative care.

I have emphasised the need for palliative-care nurses who are expert in assessing and analysing the presence and extent of suffering in dying people. They can then report that to the attending doctor to ensure adequate analgesic and sedative prescribing and sufficiently frequent administration. The old days of strict four-hourly pain relief for the dying should be long gone; the correct dose is that which abolishes the pain, and keeps it absent. The Victorian *Medical Treatment Act 1988* states that dying patients should receive maximal relief of pain and suffering: not a little, not intermittent, but maximal, which means to the greatest possible extent. Family members have an important role to bring any indication of suffering to the attention of the doctor and nursing staff and insist on its relief. Inadequate relief of such suffering is on record and is inexcusable. The sooner a doctor, nursing team or nursing home is brought to heel for failing to adequately relieve such suffering, the sooner it will cease.

I am not critical of the nursing profession, which has recognised this dilemma for years, and has represented its own members and those they care for, arguing for improved staffing levels and conditions as essential to improving basic care. I admire that profession for its efforts. The major problem for nurses is inadequate staffing levels, and a waste of their efficient nursing time on administrative paperwork rather than real care.

There are unfortunately no mandated registered-nurse staffing levels for residential care, unlike in our acute hospitals, yet residential aged care has a cohort of sick and dying patients whose adequate care depends on proper staffing. Aged-care providers have fought vigorously against mandated staff levels, for the obvious reason that more staff means less profit.

Obviously, poorer care is the result. Registered nurses need time away from their desks to spend observing their staff at work, training and encouraging them. Most importantly, they need to spend time with each resident when procedures that might be associated with pain (such as washing, dressing, wound care, moving and feeding) are being carried out. Observation to detect pain takes time, and staff should not react defensively when family members report observations of distress. Staff should not respond only that they are giving what is ordered, but should immediately assess the situation in depth, and report unrelieved pain forcefully to the treating doctor.

Both the nurses and doctors treating pain in aged care should follow the advice of Professor Bernat:

> The primary goal of therapeutics in this setting is to maintain patient comfort. Physicians traditionally have been too tentative and not sufficiently aggressive in ordering medications to suppress suffering in the dying patient. The discipline of 'aggressive palliative care' holds that physicians should exhibit the same sense of aggressiveness in prescribing palliative care for terminally ill patients as they exhibit when they treat cancer patients with chemotherapy.

It is axiomatic that to improve care we need more staff and better-trained staff, yet providers seem to persistently deny any such problems, even in the face of repeated surveys and reports to the contrary.

The bulk of the resident attention (it is euphemistically called 'care') in residential homes is provided by poorly trained staff, who are poorly paid, are overworked due to understaffing, and may lack the language and cultural background to provide the best care. Such work requires education in the recognition of subtle aspects of suffering, but it is acknowledged that such carers do not receive any education in dementia care.

So now, inevitably, we come to the vexed matter of dementia, undoubtedly the most important and complex issue of modern medicine.

Let me remind you of some quotations from chapter 6. Firstly, Robert Gray (*The Lancet*, 1990): 'Your patient will get worse no matter what you do or how well you do it.' Greg Sachs (*New England Journal of Medicine*, 2009): 'Now some 30 years after my grandmother's death from Alzheimer's disease, end of life care for many patients with dementia doesn't look all that different from the treatment she received.' Let me add the voice of John Bradshaw, professor of neuropsychology at Monash University, whose wife suffered a massive stroke, and subsequent dementia. He stated (*Ockham's Razor*, ABC, 4 April 1999): 'If I became demented, I would choose euthanasia, were it available, while I could still make the choice, as I believe quality of life is infinitely more important than life itself.' Bradshaw was anticipating the view of the Mayo Clinic (27 May 2007), which wrote in *Anticipating the Needs of People with Alzheimer's Disease* that 'Comfort, not life extension' was paramount. The Mayo people strongly advocated advance care directives, because people with end-stage Alzheimer's disease often receive too little pain medication, due to their inability to communicate that they have pain, though the signs are there if one takes the trouble to observe:

> It is a difficult task for a family to keep a person with dementia home until death. [...] Most of all, the death itself and any deterioration preceding this must be planned carefully so that the person is kept comfortable and pain-free and not rushed to hospital at the last minute. [...] It is crucial that there is good communication about issues relating to end-of-life care early in the disease, when the individual with dementia can be supported to document their wishes.

If you accept that dementia is the worst illness known to man, and the worst journey in the world, you will want to make that illness and that journey as short as possible. The inherent problem with this is that as their illness progresses a dementia sufferer loses the capacity to make decisions, and therefore the ability to control the later stages of the illness and the journey. Thus, informed decisions need to be made in the early stage of the illness, while competence is still present. Such decisions need to be made clear in carefully designed documents, so that your decisions can be effected even some years later. This can be achieved by the careful use of advance care directives (see Appendix B).

Susan Okie confirmed this view in 'Confronting Alzheimer's disease' (2011): 'People with early Alzheimer's disease are usually still competent to specify their wishes concerning medical treatment and to complete an advance directive, which can make future decisions regarding health care easier and less emotionally charged for physicians and families.'

This is supported by Ron Berghmans of the Institute of Bioethics, Maastrich, in the *Annals of New York Academy of Sciences* ('Advance directives and dementia'):

> The dominant view is that by executing an advance directive a person can exhibit so-called prospective autonomy. [...] The dominant ethical and legal point of view is that a refusal of treatment by a competent patient should be respected, even if we think that this decision is unwise, and even if this refusal may lead to an earlier death of the patient.

The American Academy of Neurology Ethics and Humanities Subcommittee stated in 1996: 'Completing and following advance directives (in dementia) is desirable ethically because it permits a type of patient self-determination even in states of incompetence.'

Professor Jennifer Abbey, in her report to Dementia Australia, stated that advance care directives 'remain the only way a person with dementia can set out a legal document which provides information about their own wishes to be followed'. However, to complete such an important document, that person needs to be fully informed about their disease and its likely progression.

Professor Bernat stated emphatically that 'only patients ultimately know and are authorized to decide what treatments satisfy their values and goals', and he reminds us that:

> It is the patient's own values and goals of treatment that should be granted primacy. The patient's ethical right to consent for or refuse therapy is not extinguished when the patient loses the cognitive or communicative capacity to make medical decisions. It is essential for physicians

to practice ideal palliative care when withdrawing life-sustaining treatment. The patient should be kept comfortable at all times through the judicious use of opiates, benzodiazepines and barbiturates.

Eminent American ethicist and legal authority Norman Cantor, in an article titled 'Changing the paradigm of advance directives to avoid prolonged dementia', opined:

> With the changing prevalence of Alzheimer's disease and similar degenerative dementias, the focus of advance directives has changed for some people. The primary spectre is neither an unavoidable looming demise nor the insensate limbo of permanent unconsciousness. Rather the emerging concern is protracted maintenance during progressively increasing cognitive dysfunction and helplessness. For some, being mired in a demented state is an intolerably degrading prospect well before the advanced stage when the person no longer recognises loved ones and is totally uncomprehending.

He noted the courts' declaration that a competent person's right to control medical intervention is not lost by onset of incompetency; he was referring to advance care directives. He cited his own directive, which states: 'I instruct that my caregivers refrain from hand feeding unless I appear receptive to eating and drinking.' Similarly, Bernat determines that:

> Limitation of medical treatment for the patient with severe dementia can be defended on the ethical grounds of respect for autonomy in cases in which an advance directive is present. In cases where no advance directive exists, medical treatment can be limited on the ethical grounds of non-maleficence and justice. Clinicians can provide appropriate treatment in patients with advanced dementia by ordering supportive or palliative care.

The fundamental principle of an advance care directive in dementia is that it prevents life-prolonging treatment and allows for a natural, palliated death. This essentially means that once competence is lost, no life-prolonging treatment is to be given for any life-threatening illness, which means no surgery or other interventions, and no antibiotics or other drugs, except analgesics and sedatives for palliation of any or all symptoms of observable or reasonably presumed suffering. Artificial hydration and assisted oral (spoon) feeding must be strictly prohibited (except if oral food and fluid continue to be readily taken and enjoyed). Appropriate palliative mouth care is essential. A peaceful death at the appropriate time can then be relied upon.

Unfortunately, there are too many reports of advance care directives being ignored, abused, or not properly honoured. In most Australian states these documents have statutory legal power, and to disobey the directions is a criminal offence. However, to be valid they must be very carefully written, and apply accurately to the situation at hand. The sooner a doctor or care institution is prosecuted for abusing such a directive, the better will care be for all Australians.

I have mentioned at length in this book the word communication, which I realise needs some further definition. I do not mean by letter, or email (which has largely replaced the letter). Email especially is a good means of conveying information, but not a good means of conversation. End-of-life communication is best face-to-face and interpersonal. Many conversations start by email or letter, progress to phone, and then to a personal meeting. And this is a dialogue, by which I mean an extended conversation over time, sometimes months or even years. A doctor should never act in an end-of-life circumstance until he or she is absolutely convinced about all aspects of the matter at hand. If in doubt, wait, and continue the dialogue.

Frances Norwood is an outstanding American anthropologist who spent two years embedded in Netherlands society studying the social consequences of euthanasia (I would prefer the term applicable in Victoria: voluntary assisted dying). She recorded her experiences and conclusion in her 2009 book *The Maintenance of Life: Preventing Social Death Through Euthanasia Talk and End of Life Care*: 'Most of the people I spoke to did not want to die, but considered euthanasia an ideal option in the event that their suffering became unmanageable. Euthanasia requests were not wishes for death, but more generally an insurance policy for the future.' In their preface to Norwood's book, Andrew Strathern and Pamela Stewart wrote:

> Talk about euthanasia may be seen as having a palliative function, even prolonging life while discussion about it goes on, and keeping the patient alive enough to think about what their life has meant and continues to mean, and the circumstances in which they would or would not be content to die.

To people, I say start these conversations early in your family life. It makes it easier to develop them later when they matter. They take away the fear of dying, and they enable you to die as you would wish. 'Bad deaths' occur when there is no conversation. These dialogues must also develop with your doctor as you age or become seriously ill; at that time you do not want a doctor who is technically brilliant, not one who only talks *to* you, or won't satisfactorily answer your questions, or give you the time to ask any, but one you can talk *with*. If your doctor won't do that, consider finding another.

My first lesson in empathy (in a medical course devoid of such matters, and of ethics) was in a ward round as a final-year student. Teaching rounds were usually conducted from the end of the bed, discussing the patient's problem in an esoteric manner. In bed 13 of Ward 5 West in the Royal Melbourne Hospital was a young woman, close to the end of her life from bronchiectasis. The consultant, Sir Clive Fitts, had known her for some years and he sat down beside her and held her hand as he sensitively talked with her and discussed her problem. I have never forgotten that moment. Great teaching, all too uncommon in those days. Sir Clive looked after my mother at the end of her life.

How your life ends is *your* responsibility – more yours than your doctor's, and more yours than your family's, though they are both extremely important – don't forget or ignore that.

In making these general criticisms of aged care, I acknowledge that many aged-care institutions – their managers, doctors, nurses and carers – have acted in an exemplary and compassionate manner. However, there is sufficient evidence, accumulated over decades of observing a failing system, that there are systemic problems that need to be remedied. I identify these systemic problems as follows.

Problems and solutions

1. There is a fundamental need to understand that the vast majority of people who are admitted to aged care do not want to be there. They would prefer to be at home, even If that entails some risk. Their requests should be heeded.
2. As a consequence of this there is a need for much-increased resources to keep people at home. Admittance to aged care should be the last resort, not the first. I am told by experienced general practitioners that the Royal District Nursing Service is withering on the vine after being subsumed into private hands.
3. Underlying these matters is the most important issue: COMMUNICATION. This needs to occur between families and their elderly parents, doctors and their older and terminally ill 'patients'. Society needs to evolve to a point where a conversation about dying is natural, open and easy. We all face it; *The Economist* wrote in 2017:

> Most people feel dread when they contemplate their mortality. As death has been hidden away in hospitals and nursing homes, it has become less familiar and harder to talk about. [...] But honest and open conversations with the dying should be as much a part of modern medicine as prescribing drugs or fixing broken bones. A better death means a better life, right to the end.

I could not agree more, but would add conversations between older parents and their children. This is vital in order to prevent unwanted and unnecessary treatment, prolonged suffering and prolonged dying, which is followed by prolonged guilt and grief. Children (and the medical profession) must understand that there is a time to 'let go'.

4. This communication should encourage the knowledge of values, wishes and needs, and should lead to the appointment of medical treatment decision

makers, and to the development of advance care plans, but more importantly, in my view, to advance care directives. The difference is important: an advance care plan (or values statement) is an indication of wishes, which can be interpreted and even ignored, but an advance care directive is exactly that, a directive that is legally binding and cannot be ignored without legal risk. An advance care plan is useful, but an advance care directive is more valuable. However, a directive must be very carefully written to be effective.

5. Sensitively prepared video documentaries should be available, to provide information about the dementia journey, and allow informed decision-making through advance care directives by still competent dementia patients.

6. Aged-care homes should be obliged to ensure that all those admitted have appointed a medical treatment decision maker and have been strongly encouraged to create an advance care directive. These documents should be prominently displayed on the front of the resident's file, and copies should accompany the resident to hospital if that is necessary.

7. The level of care for residents varies widely. Many current disappointments in aged care would be avoided if discussion of realistic expectations occurred. An initial prognostic assessment should be made by the attending doctor and discussed with the resident and family. The aims of treatment and the expectations for the family should be made clear. This prognostic assessment should be updated at least every six months; indications of a terminal stage or palliative situation should be made clear and discussed with family and staff.

8. If a terminal or palliative situation develops, with the consent of the family every effort should be made to provide palliative care *in situ*. I would recommend that a small palliative section be resourced in all reasonably sized residential care homes, that all homes have trained palliative-care nurses, and that there be a direct connection to a specialist palliative-care unit for specific advice.

9. Adequate training at all levels of aged care needs to be improved. Care staff need specific training in dementia care. Staff-to-patient ratios of nurses and basic carers need to be increased and mandated. These recommendations

apply particularly to the special area of dementia care, where higher levels are necessary.

10. There is a very sound argument that aged-care staff should, like all other health professionals, become registered, and subject to codes of conduct and investigation for misconduct or abuse.

11. For many years, the restraint of difficult (usually dementia) patients, by both physical and chemical means, has been documented as being at an unacceptable level. Restraint should be a last resort, but it must be acknowledged that circumstances can arise when it is necessary. The alternatives (of vocal engagement, building relationships, pre-emptive interventions) are time-consuming, and therefore costly, and may come at the expense of other needy residents, but these dignity-preserving methods should be the first resort, regardless of cost. Physical or chemical restraint should be monitored and reported.

12. Understanding of the concept of a completed life (and not its denial), and acceptance of the concept of incarceration and denial of freedom (the prison system) in the mind of many residents, should be recognised.

13. Counselling should be readily available, to assist many residents to adapt to residential aged care.

14. Every competent resident of aged care has a legal right to refuse fluids and food, even if such action would hasten their death. It has been judicially determined that such action is not suicide, and that any suffering of such persons should be properly palliated. Such a request should be carefully assessed and carefully planned.

15. Many aged frail people entering aged care (or threatened with entry) may have determined that they have a completed life. Some will also be terminally ill, with perhaps less than six months to live. Voluntary assisted dying is a legal request for those with less than six months to live, and should be considered as an option for others with a completed life, whose suffering cannot be palliated. Incarceration in what they consider to be a prison-like situation should not be society's only option.

In consideration of the likelihood of improvement, I make the following points.

Fresh forecasts from the Parliamentary Budget Office indicate that Australia's ageing population will mean an annual cost to the budget of about $36 billion for aged care by 2028–29 – larger than the anticipated cost of Medicare – due to a surge in demand from baby boomers. It is highly relevant that such an estimate is based on current funding adjusted for increased demand. These costs are based on the currently woeful state of aged care in Australia. What might this cost be if the royal commission were to make realistic recommendations to bring aged care up to a reasonable, safe and equitable standard – and the government of the day were to properly implement such recommendations?

I am normally an optimist, but, frankly, I am not optimistic that sufficient and adequate improvements in aged care will occur over the next decade and beyond. I predict only marginal improvement, and this will not be equitable. As usually happens in health care, the poorest and most vulnerable wait longest for assistance and get left behind in quality.

What are the consequences of the givens with which I commenced this chapter? They can be broadly described as follows:

1. No doctor wants to be responsible for his or her patient having a 'bad' death.
2. Most doctors respect the views of their patients.
3. No doctor wishes to 'kill' his or her patient.
4. Most doctors have the intention to effectively relieve pain and suffering at the end of life, even if this may involve unintentionally hastening death.
5. Many doctors have a fear of professional or criminal proceedings if they are involved in the hastening of death.
6. Doctors currently lack the means to assist a person to end their intolerable suffering in a controlled and safe manner.
7. To eliminate fear and create a reliable process needs legislation to allow for voluntary assisted dying in safe and controlled circumstances – for people in aged care as well as those clearly dying of cancer.

Again, I quote J. L. Bernat:

> Unlike other forms of palliative therapy, including nearly all appropriate opiate treatment to suppress pain and dyspnoea, terminal sedation clearly accelerates the moment of death.
>
> Medications such as morphine and benzodiazepines can be administered parenterally to reduce air hunger, suffering and level of consciousness. Doses should be chosen to comfort the patient during the dying process without purposely accelerating the moment of death. The ideal use of morphine and benzodiazepines is the smallest dose that induces adequate patient comfort. It is acceptable to risk accelerating the moment of death as long as the intent of therapy and the dosage prescription are designed for and appropriate to provide patient comfort.

However, it may be rational for a patient to wish to escape a life of intractable suffering, rather than to continue living in a locked-in state. The mere presence of depression alone does not automatically invalidate a patient's refusal of treatment.

With respect to refusal of treatment: 'The Courts [in the USA] have ruled that a citizen's tangible right to self-determination was more compelling than the state's abstract right to preserve life.'

CHAPTER 11

Conclusions

D ementia is the worst disease known to man. It is the worst journey in the world. It is a progressive terminal illness that has no cure and that lasts from five to fifteen years, gradually stripping away all those assets that make us human, reducing us to a vegetative state, and is often accompanied by unrecognised significant physical suffering. In the early – still cognitive – stage, psychological and existential suffering can occur from the contemplation of the future. In the middle – diminished but confusional – stage, awareness of losses is painful, and psychosis may develop. The terminal – vegetative – stage is to be avoided at all costs.

The cost to family carers is enormous, such that it can be borne no longer, and aged-care placement becomes unavoidable. This institutional care is barely adequate, and sometimes quite inadequate. It comes at great financial cost to families and to the community at large. Dementia is now the second-leading cause of death in Australia, and no cure is in sight. It is heading to be the predominant illness facing the developed world, unless a resurgence of infectious illnesses of plague proportions develops.

There is no accepted approach to management except 'care'. This is understandable, because from an ethical point of view any other treatment suggestion is currently untenable. However, a doctor confronting a patient with an incurable terminal illness has a duty to inform that person of the consequences of the illness, its likely course and complications. Currently that is probably rarely done with dementia. This denies that person the opportunity to make refusal of treatment decisions in an advance care directive. In my opinion they should be shown a sensitive video of the dementia journey so that they are fully informed about what lies ahead for them. Doctors are legally obliged to fully inform their patients who have cancer – why not those who have dementia? It borders on the unethical to not at least offer more information about the diagnosis and the reasons why.

However, in the Netherlands, due to that country's end-of-life law based on intolerable suffering rather than terminal illness, and its 35-year history of discussing and assessing end-of-life practice (and more liberal and pragmatic attitudes), it has been gradually accepted that people diagnosed with dementia can be given assistance in dying while they remain competent. The difficulty here is the timing of such a decision. Occasional episodes of assistance via advance directives when the person has become incompetent have not gone well. At this stage, Australia is 30 years behind the Netherlands in considering this problem, but I believe we will have to seriously address it within 20 years.

Currently, however, there is one important action that competent people can take. If you are concerned about the possibility of dementia on the basis of family history, if you are living to an age where the incidence of dementia is considerable (over 80), or you have been diagnosed with early dementia but are still competent, then it is essential that you complete a watertight advance care directive. Such a directive must make it clear that if you become incompetent to make your own decisions, then no life-prolonging treatment is to be administered to you, and that maximal palliation of any suffering as a consequence of refusal is to be provided. This must include the refusal of assisted spoon-feeding, the most devastating prolonger of demented life. This directive is to allow natural dying without unwanted medical intervention, and prevent the prolonging of life into the late stages of dementia.

The wonders of medical science have now advanced the average life expectancy in Australia into the early eighties, and it is rising. While beneficial in many respects, it also means that as we age we will suffer from a number of crippling degenerative diseases that can lead to dependency – the inability to look after ourselves, which opens the door to the aged-care home. There is no doubt that the vast majority of Australians view such an outcome with horror. Only 1 per cent of Australians express a wish to die in aged care, yet 90 per cent of Australians who enter aged care die there, while the remaining 10 per cent die after acute transfer to hospital. Palliation of dying in aged care is not complex: it requires a consenting patient, sympathetic staff and attending doctor, and appropriate medications. Yet palliation in aged care is poorly managed and resisted by some managements.

Some find the aged-care experience to be better than they anticipated, some tolerate it since they have no alternative, but a number rail against it, while a very few end their own lives to escape it. My own counselling indicates that many more would take this last option if they had a dignified and secure way of doing so.

Why do they consider this? Because by the time they have reached a state of dependence requiring such care, they have reached a stage of completed life. As Frances Norwood puts it so poignantly, they have reached a point of social death, where all purpose and pleasure in life have gone before the time of their biological death. As the Dalai Lama would describe it, their lives have lost meaning.

The concept of a completed life is not difficult to comprehend, but for many who are not yet there it is difficult to accept, so the frail aged find themselves exhorted to keep going, despite the varying combinations of blindness, deafness, loss of (or painful) mobility, incontinence and declining cognition, not to mention poor food, boredom and loneliness. They are exhorted to keep going because there is no alternative – except the deliberate cessation of fluids and food. It is astonishing that this should be a legal option for people with completed lives, but a rational, carefully considered, medically discussed and supervised peaceful death remains illegal.

If a person's journey is complete, why do we determine that they must go all the way to the terminus? Why can they not elect to get off one or two stops before the end? Who is disadvantaged if this option has been carefully discussed over time with the family, and the doctor who has taken care and time to assess competence? Good, open communication and time are the essentials. There need not be encouragement of such discussions, but certainly no discouragement. Through such discussions, problems may be uncovered which, if effectively dealt with, may resolve the request.

Underlying such discussions there needs to be a law that allows competent consenting adults, in this particular instance the frail aged, to request assisted dying. In Victoria, there is a law that allows requests for assistance by competent adults with a progressive terminal illness with a prognosis of less than six months, and whose suffering cannot be acceptably relieved.* These circumstances can apply to some residents of aged care, but many frail aged people do not have a specific terminal illness. (Frailty is not a recognised terminal illness, nor is age, but the combination is often predictive.) Prognosis in aged care is sometimes simple, but more often unpredictable. So, although this law can apply to the frail aged, it is unlikely that many doctors will comply. Moreover, because of the relative isolation of most frail aged people, the majority will not be aware of its existence, and therefore will not make the necessary specific request for assistance.

The number of frail aged likely to use such a law would be very small. In the Netherlands, where assistance for such people has been available for more than 30 years, only approximately 0.15 per cent of all assisted deaths occur in nursing homes. In Australian medicine a slow evolution of thinking has occurred over the last 30 years in attitudes to dying, but it needs to become more of a *revolution*. People, a mass of people, create revolutions, but unfortunately those affected by dying do not have the energy or the platform to mount a revolution.

It takes a special form of courage and determination to face one's own mortality. Most studies show that it is predominantly people of higher education and a very strong sense of autonomy, and a desire for control, who do so. Facing one's own mortality: Albert Camus wrote, 'There is only one serious philosophical problem and that is suicide.' Shakespeare's Hamlet contemplated it in 'To be or not to be', and ducked, but he did not have a completed life.

Which brings me to the fundamental reason for this book. How often do you encounter someone with dementia in the community? They commonly shun society because of their embarrassment at being unable to follow conversation or contribute sensibly. They spend most of their time in care – either at home or in residential aged care. And of course, they are largely silent – not entirely of course, but what they have to say is often irrelevant and unintelligible as time goes on. Only those who have personally cared for or closely shared care at

---

* Publisher's note: the *Voluntary Assisted Dying Act 2017* (Vic) allows for a prognosis of 12 months in the case of neurodegenerative conditions.

home have a deep understanding of this disease – more so than many so-called experts, who often only share short times with sufferers. They do not share the intimate moments of grief, boredom, pain and suffering, or the all-too-brief moments of joy. These moments need to be seen and shared to fully experience the dementia journey. They do not occur in the consulting room or the short consultation.

The frail aged are in a slightly more advantageous position, but, as Nicholas Christakos said, you do not see marches of protesters in wheelchairs descending on parliament. It is very important to distinguish people with disability from frail aged people. You will see disabled people in their often-elaborate wheelchairs at Melbourne Symphony Orchestra concerts, or shopping in supermarkets. They demonstrate, despite their disability, a considerable degree of independence and they do vocally defend it. The frail aged are taken out by carers in their wheelchairs – one can see them in supermarkets, shops and parks, but the involvement in the outing seems different – more passive, they are being taken out rather than demanding or organising the event. I understand it can be making a grave mistake in this generalisation, so I apologise for any offence to anyone to whom it does not apply.

I doubt that any of the frail aged cohort write letters to the editor, or even read a newspaper. They are not only largely hidden from us, but they are divorced from society. I am not frail or aged (I am 84) but a few years ago I read the daily newspaper, and would not miss the ABC 7 pm news or *7.30 Report*. Now retired and living in the country as a virtual full-time carer, I rarely see the news and read a weekend newspaper only. To my amazement I do not seem to miss the all-too-common bad news; perhaps the frail aged have some advantages. But replacing those previous pursuits are music and books – advantages that the frail aged are unlikely to have. Bingo and clapping hands to music once or twice a week is not quite the same. Not being aware of what is happening in the world gives one little to complain about except one's own misery. As a result, these people remain invisible and unheard – a silent, suffering group with no voice. Professor Stephen Post wrote of individuals affected by dementia 'who, with waning powers of articulation and will, are politically voiceless and vulnerable'.

Most frail aged bear their misery stoically. Their complaints to family create embarrassment and a sense of guilt. Providing assistance in dying in aged care is virtually impossible. The only legal alternative is voluntary cessation of fluids and food – not attractive to the frail aged, usually abhorrent to family, and poorly understood or supported by doctors or administration.

It is impossible not to ask the question: If a competent, frail aged person can end their life legally by deliberately dehydrating to death, why should they not have the more compassionate, and I would argue moral, right to voluntary assisted dying?

Do you think you are providing benefit to your frail aged or cognitively impaired relative when you commit them to residential aged care, particularly if they have expressed a clear and persistent wish not to enter that prison (of course, that is probably not how she or he would express it)? It commonly happens because you, and your loved one, have no other choice, and over the past 60 years it has become culturally accepted without scrutiny. If you have recently visited someone in residential aged care, ask yourself: Is this where I want to end my life? If the answer is *no*, isn't it time to start raising hell for an alternative, a choice?

Do you think it is caring to force a frail aged person against their will into a situation they regard as imprisonment?

Do you think people with early dementia, who still have decision-making capacity, should be denied the opportunity to make decisions about the rest of their dementia journey?

To effectively answer these questions will require some major cultural shifts.

The first is to alter our understanding of suicide as it is currently applied to the frail aged, and our attempt to prevent it at all costs.

The second is to recognise that confining competent frail aged people to prison against their will is not caring.

Third is to recognise that competent people can reach a stage in life of a completed life, and can be ready to die. We should respect them and be prepared to let go.

Fourth, if such a person with a completed life has reached their time to die, they should be allowed to choose to request voluntary assisted dying, in order to die peacefully and with dignity, at a time and place of their choice, surrounded by those they love.

Rodney Syme makes us think from beyond the grave

Michael Bachelard

When my father entered the last weeks of his life, he was admitted to hospital. He had late-stage bowel cancer, for which he'd undergone various invasive treatments. We, his family, knew he could not be cured, but we had no idea how to navigate the path from that point to his eventual death. Like most people, we looked to the medical system for help.

In hospital he was impatient, confused, sometimes angry. The pain, the drugs, the unfamiliar surroundings, disorientated him. It was agonising to watch. I remember one night coming to see him just after dinner. He'd barely touched his food. His appetite had disappeared. As I came in a nurse was scolding him saying, 'Now Eric, don't you want to get better?'

When a palliative doctor visited Dad days later, he was quickly sent to Canberra's dedicated hospice, a lovely place on the banks of Lake Burley Griffin, where he was put under heavy sedation. In that state he died peacefully not long afterwards, surrounded by his family.

I tell this story – it's momentous for our family, but otherwise a run-of-the-mill end of life experience – because I was struck by the difference between the palliative approach to my father's illness and the medical approach. It's as much a philosophical difference as anything. One expects death, even welcomes it; the other (standing heroically against the evidence provided by every living organism) denies it.

Dr Rodney Syme expected death. He was unflinching in its face. For decades, knowing its inevitability, he tried to convince us to see it clearly, looking for ways to ease our transition through it. And he did it with compassion. I have been angry at times with the nurse who berated my father. Dr Syme's words suggest I should be more forgiving.

'One of the difficulties of being a doctor is to decide the point where being cheerful and hopeful should give way to being realistic,' he writes in this book. The conflict between hope and realism is 'the essence of the dying debate'.

As a Victorian and a journalist at *The Age* I found it impossible for two decades to ignore the 'dying debate', or the name Rodney Syme with which it was inextricably linked. He was by far the most powerful local proponent for a cause, voluntary assisted dying, which has achieved nationwide success. He was also a hero of my mother-in-law, who for years reminded us of her advance care directive, and ultimately benefited from the voluntary assisted dying laws to bring on her own peaceful death in the face of lung cancer.

This book shows that Dr Syme was still thinking about death, and still unflinching, to the end of his own life. It is magnificent: compassionate and compelling. It was written as he nursed his beloved wife, Meg, through dementia, so when he describes that disease as 'the worst illness known to man and the worst journey in the world', you know he knows what he's talking about.

He eviscerates the aged-care system and describes vividly the existential dread of confronting the loss of capacity and independence that goes with great old age. He sharpens the terms of the debate with the doctors and nursing home managers in a long and serious discussion about the legality and morality of withdrawing food and fluids from people to hasten their death.

And he asks perhaps the hardest question of all: Can people with dementia be given a dignified death when they can no longer clearly express their wishes?

The ultimate challenge Dr Syme lays out is for us to question the adequacy of Victoria's *Voluntary Assisted Dying Act*. This was a progressive policy conservatively enacted. He asks us from beyond the grave to look again and conclude that an easier death should be available to the frail aged and those with dementia, inside and outside the aged-care system.

The mental anguish of being assailed by the Six Horsemen of the Ageing Apocalypse, he tells us, is not a psychological disorder — or not usually — but a rational response by the elderly to the horrors that confront them.

In making these arguments, Dr Syme gives us another philosophical notion to chew over: that of a 'completed life'. He describes this as a life 'without pleasure and purpose [...] usually accompanied by physical, intellectual and existential losses. It is usually present when a person is "ready to die": they have come to terms with their mortality and would be content if they went to sleep and did not wake up.'

People who believe their life to be complete, he argues, should have access to the voluntary assisted dying laws. It would be no small thing to extend the scope of these laws beyond those whose death is inevitable within six months. To adopt Dr Syme's prescription would mean the state providing the means for people to shorten their lives when, medically at least, they might be capable of many more years on this earth.

'How does one assess whether someone has a completed life?' Dr Syme asks. 'What objective criteria are there to measure? The answer is none. How do you determine that someone has a completed life? The answer is simple: ask them.'

As our society ages and gets less religious it's time we have this argument again. We should be grateful to Dr Syme and this book that he has given us the anecdotal and scientific evidence, as well as the moral language, to conduct that debate.

Rodney Syme died in 2021, four months after Meg. He had a stroke. Not for him the lingering death of dementia or the depredations of the nursing home.

We can't be sure whether, at the end, he felt his life to be complete in the sense that, 'a completed purpose can bring untold pleasure'. But we can say with confidence that he made our society a better, more compassionate place. This book, at least, completes his work.

Now it's up to others to carry it forward.

Voluntary refusal of fluid and food

Publisher's note: This information about voluntary refusal of fluid and food, or VRFF, was prepared by Dr Syme as general information only. It is not intended to constitute medical advice for any specific situation. It is provided for public interest to increase understanding of VRFF, and to contribute to the conversation about potential future developments of voluntary assisted dying. DWDV does not intend that this material be used for the purposes of suicide, or to counsel or incite suicide. We make Dr Syme's information available to assist those who have already chosen to embark upon VRFF in the hope that their suffering during the process will be minimised.

Protocol for voluntary refusal of fluid and food (VRFF), also known as voluntary stopping of eating and drinking (VSED)

During the 1990s and later, there was a significant reference in the esteemed medical literature around the merits of refusal of treatment, voluntary assisted dying (VAD) and voluntary refusal of food and fluids (VRFF) as a means of controlling the end of life. This literature has diminished in the USA following VAD law in Oregon (1997) and its consequent spread into other states. Even in the Netherlands, where voluntary euthanasia has been legal since 2001, it has remained a topic of significance for people who do not comply with the strictures of the law. There has been virtually no discussion about it in Australian medical literature.

It should be very clear that death occurs by dehydration, not starvation.

Refusal of artificial nutrition and hydration is legal, and withdrawal of oral food and fluids is commonly used in palliative care (in association with terminal sedation). There are judicial determinations in Australia that a competent person can refuse artificial hydration, and can also refuse oral food and fluids. Forced feeding is illegal and this is endorsed by the AMA.

As an alternative to VAD, VRFF suffers from the common belief that such a process would be very distressing and painful. There is much literature to confirm that this need not be the case, though for people with extreme suffering, who have only a short time to live, it is not an attractive option.

Its acceptance may be found in a significant group of people who are dying slowly, and do not qualify for VAD. Many are aged and frail, living alone at home or in aged-care institutions.

It is CRITICALLY IMPORTANT to understand that this approach should occur only after careful discussion with family or carers, and the strong and educated support of the doctors and nurses involved in care. Engagement with community palliative-care services can be valuable. Additional expert nursing care can be arranged in aged care.

It should be stressed that this can be a completely legal decision by any competent person, and it can be included in advance care plans and advance directives. Having a medical enduring power of attorney or medical treatment decision maker is highly advisable. It is not considered as suicide in judicial judgements. Because of the serious nature of the decision, some doctors may request an expert psychiatric assessment of competence.

The key issues are good communication in preparation, followed by a graduated process involving control of thirst, management of bowel and bladder, social support, and appropriate medication.

All life-sustaining medications should be ceased, and only palliative medications for the relief of symptoms (essentially sedatives and pain-control medications) prescribed.

Sequence of events in voluntary refusal of fluid and food

1. Initially some hunger may be appreciated, but usually rapidly disappears as ketones increase in the blood.

2. Thirst develops after 24–48 hours and is appreciated as a dry mouth and dry lips.
3. Some confusion develops after 3–5 days, followed by drowsiness.
4. Physical weakness makes mobility difficult/dangerous (falls) after 3–4 days.
5. Coma ensues after 5–7 days, depending on original state of health, and medication.
6. Death occurs in 5–10 days, occasionally more, depending on the rigour of the cessation of fluids (and, to a lesser extent, food).

Management of bowel

Distressing bowel incontinence, and the need to mobilise to the toilet, can be avoided by emptying the bowel prior to ceasing fluids. Start by ceasing eating solids, combined with a mild laxative, to empty the bowel BEFORE commencing cessation of fluids. At the same time, gradual reduction of fluid intake can start. The fluids taken at this time can be energy-rich to diminish hunger.

Management of bladder

Once fluid restriction commences, urine output will diminish, but the need to void will continue up to 5–6 days after fluid cessation. A commode chair beside the bed is valuable while mobilisation is still possible. A catheter avoids the need to mobilise to toilet but is invasive, and to be avoided if possible. In the later stages, absorbent incontinence pads avoid wet clothes and bed, or voiding can occur into a towel, or bottle for a man.

Management of thirst

A gradual reduction of fluid intake can precede complete cessation. Start with 2000 ml/day, then 1,500 ml, then 1,000 ml, then 500 ml, before complete cessation (with minimal exceptions for essential palliative medication and oral care).

The more complete the cessation of oral fluids the better, as it shortens the process.

A dry mouth is the principal symptom of thirst, and dry lips follow and can be painful.

Dry lips can be easily avoided by regular application of a lip balm.

There are various ways to alleviate a dry mouth:

1. A mouth spray of water can be used as needed.
2. Ice chips can be sucked.
3. There are proprietary products for keeping the mouth moist (Biotene).
4. Moist gauze swabs are used in nursing to moisten the tongue and mouth.
5. Small quantities of lemon/grapefruit/orange juice will stimulate saliva.

Medication

Pain is not necessarily an issue for VRFF *per se*, but may be present for other reasons. Pain relief can be obtained without significant fluid by using oral morphine (2–10 mg/ml – Ordine). Sedation can be provided orally, rectally, or by injection if desired, or if indicated by restlessness/confusion.

Oral medication for fungal infection of the mouth may be needed.

Social support

Perhaps the hardest part of this journey is the psychological and existential aspect.

People need to be accompanied as much as possible: engagement with family and friends, shared memories, care and love. Soft, familiar music in the background may be valuable.

Many people would reject this option from an emotional perspective. Yet for those who have no other option, there is clear evidence that, properly managed, it can be without physical suffering, and for some, the slow nature of the process allows for a surprisingly positive farewell.

APPENDIX B

Advance care directives

Considerations if you wish to create a values advance care directive*

Give careful thought to each of the issues raised in the 15 sections of this document. Try to be as clear and concise as you can in your discussion about each of them. Study the notes describing each section, and reflect on what your own position is; it may be nothing like the examples which are given here to illustrate the kinds of factors you might think about. In some cases you might not even know what you think! In that case, continue to reflect, and consider talking things over with trusted others to help establish your position. Once you have sorted out your thoughts, write them out as simply and clearly as you can. Then, neatly draw a strike-through line across the remainder of the answer space for the section if you did not completely fill it with your points.

1. What gives my life meaning and purpose

This is a broad, philosophical section intended to give your agent a clear picture of what creates purpose and meaning to your life overall, and the absence of which may mean that life is of significantly diminished value to you. Items may include religious faith, family, making a contribution to society, personal challenge, relationships, learning, teaching, exercise of intellect and reflection, personal peace, etc. Do you believe in a God, an afterlife, heaven or hell, the

---

* In addition to a Values Advance Care Directive, an Instructional Directive which allows for specific requests or refusals of medical treatment may be found on the DWDV website.

importance of and medically relevant pathways to redemption, or perhaps that there is nothing after death? Do you believe that it is God's will alone that ought to determine your time of death, even if life is burdensome, or is your view that God is compassionate and would not want you to suffer unnecessarily?

If you are already near the end of life and believe that your life has been a good one but you have no wish to extend it through further – and especially through burdensome – medical interventions which would be meaningless to you even if life-saving, say so.

2. What brings pleasure and joy to my daily existence

This is a more practical, experiential section. Describe which factors provide you with pleasure on a more immediate basis, such as reading, conversation, listening to music, walking, gardening, dancing, exercise and sports (which kinds and how often), making a contribution to grand/children's development, cooking, foods, intimate relations, hobbies, clubs or specific regular outings or meetings with friends, a sense of connectedness and community, personal autonomy and independence, a degree of solitude, etc. This helps inform your agent about what aspects of daily living are most important, and may assist decision-making should your medical prognosis indicate that any of these factors might be adversely affected on the basis of consenting to or refusing medical treatments.

3. Senses and capacities that are important to me

As in section 2, answers may help inform your agent's decision-making if your prognosis suggests that any sense or physical capacity might be seriously compromised. Think of the five senses: sight, hearing, touch, taste and smell. Some of them may be relatively unimportant if lost; you could readjust your life and cope. On the other hand, you may believe that the loss of sight or hearing, for example, would be a tortured and distressing blow to the remainder of your life. For any of these, state your views clearly.

Your views on capacities are important too. Would you accept a loss of ability to feed yourself, to toilet yourself, to keep a home and cook for yourself, to change a colostomy bag yourself, to understand the world around you, to engage in meaningful conversation, to move around your home (unaided, walker, crutches, wheelchair?) and other general forms of autonomy, or to recognise and remember your nearest and dearest? Or does the thought of losing a particular capacity seriously affect your opinion of the value of continuing medical treatment or an attempt to extend your life?

Make your notes first on a separate sheet before filling in the form. When you have made your notes, carefully reflect on whether you really would find loss of a particular sense or capacity so calamitous, particularly in the context of support from family, friends and health-care specialists. People often find themselves able to adjust to new circumstances, to their surprise. For example, a hiker with cancer initially decided he would prefer to die than to no longer be able to go out hiking with his friends. When that became his reality, his perspective adjusted to preferring to die if he could no longer move around his country home and bask in the glow of his roaring log fire. When that became his reality, his perspective adjusted to preferring to die if he could no longer move between his bed and his bathroom without too much difficulty. Finally, that became his reality and he decided to refuse all medical treatment and to receive maximum palliation, which had the consequence of shortening his life.

Are there differences in your views about impairment of sense or capacity between those that would allow you to stay at home, even if requiring care by loved ones, and those that would almost certainly need your transfer to a nursing home or other special-care facility?

Once you have reflected deeply on diminished senses and capacities, fill in the form.

4. My attitudes about medical estimates and opinion

The human body is organic, and as such can change in unexpected ways and sometimes with unexpected speed. It can react well or badly to treatment attempts. Doctors can in many cases make a fair estimate of your likely health in the foreseeable future, such as deterioration of breathing capacity, ability to walk, or response to medication. They are also reasonably good at predicting your death when it is imminent – which means within a week or a few days.

However, doctors' predictions about your likely remaining time to death given your current illness, or response to medication or other procedures, can sometimes be wrong by a wide margin. You may begin to deteriorate suddenly and unexpectedly, or your condition may continue in its current state, perhaps even with some improvement, for a long time, perhaps many months or some years.

It is normal in these 'organic' and uncertain circumstances for doctors to make estimates of a likely path or outcome. For example, a doctor may assess that you are likely to die in around three months, with 80 per cent probability of that outcome; or assess that you have a 50 per cent chance of making a reasonable recovery from the serious illness that has rendered you unable to participate in your own health-care decisions; or assess that you have a 30 per cent chance of surviving but with significant brain damage, making it unlikely you will be able to recognise or interact with your loved ones again.

In this section, do your best to describe your attitude to this kind of chance: to what degree is certainty of recovery needed in order for you to endure aggressive (or any) medical treatment or rehabilitation, or prefer only comfort care until death? Conversely, to what degree do you need certainty of a poor prognosis before wanting to refuse medical treatment? To what degree, especially in 'chancy' or burdensome-treatment circumstances, do you wish your agent to seek several medical opinions? For example, are you comfortable with the determination of your own treating doctor – whom you might have been seeing for decades –or would you prefer other specialist opinions before giving up hope of an acceptable life, or accepting intensive and burdensome health care? You may be relatively young and healthy, and want multiple opinions before any significant decision is made to refuse treatment or life support. On the other hand, you may be elderly or frail and need only one or even no medical opinion about outcomes in order to refuse all and any treatment.

What is your own approach to decision-making if medical opinions differ? Do you lean more towards your own doctor's opinion, towards an independent specialist's opinion, or prefer to have multiple opinions until a majority opinion reveals itself? Be as clear and straightforward as you can. If you simply want your agent to 'decide as best they personally can in the circumstances and that you trust their judgement', say so.

5. *My attitudes about resuscitation and life support*

Describe your attitudes towards the use of resuscitation, life support – for example, artificial feeding and hydration (tubes to your stomach), artificial ventilation, dialysis, and potentially life-saving surgery – and trial treatments. Be sure to compare and contrast your attitudes in situations where there is a good chance of recovery versus little chance, if the difference is important to you. How would you take into account the likely burdensomeness of such interventions, if at all?

Thinking about the potential to have a serious health episode in the street or other public place, as well as at home, with the attendance of an ambulance emergency crew, what is your position on receiving resuscitation? For example, you may want none at all (just maximal relief from pain and suffering), all available measures even if heroic and burdensome, or moderate measures (such as non-invasive treatments) for a certain period of time, after which you believe it would be better to discontinue attempts to resuscitate you.

Do you personally lean towards erring on the side of continuing life support, or refusing or withdrawing it when there is doubt about either the degree of recovery or severity of continuing illness? Reflect on your answers to sections 1, 2 and 3 to help inform this section. Would you want a pre-determined period of life-support trial such as a few days, weeks or months, after which you would want life support discontinued if there was no or little improvement? Would you want all reasonable support continued, regardless? Would you refuse life support altogether?

6. *My attitudes about surgery*

Would you want all offered surgery? Would you want any and all surgery if it was life-saving? Would you agree to minor surgery but refuse major (risky, burdensome) surgery? Would you refuse surgery altogether? Try to weigh and balance your considerations between burdensomeness of surgery and recovery, versus potential benefits of having it.

7. *My attitudes about trial treatments*

To what degree would you want to participate in trial or experimental treatments if any were available, given their unestablished effectiveness but potential for hope? For example, what is your disposition towards being enrolled in a treatment regime in which you could receive either the real drug or a placebo ('fake', inert drug)? That would mean you had either no potential benefit (placebo) or an unknown chance of improvement (real drug), but at the very least would be contributing to the body of medical knowledge for the treatment of patients following in your footsteps in the future. Would you want to participate in an experimental procedure with unknown likelihood of success? What degree of burdensomeness would you accept to participate, and for how long, if at all?

8. My attitudes about maximal palliation and assisted dying

In this section it is important to inform your agent about your attitudes towards the transition between medical care (treatment and potential cure) and palliative care (keeping you comfortable until your death). You should understand that some forms of comfort care, such as elevated levels of morphine to keep you unconscious and unaware of your pain ('terminal sedation'), may result in accelerating your death (in the case of morphine by depressing your breathing). Are you averse to any care that might potentially shorten your life, or do you lean more towards terminal sedation and fuller comfort? Is it more important to you both for yourself and your loved ones to see out your final days in relative peace (terminal sedation), or have the chance to potentially awaken and interact with your loved ones (light sedation) but with the chance of significant suffering? If there is a chance, even with significant suffering, would you want one final short period of lighter sedation so you might have a chance to wake up and say your goodbyes, and even participate in decision-making, or would you just prefer to remain unconscious?

What is your attitude towards physician-assisted dying? If your health circumstances are dire and doctors believe there is no realistic hope of you recovering or improving, and it is legal to do so at the time, would you want medical assistance to die peacefully in the presence of your loved ones, or is the mere thought of that a vile travesty against your beliefs – in which case you may prefer to 'let nature take its course' with minimal support?

Reflect carefully about the agent you are appointing or have appointed, and whether they are willing to act according to the advice you are giving here to actually make decisions that you firmly believe are in your best interests. For example, if you would want maximal palliation, and shortening of your life should it be available, is your agent willing to take those decisions if the circumstances arose? On the other hand, if you want any and all treatments, even those that are heroic, aggressive and burdensome, would your agent continue to request them even if doing so causes your agent distress? Are your beliefs and values around these difficult matters reasonably compatible? If you are unsure, talk with your agent about your views in this section and assure yourself that they would be willing to take the tough decisions in a manner you would like.

9. Important experiences for loved ones

Describe what is important to you for loved ones to experience and to hold as memories of you and your final life chapter. For example, you may wish your loved ones to remember you as a coherent, competent and intelligent person, in which case in life-threatening circumstances your agent may make decisions that partly result in a shortening of your life so that you do not have a prolonged period of incoherence and incompetence. On the other hand, you may prefer your family to experience your final chapter as someone who always allowed God's will to guide your end, regardless of your condition leading up to death. Describe as best you can the experiences and memories you would like your loved ones to be left with.

10. People to consult

Good decisions are rarely made in a vacuum, and a good experience for loved ones who survive you usually includes the opportunity to be heard and to be understood at times of trauma and significant decision-making. That does not mean your agent will act on the opinions of relatives if they differ from yours. It simply means your agent can have the opportunity to hear out loved ones, adding their experience and memories of you and your wishes to the mix of information they bring to bear when deciding about medical treatment and care. If you want consultation, list the people you would like your agent to take reasonable efforts to consult, and, if appropriate, what aspects and to what reasonable extent you would like them consulted. Remember to include philosophical, ethicist, spiritual or religious advisors if appropriate.

Mention anyone you would like your agent to keep informed, even if not initially consulted.

If you are in a personal relationship of which your relatives disapprove (for example, a same-sex or wide-age-difference relationship) and you want your partner's attendance, views and wishes to take precedence – rather than those of your blood relatives, be sure to spell that out.

If you believe that your best interests would be served by deferring or relinquishing decision-making to your family (for instance, in some Asian cultures), to your community elders (for example, traditional Aboriginal culture), or to other individuals or classes of people, then say so, being clear and unambiguous about who those people are and the extent to which you defer or relinquish.

Also reflect on your responses to section 9 above. Would you, for example, despite wanting to have any life-supporting machines switched off sooner rather than later, still want to give, say, two or three days for far-flung relatives or friends to attend your bedside in order to have the opportunity to say their farewells while you are alive, even if you can't respond? Or is your earlier death something you believe they will simply have to cope with?

11. People not to consult

In some families, difficult or estranged relatives can become vocal and active once your mental capacity is compromised. If there are relatives or others, such as past carers or neighbours, whom you would prefer *not* to be consulted, or perhaps even to be excluded from attending your bedside or interfering with relatives or friends (especially those you've nominated in section 10 above) during decision-making, state your wishes clearly in this section. This can help your agent authoritatively (but not officiously) smooth difficult circumstances, focus their consultation attentions where *you* think it's appropriate, and even inform security if an abusive person exhibits inappropriate behaviour that causes serious distress to your nearest and dearest. Try to neither over- nor under-estimate potential serious conflict. (A degree of conflict is natural and can be healthy; try not to avoid it altogether. Moderate and reasoned discussion with mutual respect is important.)

12. Specific time-based goals
If your health is in serious peril and medical treatment or rehabilitation (perhaps even if it is aggressive) is required for you to regain consciousness and improve, are there specific time-based goals that are important to you? For example, do you treasure the opportunity to see a grandchild born, a nephew graduate, a cousin married, observe your diamond wedding anniversary, or other important event which would mean you would accept greater medical intervention than you would without such goals? List any specific goals in this section and try to describe the degree to which you would accept more burdensome challenges in order to reach the goal. Is there a difference between simply observing the goal (such as from a wheelchair, or in photos after the event) and actively participating in it?

If a goal you describe here has already been reached before your agent has to act on your behalf, then that goal would automatically be irrelevant to the scheme of advice about decision-making.

If you have no such specific goals, simply write 'None' and rule a line through the remainder of this section.

13. Other relevant information
If there are any other important aspects to your agent's decision-making that are not already covered in this document, add them here. Otherwise write 'None' and rule a line through this section.

Addendum
The following two sections are about organ donation and funeral arrangements. Keep in mind that your agent has no authority to speak or decide on your behalf in regard to these matters – only about your health care while you are alive. However, documenting your wishes here can help families and authorities act in a timely manner with reduced stress, once you have passed away.

14. Organ donation and research

Briefly discuss your attitude towards donating your organs and body. Do you prefer not to donate under any circumstances, or to donate for transplant to another living person for their benefit, for example organs such as heart, liver and kidneys, retinas – greatly improving, if not saving, another life? (Only organs in good health that will benefit another person at the time of your death would be donated this way.)

What is your attitude towards donating organs for medical research? For example, a person dying of motor neurone disease may wish to donate their brain and spinal cord for research towards developing new treatments that could benefit future sufferers. Do you want to decline all donations, to donate specific organs for research in a particular disease or syndrome, or to donate whatever may be useful to medical science?

Do you wish to donate your body (or the remainder after specific donations above) to training for medical students so that they may improve their skills in becoming doctors?

15. Funeral arrangements

Describe your preferences as to your funeral arrangements. Would you rather burial or cremation? If burial, do you want to be buried in a particular location (such as next to loved ones), and do you prefer a well-dressed grave (perhaps like other family members already buried) or something modest and simple? If cremation, would you like to have your ashes scattered, or kept, and in a particular place? If scattered, is there a particular person or perhaps a group of people you would like to do the scattering?

Do you want faith-based post-death observance and funeral service of a single religion or denomination, or perhaps a blended one to reflect the shared values of an extended family and past? Alternatively, do you request a secular, non-faith-based service with a civil celebrant? Would you prefer a particular venue for the service?

Are there any personal effects or symbols you would like at the service, such as a favourite hat, flowers or photos, or particular music or instrument to be played or poetry or verse read out? Would you like to leave the legacy of a written message of love and thanks to your bereaved? (If so, write it separately.)

Are there any special people you would like notified of your death and funeral so that they might be able to attend? Are there people you would prefer not attend?

If you would prefer to leave some or all of these decisions to your loved ones or a particular person, say so.

Before you start writing

Now that you have read the preceding information, you are ready to fill in the sections of the following form with your views. It is recommended that you complete each section, one by one, after re-reading the information for the section you are completing.

If you are not clear in your mind about what you want to write in a section, don't write anything yet: it's important not to create any potential confusion or conflicts of information with sections you have completed, or with your advance care directive. Therefore, complete a section only after giving the section's issues serious deliberation and feeling comfortable that you know what you want.

You may choose to fill out the form in handwriting. However, especially if the space provided is inadequate, hand-write, type or word-process on your computer an equivalent document of your own. If you create your own document, be sure to include the commencing and ending sections of the form printed here.

It is also recommended that you attach this preamble to your signed form as evidence of the extent of your thinking and preparation of advice to your agent and other decision-makers about what you believe is in your best interests.

After you have completed this document, it is recommended that you review your advance care directive to ensure that what you have said in each is consistent and doesn't create any conflict or ambiguity for those who would have to interpret and implement your wishes.

Also, it is recommended that you discuss both this and your advance care directive with your agent, so that he or she may ask any questions necessary to understand what you mean, and potentially even make amendments that help clarify your intentions.

Documenting your wishes may not be quick, but can be rewarding – not only in settling in your own mind what you want, but in having your wishes honoured and respected. Research shows that 86 per cent of people who document their end-of-life treatment wishes have those wishes honoured, a rate twice that of people who don't document their wishes. So, if you find that a section or two give you pause for thought, don't give up. Instead, accept the pause as natural, and come back to the document as often as necessary to complete it.

The more simply, clearly and fully you write down what's important to you, the more informed your agent, your loved ones, your doctors and other carers will be. That can lift from their shoulders a tremendous burden of decision-making caused by trying to guess what you would have wanted, or worse, people of different opinions arguing over alternatives.

Now it's time to commence your reflections on each section and write down what you believe is in your own best interests.

Informing my Agent

I, ...(your full name) of
... ...
.... (your address)
have prepared the following statements of my beliefs, values, opinions, pref-
erences and wishes about medical interventions and health care to assist my
Enduring Power of Attorney (Medical Treatment) ('Agent') and others to make
informed decisions at such time as I lack capacity to participate in such decision-
making. I attest and affirm my strong and enduring belief that decisions made
which are consistent with the statements herein are in my best interests, and I
hereby reject fundamentally conflicting assessments of my best interests.

1. What gives my life meaning and purpose
2. What brings pleasure and joy to my daily existence
3. Senses and capacities that are important to me
4. My attitudes about medical estimates and opinion
5. My attitudes about resuscitation and life support
6. My attitudes about surgery
7. My attitudes about trial treatments
8. My attitudes about maximal palliation and assisted dying
9. Important experiences for loved ones
10. People to consult
11. People not to consult
12. Specific time-based goals
13. Other relevant information.

Addendum: After-death wishes and preferences

14. Organ donation and research
15. Funeral arrangements.

→━● ●━←

I RESERVE the right to revoke this information document at any time, but unless I do so it should be taken to represent my continuing beliefs about my best interests in medical treatment and health care, end-of-life issues, and after-death wishes and preferences. Should I after signing this document express an opinion or exhibit behaviour at odds with the views I have recorded in this document, then such change of best interests shall be limited to the opinion or behaviour so expressed, and the remainder of my views contained in this document shall continue to stand and endure as my continuing beliefs about my best interests, unless I revoke this document in its entirety.

SIGNED BY ME: .... (signature)
this .... day of .... 20......
in the presence of
.... (signature of witness)
.... (name of witness)
of ....
....
.... (address of witness)

References

Introduction

Metcalfe, D. (1998). Doctors and patients should be fellow travellers. *British Medical Journal, 316*(7148), 1892–3. http://www.jstor.org/stable/25179586

Royal Commission into Aged Care Quality and Safety. (2021). *Final Report: Care, Dignity and Respect.* Commonwealth of Australia. https://agedcare.royalcommission.gov.au/

Chapter 1 – The problems of ageing

Martin, D. K., Emanuel, L. L., & Singer, P. A. (2000). Planning for the end of life. *The Lancet, 356*(9242), 1672–6. https://doi.org/10.1016/s0140-6736(00)03168-8

Quill, T. (1991). Death and dignity: A case of individualized decision making. *New England Journal of Medicine, 324*(1), 691–4. https://doi.org/10.1056/NEJM199103073241010

Chapter 2 – Mortality

Enkin, M., Jadad, A. R., & Smith, R. (2011). Death can be our friend: Embracing the inevitable would reduce both unnecessary suffering and costs. *British Medical Journal, 343*(7837), 1277–8. https://doi.org/10.1136/bmj.d8008

Hitchens, C. (2012). *Mortality.* Allen & Unwin.

Chapter 3 – The phenomenon of old age

Ariès, P. (1981). *The Hour of Our Death* (H. Weaver, trans.). Allen Lane. (original work published 1977).

Bookwala, J., & Lawson, B. (2011). Poor vision, functioning, and depressive symptoms: A test of the activity restriction model. *The Gerontologist, 51*(6), 798–808. https://doi.org/10.1093/geront/gnr051

Cardona-Morrell, M., Kim, J., Turner, R. M., Anstey, M., Mitchell, I. A., & Hillman, K. (2016). Non-beneficial treatments in hospital at the end of life: A systematic review on extent of the problem. *International Journal for Quality in Health Care, 28*(4), 456–69. https://doi.org/10.1093/intqhc/mzw060

Carter, H. E., Winch, S., Barnett, A. G., Parker, M., Gallois, C., Willmott, L., White, B. P., Patton, M. A., Burridge, L., Salkield, G., Close, E., Callaway, L., & Graves, N. (2017). Incidence, duration and cost of futile treatment in end-of-life hospital admissions to three Australian public-sector tertiary hospitals: A retrospective multicentre cohort study. *BMJ Open, 7*(10), e017661. https://doi.org/10.1136/bmjopen-2017-017661

Corke, C. (2010). *Saving Life … or Prolonging Death: Finding the Way in the World of Medical Technology.* Erudite Medical Books.

Cushman, R. (2007, October 31). Think care, not just cure, for ill seniors. *Ottawa Citizen.*

Osler, W. (1898). *The Principles and Practice of Medicine: Designed for the Use of Practitioners and Students of Medicine* (3rd edn). Young J. Pentland.

Royal Australian College of General Practitioners. (2006). *Medical Care of Older Persons in Residential Aged Care* Facilities (4th edn). https://www.racgp.org.au/FSDEDEV/media/documents/Clinical%20Resources/Guidelines/

Silverbook/Medical-care-of-older-persons-in-residential-aged-care-facilities.pdf

Wachterman, M. W., Pilver, C., Smith, D., Ersek, M., Lipsitz, S. R., & Keating, N. L. (2016). Quality of end-of-life care provided to patients with different serious illnesses. *JAMA Internal Medicine, 176*(8), 1095. https://doi.org/10.1001/jamainternmed.2016.1200

Chapter 4 – Aged care: Our second prison system

Anonymous. (2017, September 29). [Letter in] Readers respond: Your experiences of nursing homes in Australia. *Sydney Morning Herald*. https://www.smh.com.au/national/readers-respond-your-experiences-of-nursing-homes-in-australia-20170928-gyqlo0.html

Appel, J. M. (2009, November 25). 'Mercy killing': When love and law conflict. *HuffPost*. https://www.huffpost.com/entry/mercy-killing-when-love-l_b_299726

Australian Government Department of Health and Aged Care. (2020). *2019–20 Report on the Operation of the Aged Care Act 1997*. https://www.gen-agedcaredata.gov.au/Resources/Reports-and-publications/2020/November/2019%E2%80%9320-Report-on-the-Operation-of-the-Aged-Care-A

Australian Government Productivity Commission (2011). *Caring for Older Australians* (Report No. 53, Final Inquiry Report). https://www.pc.gov.au/inquiries/completed/aged-care/report

Australian Institute of Health and Welfare. (2013). *Depression in Residential Aged Care 2008–2012* (Aged Care Statistics Series No. 39, Cat. No. AGE 73). https://www.aihw.gov.au/reports/aged-care/depression-in-residential-aged-care-2008-2012

Bachelard, M. (2017, September 23). Jyl's journey to aged care: 'I feel like part of me is lost. *Sydney Morning Herald.* https://www.smh.com.au/national/jyls-journey-to-aged-care-i-feel-like-part-of-me-is-lost-20170922-gymj83.html

Bachelard, M. (2018, May 1). 'Big nursing home' industry is aggressively minimising tax. *Sydney Morning Herald.* https://www.smh.com.au/politics/federal/big-nursing-home-industry-is-aggressively-minimising-tax-20180501-p4zcq9.html

Bachelard, M., & Browne, R. (2017, May 28). Aged care: Preventable nursing home deaths surge. *The Age.* https://www.theage.com.au/national/aged-care-preventable-nursing-home-deaths-surge-20170526-gwdx2q.html

Bachelard, M., & Tomazin, F. (2017, September 24). Nursing home accused of being like Guantanamo Bay. *Sydney Morning Herald.* https://www.smh.com.au/national/nursing-home-accused-of-being-like-guantanamo-bay-20170922-gyn0a2.html

Bernoth, M. (2010, July). *Submission to the Productivity Commission Inquiry into Caring for Older Australians.* https://www.pc.gov.au/inquiries/completed/aged-care/submissions/sub253.pdf

Brodaty, H. (2019, May 17). *Statement to the Royal Commission into Aged Care Quality and Safety* (Exhibit 3–80 – WIT.0116.0001.0001). https://agedcare.royalcommission.gov.au/media/4866

Buckwalter, K., Smith, M., & Martin, M. (1993, February 3). Ageing Matters. Attitude Problem. *Nursing Times* 89(5), 54–7.

Claire, Marie. (2017, September 29). A resident's lament. *Sydney Morning Herald.* https://www.smh.com.au/national/readers-respond-your-experiences-of-nursing-homes-in-australia-20170928-gyqlo0.html

Elliston, B. Urgent need for money. *The Age*. https://www.theage.com.au/national/aiia-maasarwe-a-world-where-women-are-respected-and-valued-20190118-h1a760.html

Fiveash, B. (1998). The experience of nursing home life. *International Journal of Nursing Practice, 4*(3), 166–74. https://doi.org/10.1046/j.1440-172X.1998.00062.x

Fleming, J., Farquhar, M., Cambridge City over-75s Cohort (CC75C) Study Collaboration, Brayne, C., & Barclay, S. (2016). Death and the oldest old: Attitudes and preferences for end-of-life care: Qualitative research within a population-based cohort study. *PloS ONE, 11*(4), e0150686. https://doi.org/10.1371/journal.pone.0150686

Foreman, L. M., Hunt, R. W., Luke, C. G., & Roder, D. M. (2006). Factors predictive of preferred place of death in the general population of South Australia. *Palliative Medicine, 20*(4), 447–53. https://doi.org/10.1191/0269216306pm1149oa

'Former national operations manager'. (2017, September 29). Staff speak out. *Sydney Morning Herald*. https://www.smh.com.au/national/readers-respond-your-experiences-of-nursing-homes-in-australia-20170928-gyqlo0.html

Hamilton, M., & Thomson, C. (2016). Recognising unpaid care in private pension schemes. *Social Policy and Society, 16*(4).

Kayser-Jones J. (2002). The experience of dying: An ethnographic nursing home study. *The Gerontologist, 42*, Spec. No. 3, 11–19. https://doi.org/10.1093/geront/42.suppl_3.11

Kot, T. (2017, September 29). Readers respond: Your experiences of nursing homes in Australia. *Sydney Morning Herald*. https://www.smh.com.au/national/readers-respond-your-experiences-of-nursing-homes-in-australia-20170928-gyqlo0.html

Legislative Council Legal and Social Issues Committee. (2016). *Inquiry into End of Life Choices: Final Report*. Parliament of Victoria. https://www.parliament.vic. gov.au/file_uploads/LSIC_pF3XBb2L.pdf

Lee, Jane. (2016, April 9). The workers we trust to look after our mums and dads are changing – and struggling. *Sydney Morning Herald*. https://www.smh.com. au/politics/federal/just-who-are-the-people-we-increasingly-trust-look-after-our-mums-and-dads-20160406-gnzcz8.html

Lloyd-Williams, M., Kennedy, V., Sixsmith, A., & Sixsmith, J. (2007). The end of life: A qualitative study of the perceptions of people over the age of 80 on issues surrounding death and dying. *Journal of Pain and Symptom Management, 34*(1), 60–6. https://doi.org/10.1016/j.jpainsymman.2006.09.028

Mahoney, P. (2017, September 29). Letter to the editor. In Readers respond: Your experiences of nursing homes in Australia. *Sydney Morning Herald*. https:// www.smh.com.au/national/readers-respond-your-experiences-of-nursing-homes-in-australia-20170928-gyqlo0.html

McCallum, J., Simons, L. A., & Simons, J. (2007). Private lives and public programs: An Australian longitudinal study of the elderly [known as the Dubbo longitudinal study of older Australians]. *Journal of Aging and Social Policy, 19*(4), 87–103. https://doi.org/10.1300/J031v19n04_05

McCredie, Jane. (2009, August 20). Aged care: The depressing reality. *ABC Health & Wellbeing*. https://www.abc.net.au/health/features/stories/2009/08/20/ 2661451.htm

Melding, P. S. (2002). Can we improve pain management in nursing homes? *Medical Journal of Australia, 177*(1), 5–6. https://doi.org/10.5694/j.1326-5377.2002. tb04610.x

Mitchell, M. (2019, May 11). I live in aged care but it's not home: an insider's story. *The Age*. https://www.theage.com.au/national/i-live-in-aged-care-but-it-s-not-home-an-insider-s-story-20190510-p51lym.html

Moore, A. (2016, March 24). Dear kids, don't ever shove me in an old people's home. *The Age*. https://www.theage.com.au/opinion/instructions-for-our-children-to-let-their-parents-stay-at-home-to-the-end-20160324-gnq4b1.html

Nay, R. (1995). Nursing home residents' perceptions of relocation. *Journal of Clinical Nursing, 4*, 319–25. https://doi.org/10.1111/j.1365-2702.1995.tb00030.x

Office for Senior Victorians, Department for Victorian Communities. (2005). *Strengthening Victoria's Response to Elder Abuse: Report of the Elder Abuse Prevention Project*. Victorian Government.

Parliamentary Budget Office. (2019). *Australia's Ageing Population: Understanding the Fiscal Impacts Over the Next Decade* (Report 02/2019). Australian Government. https://www.aph.gov.au/-/media/05_About_Parliament/54_Parliamentary_Depts/548_Parliamentary_Budget_Office/Reports/2018-19/02_2019_Australias_ageing_population/Australias_Ageing_Population_PDF.pdf

Phillips, T. M. (2017, September 29). Readers respond: Your experiences of nursing homes in Australia. *The Sydney Morning Herald*. https://www.smh.com.au/national/readers-respond-your-experiences-of-nursing-homes-in-australia-20170928-gyqlo0.html

Rabow, M. W., Hauser, J. M., & Adams, J. (2004). Supporting family caregivers at the end of life: 'They don't know what they don't know'. *JAMA, 291*(4), 483–91. https://doi.org/10.1001/jama.291.4.483

Richards, N. (2012). The fight-to-die: Older people and death activism. *International Journal of Ageing and Later Life, 7*(1), 7–32. https://doi.org/10.3384/ ijal.1652-8670.11153

River, A. (2017, September 29). Staff speak out. *Sydney Morning Herald.* https:// www.smh.com.au/national/readers-respond-your-experiences-of-nursing-homes-in-australia-20170928-gyqlo0.html

Ruppanner, L., & Bostean, G. (2015, January 5). Counting the costs of caregiving: Is there a better way forward? *The Conversation.* https://theconversation. com/counting-the-costs-of-caregiving-is-there-a-better-way-forward-33181

Russell, S. (2016, July 5). Reverse the aged care cuts. *Aged Care Matters.* https:// www.agedcarematters.net.au/reverse-the-aged-care-cuts/

Salkeld, G., Cameron, I. D., Cumming, R. G., Easter, S., Seymour, J., Kurrle, S. E., & Quine, S. (2000). Quality of life related to fear of falling and hip fracture in older women: A time trade off study. *British Medical Journal, 320*(7231), 341–6. https://doi.org/10.1136/bmj.320.7231.341

Saltarelli, L. (2007, November 19). Vulnerable elderly deserve better care. *The Age.* https://www.theage.com.au/national/vulnerable-elderly-deserve-better-care-20071119-ge6c6h.html

Saul, P. (2013, April 29). A conversation that promises savings worth dying for. *The Conversation.* https://theconversation.com/a-conversation-that-promises-savings-worth-dying-for-13710

Short, M. (2013, October 29). The Zone transcript: Greg Evans. *Sydney Morning Herald.* https://www.smh.com.au/national/the-zone-transcript-greg-evans-20131029-2weg9.html

Singer, P. A., Martin, D. K., & Kelner, M. (1999). Quality end-of-life care: Patients' perspectives. *JAMA, 281*(2), 163–8. https://doi.org/10.1001/jama.281.2.163

Spriggs, B. (2019, February 11). *Statement to the Royal Commission into Aged Care Quality and Safety* (Exhibit 1–1 – WIT.0025.0001.0001). https://agedcare.royalcommission.gov.au/media/8166

StewartBrown. (2019). *Aged Care Financial Performance Survey: Sector Report.* https://www.stewartbrown.com.au/images/documents/StewartBrown---ACFPS-Sector-Financial-Performance-Report-September-2019.pdf

Swerissen, H., & Duckett, S. (2014, September). *Dying Well.* Grattan Institute. Report No. 2014–10. https://grattan.edu.au/report/dying-well/

Syme, R. (2008). *A Good Death.* Melbourne University Press.

Triggs, G. (2018). Humanism in a post-truth world [acceptance speech for Australian Humanist of the Year 2018]. *Australian Humanist, 130,* 3–6. https://static1.squarespace.com/static/59b4e4953e00be04abab9d89/t/5c56724108 5229a138aff646/1549169225948/Australian-Humanist-130-MayJul2018.pdf

Valente, S. M. (2004). End-of-life challenges: Honoring autonomy. *Cancer Nursing, 27*(4), 314–19. https://doi.org/10.1097/00002820-200407000-00008

Chapter 5 – Remember me, Mrs V?

Halliday, C. (2010, December 8–14). *The Weekly Review.* https://issuu.com/theweeklyreview.com.au/docs/twr-stonington-20101208-edition33_all_web.

Manfredi, P. L., Breuer, B., Meier, D. E., & Libow, L. (2003). Pain assessment in elderly patients with severe dementia. *Journal of Pain and Symptom Management, 25*(1), 48–52. https://doi.org/10.1016/s0885-3924(02)00530-4

Morrison, R. S., & Siu, A. L. (2000). A comparison of pain and its treatment in advanced dementia and cognitively intact patients with hip fracture. *Journal of Pain and Symptom Management, 19*(4), 240–8. https://doi.org/10.1016/s0885-3924(00)00113-5

Teno, J.M., Weitzen, S., Wetle, T., & Mor, V. (2001). Persistent pain in nursing home residents. *Journal of the American Medical Association, 285*(16), 2081. https://jamanetwork.com/journals/jama/articlepdf/193765/jcx10004.pdf

Valenta, T. (2007). *Remember Me, Mrs V? Caring For My Wife: Her Alzheimer's and Others' Stories.* Michelle Anderson Publishing.

Chapter 6 – Dementia

Abbey, J. (2013). *Wrestling with Dementia and Death: A Report for Alzheimer's Australia.* Alzheimer's Australia Inc. https://agedcare.royalcommission.gov.au/system/files/2020-06/JAB.0001.0001.0001.pdf

Abbey, J., Piller, N., De Bellis, A., Esterman, A., Parker, D., Giles, L., & Lowcay, B. (2004). The Abbey pain scale: A 1-minute numerical indicator for people with end-stage dementia. *International Journal of Palliative Nursing, 10*(1), 6–13. https://doi.org/10.12968/ijpn.2004.10.1.12013

Age. (2004, March 1). Assault a daily hazard for nursing home workers. *The Age.* https://www.theage.com.au/national/assault-a-daily-hazard-for-nursing-home-workers-20040301-gdxepl.html

Bachelard, M. (2017, September 21 and 23). Dawn's final days reveal aged care horror. *The Age.* https://www.theage.com.au/national/dawns-final-days-reveal-aged-care-horror-20170921-gylvaj.html

Ballard, C., Smith, J., Corbett, A., Husebo, B., & Aarsland, D. (2011). The role of pain treatment in managing the behavioural and psychological symptoms of dementia (BPSD). *International Journal of Palliative Nursing,17*(9), 420–4. https://doi.org/10.12968/ijpn.2011.17.9.420

Boulton, L. (2021). *Pas de Deux: A Carer's Story.* Ginninderra Press.

Brett, J. (2017). *The Enigmatic Mr Deakin.* Text Publishing.

Brodaty, H., & Rees, G. (2011, September 21). Alzheimer's disease a scourge we can't afford to forget. *Sydney Morning Herald.*

Campbell, D. (2016, January 27). Dementia takes the choice out of death decisions. *The Age.* https://www.theage.com.au/opinion/dementia-takes-the-choice-out-of-death-decision-20160127-gmew1d.html

Campion, E. W. (1996). When a mind dies. *New England Journal of Medicine, 334*(12), 791–2. https://doi.org/10.1056/nejm199603213341209

Clare, L., Rowlands, J., Bruce, E., Surr, C., & Downs, M. (2008). The experience of living with dementia in residential care: An interpretative phenomenological analysis. *The Gerontologist, 48*(6), 711–20. https://doi.org/10.1093/geront/48.6.711

Corderoy, A. (2015, July 22). One in 10 dementia carers think about killing a loved one: study. *The Age.* https://www.theage.com.au/healthcare/one-in-10-dementia-carers-think-about-killing-a-loved-one-study-20150722-gi-i5fw.html

Cunningham, S. (2020). *City of Trees: Essays on Life, Death and the Need for a Forest.* Text Publishing.

D'Agata, E., & Mitchell, S. L. (2008). Patterns of antimicrobial use among nursing home residents with advanced dementia. *Archives of Internal Medicine, 168*(4), 357. https://doi.org/10.1001/archinternmed.2007.104

Feast, A. R., White, N., Lord, K., Kupeli, N., Vickerstaff, V., & Sampson, E. L. (2018). Pain and delirium in people with dementia in the acute general hospital setting. *Age and Ageing, 47*(6), 841–6. https://doi.org/10.1093/ageing/afy112

Gray, R. (1990). The carer's view [occasional book review of *Dementia Care: Patient, Family and Community*, edited by N. L. Mace]. *The Lancet, 336*(8715), 614. https://doi.org/10.1016/0140-6736(90)93404-D

Harrison, A. (1996, June 3). *Australian Medicine: News Magazine of the Australian Medical Association.*

Kovach, C. R., Weissman, D. E., Griffie, J., Matson, S., & Muchka, S. (1999). Assessment and treatment of discomfort for people with late-stage dementia. *Journal of Pain and Symptom Management, 18*(6), 412–19. https://doi.org/10.1016/s0885-3924(99)00094-9

Lancet. (2008). Editorial: This unremembered state. *The Lancet, 372*(9634), 177. https://doi.org/10.1016/s0140-6736(08)61043-0

Lyketsos, C. G., & Alzheimer's Australia. (2009). *Dementia: Facing the Epidemic* [presentation to the National Press Club, Canberra]. Alzheimer's Australia. https://www.dementia.org.au/sites/default/files/20090923_Nat_NP_NP18LyketsosFacingDemEp.pdf

Medew, J. (2014, March 13). A son's plea to Denis Napthine: This is no way for my mother to live. *The Age.*

Mitchell, S., Kiely, D., & Hamel, M. (2004). Dying with advanced dementia in the nursing home. *Archives of Internal Medicine, 164*(3), 321–6. https://doi.org/10.1001/ARCHINTE.164.3.321

Mitchell, S. L., Miller, S. C., Teno, J. M., Davis, R. B., & Shaffer, M. L. (2010). The advanced dementia prognostic tool: A risk score to estimate survival in nursing home residents with advanced dementia. *Journal of Pain and Symptom Management, 40*(5), 639–51. https://doi.org/10.1016/j.jpainsymman.2010.02.014

Moore, A. (2016, March 24). Dear kids, don't ever shove me in an old people's home. *The Age.* https://www.theage.com.au/opinion/instructions-for-our-children-to-let-their-parents-stay-at-home-to-the-end-20160324-gnq4b1.html

Morris, S. (2005). The experience of the Victorian Civil and Administrative Tribunal in relation to the Victorian Medical Treatment Act. *Australasian Journal on Ageing, 24*, S36–S41. https://doi.org/10.1111/j.1741-6612.2005.00096.x

Norwood, F. (2009). *The Maintenance of Life: Preventing Social Death Through Euthanasia Talk and End-of-Life Care: Lessons from the Netherlands.* Carolina Academic Press.

O'Dwyer, S. T., Moyle, W., Taylor, T., Creese, J., & Zimmer-Gembeck, M. J.. (2016). Homicidal ideation in family carers of people with dementia. *Aging & Mental Health, 20*(11), 1174–81. https://doi.org/10.1080/13607863.2015.1065793

O'Dwyer, S. T., Moyle, W., Zimmer-Gembeck, M., & De Leo, D. (2013). Suicidal ideation in family carers of people with dementia: A pilot study. *International Journal of Geriatric Psychiatry, 28*(11), 1182–8. https://doi.org/10.1002/gps.3941

Osler, W. (1898). *The Principles and Practice of Medicine: Designed for the Use of Practitioners and Students of Medicine* (3rd edn). Young J. Pentland.

Post, S. G. (2000). *The Moral Challenge of Alzheimer Disease: Ethical Issues from Diagnosis to Dying* (2nd edn). Johns Hopkins University Press.

Sachs, G. A. (2009). Dying from dementia. *New England Journal of Medicine, 361*(16), 1595–6. https://doi.org/10.1056/NEJMe0905988

Sklovsky, J. (2014, November 12). Euthanasia: A question of trust. *The Age.* https://www.theage.com.au/healthcare/euthanasia-a-question-of-trust-20141112-11kyew.html

Van Der Steen, J. T., Ooms, M. E., Van Der Wal, G., & Ribbe, M. W. (2002). Pneumonia: The demented patient's best friend? Discomfort after starting or withholding antibiotic treatment. *Journal of the American Geriatrics Society, 50*(10), 1681–8. https://doi.org/10.1046/j.1532-5415.2002.50460.x

Van Der Steen, J. T., Pasman, H. R. W., Ribbe, M. W., Van Der Wal, G., & Onwuteaka-Philipsen, B. D. (2009). Discomfort in dementia patients dying from pneumonia and its relief by antibiotics. *Scandinavian Journal of Infectious Diseases, 41*(2), 143–51. https://doi.org/10.1080/00365540802616726

Waite, L. (2015). Treatment for Alzheimer's disease: Has anything changed? *Australian Prescriber, 38*(2), 60–3. https://doi.org/10.18773/austprescr.2015.018

Wolff, M. (2012, May 18). A life worth ending. *New York Magazine.* https://nymag.com/news/features/parent-health-care-2012-5/

Zwakhalen, S. M., Hamers, J. P., Abu-Saad, H. H., & Berger, M. P. (2006). Pain in elderly people with severe dementia: A systematic review of behavioural pain assessment tools. *BMC Geriatrics, 6*(1). https://doi.org/10.1186/1471-2318-6-3

The worst disease known to man – Helga Kuhse

Kuhse, H. (2023, May 11). Letters: Escaping the monster. *The Age.* https://www.theage.com.au/national/victoria/when-will-labor-make-the-fair-decisions-if-not-now-20230511-p5d7sv.html

I'm sorry, Mum – Guy Pearce

Johnson, S. (ed.) 2021. *Dear Mum*. Hachette.

Pearce, G. (2021, March 27–28). What would you say to your mother? *The Weekend Australian.*

Chapter 7 – A completed life

Bilefsky, D., & Schuetze, C. F. (2016, October 13). Dutch law would allow assisted suicide for healthy older people. *New York Times.* https://www.nytimes.com/2016/10/14/world/europe/dutch-law-would-allow-euthanasia-for-healthy-elderly-people.html

Brody, E. M. (2010). On being very, very old: An insider's perspective. *The Gerontologist, 50*(1), 2–10. https://doi.org/10.1093/geront/gnp143

Drion, Huib. (1991, October 19). Het zelfgewilde einde van oudere mensen [The self-willed end of older people]. *NRC Handelsblad.*

Hallberg I. R. (2004). Death and dying from old people's point of view: A literature review. *Aging Clinical and Experimental Research, 16*(2), 87–103. https://doi.org/10.1007/BF03324537

Hillman, K. (2013, September 16). How the care conveyor belt tortures people back to life. *The Conversation.* https://theconversation.com/how-the-care-conveyor-belt-tortures-people-back-to-life-18188

Medew, J. (2016, January 15). The big sleep. *The Age.* https://www.theage.com.au/interactive/2016/the-big-sleep/

Medew, J. (2013, April 3). A time to live, a time to die, a time to debate. *The Age.* https://www.theage.com.au/politics/federal/a-time-to-live-a-time-to-die-a-time-to-debate-20130402-2h53h.html

Sacks, O. (2019). *Everything in its Place: First Loves and Last Tales*. Knopf.

Sears, L. (2012, May 9). World-weary Swiss seniors seek suicide help. *The Local Switzerland*.

Sharp, T., Moran, E., Kuhn, I., & Barclay, S. (2013). Do the elderly have a voice? Advance care planning discussions with frail and older individuals: A systematic literature review and narrative synthesis. *British Journal of General Practice, 63*(615), e657–e668. https://doi.org/10.3399/bjgp13x673667

Syme, R. (2013, April 8). Beverley's legacy: Society dying for the right to die. *The Age*. https://www.theage.com.au/opinion/beverleys-legacy-society-dying-for-the-right-to-die-20130408-2hhqy.html

Syme, R. (2016, January 18). Letter: Presence is not a crime. *The Age*. https://www.theage.com.au/national/victoria/society-what-do-we-stand-for-as-a-nation-of-consumers-20160118-gm8c65.html

Syme, R. (2016). *Time to Die*. Melbourne University Press.

You, J. (2018, April 19). Poor communication is compromising care for the dying. *The Conversation*. https://theconversation.com/poor-communication-is-compromising-care-for-the-dying-93783

Chapter 8 – Voluntary refusal of fluids and food

Abbey, J. (2013). *Wrestling with Dementia and Death: A Report for Alzheimer's Australia*. Alzheimer's Australia Inc. https://agedcare.royalcommission.gov.au/system/files/2020-06/JAB.0001.0001.0001.pdf

Andrews, K. (1996). Euthanasia in chronic severe disablement. *British Medical Bulletin, 52*(2), 280–8. https://doi.org/10.1093/oxfordjournals.bmb.a011542

Australian Medical Association. (2013, March 27). *Medical Ethics in Custodial Settings* [position statement]. https://www.ama.com.au/position-statement/medical-ethics-custodial-settings-2013

Bernat, J. L., Gert, B., & Mogielnicki, R. P. (1993). Patient refusal of hydration and nutrition: An alternative to physician-assisted suicide or voluntary active euthanasia. *Archives of Internal Medicine, 153*(24), 2723–31. Doi:10.1001/archinte.1993.00410240021003

Brightwater Care Group (Inc.) v Rossiter. (2009). Western Australian Supreme Court 229 [decision of Martin CJ].

Cox, S. S. (1987). Is dehydration painful? *Ethics & Medics, 12*(9), 1–2.

Eddy, D. M. (1994). A conversation with my mother. *Journal of the American Medical Association, 272*(3), 179–81. https://doi.org/10.1001/jama.1994.03520030013005

Ganzini, L. (2016). Legalised physician-assisted death in Oregon. *QUT Law Review, 16*(1), 76–83. https://doi.org/10.5204/qutlr.v16i1.623

Gardner; re BWV (2003). Victorian Supreme Court 173; 7 VR 487 [decision of Morris J]. https://jade.io/article/75030

H. Ltd. V J. & Anor. (2010). Supreme Court of South Australia 176 [decision of Kourakis J]. https://jade.io/article/181738

Hamilton, M., & Thomson, C. (2016). Recognising unpaid care in private pension schemes. *Social Policy and Society, 16*(4)

Heath, I. (2010). What do we want to die from? *British Medical Journal, 341*, c3883. https://doi.org/10.1136/bmj.c3883

Hunter and New England Health Service v A. (2009). New South Wales Supreme Court 761 [decision of McDougall J].

Institute of Medical Ethics Working Party on the Ethics of Prolonging Life and Assisting Death. (1991). Withdrawal of life-support from patients in a persistent vegetative state. *The Lancet, 337*(8733), 96–8. https://doi.org/10.1016/0140-6736(91)90748-E

Jacobs, S. (2003). Death by voluntary dehydration: What the caregivers say. *New England Journal of Medicine, 349*(4), 325–6. http://dx.doi.org/10.1056/NEJMp038115

Morris, S. (2005). The experience of the Victorian Civil and Administrative Tribunal in relation to the Victorian Medical Treatment Act. *Australasian Journal on Ageing, 24*, S36–S41. https://doi.org/10.1111/j.1741-6612.2005.00096.x

Pasman, H. R. W., Onwuteaka-Philipsen, B. D., Kriegsman, D. M. W., Ooms, M. E., Ribbe, M. W., & Van Der Wal, G. (2005). Discomfort in nursing home patients with severe dementia in whom artificial nutrition and hydration is forgone. *Archives of Internal Medicine, 165*(15), 1729–35. https://doi.org/10.1001/archinte.165.15.1729

Preston, T. A., & Mero, R. (1996). Observations concerning terminally ill patients who choose suicide. *Journal of Pharmaceutical Care in Pain & Symptom Control, 4*(1–2), 183–92. https://doi.org/10.1300/J088v04n01-2_02

Printz, L. A. (1992). Terminal dehydration: A compassionate treatment. *Archives of Internal Medicine, 152*(4), 697–700. http://hdl.handle.net/10822/737519

Raina, R. S. (2010). Refusing medical treatment in advance. *Law Society Journal: The Official Journal of the Law Society of New South Wales, 48*(1), 62–5. https://search.informit.org/doi/10.3316/agispt.20100688

Rogers v Whitaker (1992) High Court of Australia 58 – 175 CLR 479.

Royal Dutch Medical Association (KNMG), & Dutch Nurses' Association (V&VN). (2014). *Caring for People Who Consciously Choose Not to Eat and Drink so as to Hasten the End of Life.* https://www.knmg.nl/web/file?uuid=dacf5d4a-da2f-4a5b-94ca-f5913ad1488b&owner=5c945405-d6ca-4deb-aa16-7af2088aa173&contentid=694

Vacco v Quill. (1997). 521 United States Supreme Court 793 [transcript of proceedings]. https://www.supremecourt.gov/pdfs/transcripts/1996/95-1858_01-08-1997.pdf

White, B., Willmott, L., & Savulescu, J. (2014). Voluntary palliated starvation: A lawful and ethical way to die? *Journal of Law and Medicine, 22*(2), 376–86. https://eprints.qut.edu.au/79897/

Chapter 9 – Ending one's own life, or suicide?

Baird, C. (2018, May). Case #1: Nothing seemed out of the ordinary. *Victorian Institute of Forensic Medicine Residential Aged Care Communique, 13*(2), 3–5. https://www.thecommuniques.com/post/residential-aged-care-communiqu%C3%A9-volume-13-issue-2-may-2018

Cassell, E. J. (1999). Diagnosing suffering: A perspective. *Annals of Internal Medicine, 131*(7), 531–4. https://doi.org/10.7326/0003-4819-131-7-199910050-00009

Cunningham, M. (2019, June 18). Catholic Church restates staunch opposition to voluntary assisted dying laws. *The Age.* https://www.theage.com.au/national/victoria/catholic-church-restates-staunch-opposition-to-voluntary-assisted-dying-laws-20190618-p51yt4.html

de Ropp, R. S. (1968). *The Master Game: Beyond the Drug Experience.* Delacorte.

Edelman, S. (2013, October 3). Aina's sad story: How system blocked her wishes to end a life of pain and suffering. *Sydney Morning Herald*. https://www.smh.com.au/opinion/ainas-sad-story-how-system-blocked-her-wishes-to-end-a-life-of-pain-and-suffering-20131002-2usr3.html

Franklin, J. (2018, June 9). Why predicting suicide is a difficult and complex challenge. *The Conversation*. https://theconversation.com/why-predicting-suicide-is-a-difficult-and-complex-challenge-98052

Glover, J. (1990). *Causing Death and Saving Lives: The Moral Problems of Abortion, Infanticide, Suicide, Euthanasia, Capital Punishment, War and Other Life-or-Death Choices*. Penguin.

H. Ltd. V J. & Anor. (2010). Supreme Court of South Australia 176 [decision of Kourakis J]. https://jade.io/article/181738

Holmes, A., Ibrahim, J. et al. (2018, November). *Victorian Institute of Forensic Medicine: Residential Aged Care Communiqué, 13*(4). https://www.thecommuniques.com/post/residential-aged-care-communiqu%C3%A9-volume-13-issue-4-november-2018-1

Jain, B. (2018, May). Guest editorial. *Victorian Institute of Forensic Medicine Residential Aged Care Communique, 13*(2), 2. https://www.thecommuniques.com/post/residential-aged-care-communiqu%C3%A9-volume-13-issue-2-may-2018

Re JS [2014] NSWSC 302 [decision of Darke J]. https://jade.io/article/317819?at.hl=Re+JS+%255B2014%255D+NSWSC+302

Lieberman, V. (2010, September 28). Physician aid for dying is not euthanasia. *Missoulian*. https://missoulian.com/mobile/article_1037a8b8-cb0a-11df-a3d6-001cc4c002e0.html

McGorry, P. (2012, September 10). A deadly silence that has to end. *Sydney Morning Herald*.

Ministerial Advisory Panel on Voluntary Assisted Dying. (2017, July). *Final Report*. Victorian Government. https://content.health.vic.gov.au/sites/default/files/migrated/files/collections/research-and-reports/m/ministerial-advisory-panel-on-voluntary-assisted-dying-final-report-pdf.pdf

Murphy, B. J., Bugeja, L. C., Pilgrim, J. L., & Ibrahim, J. E. (2018). Suicide among nursing home residents in Australia: A national population-based retrospective analysis of medico-legal death investigation information. *International Journal of Geriatric Psychiatry, 33*(5), 786–96. https://doi.org/10.1002/gps.4862

O'Connell, H., Chin, A.-V., Cunningham, C., & Lawlor, B. A. (2004). Recent developments: Suicide in older people. *British Medical Journal, 329*(7471), 895–9. https://doi.org/10.1136/bmj.329.7471.895

Quill, T. E., Cassel, C. K., & Meier, D. E. (1992). Care of the hopelessly ill: Proposed clinical criteria for physician-assisted suicide. *New England Journal of Medicine, 327*, 1380–4. https://doi.org/10.1056/NEJM199211053271911

Sokol, D. K. (2008). Clarifying best interests. *BMJ (Clinical Research ed.), 337*, a994. https://doi.org/10.1136/bmj.a994

Van der Maas, P. J., Van Delden, J. J. M., Pijnenborg, L., Looman, C. W. M., & Central Bureau of Statistics, The Hague. (1991, September 14). Euthanasia and other medical decisions concerning the end of life. *The Lancet, 338*(8768), 669–74. https://doi.org/10.1016/0140-6736(91)91241-L

Young, C. (2018, May). Case #2: A pain in the back. *Victorian Institute of Forensic Medicine Residential Aged Care Communique, 13*(2), 5. https://www.thecommuniques.com/post/residential-aged-care-communiqu%C3%A9-volume-13-issue-2-may-2018

Chapter 10 – Solutions

Abbey, J. (2013). *Wrestling with Dementia and Death: A Report for Alzheimer's Australia.* Alzheimer's Australia Inc. https://agedcare.royalcommission.gov.au/system/files/2020-06/JAB.0001.0001.0001.pdf

AMA (Australian Medical Association). (2016, March 10). *AMA Submission to the Standing Committee on Community Affairs: Inquiry into the Future of Australia's Aged Care Sector Workforce.* https://www.ama.com.au/submission/ama-submission-senate-community-affairs-inquiry-future-australia%E2%80%99s-aged-care-sector

American Academy of Neurology Ethics and Humanities Subcommittee. (1996). Ethical issues in the management of the demented patient. *Neurology, 46*(4), 1180–3. https://doi.org/10.1212/wnl.46.4.1180

Berghmans, R. (2000). Advance directives and dementia. *Annals of the New York Academy of Sciences, 913*, 105–10. https://doi.org/10.1111/j.1749-6632.2000.tb05165.x

Bernat, J. L. (2002). *Ethical Issues in Neurology* (2nd edn). Butterworth-Heinemann.

Bernat, J. L. (2008). *Ethical Issues in Neurology* (3rd edn). Lippincott Williams & Wilkins.

Cann, P. (2006, April 12). Past caring. *The Guardian.* https://www.theguardian.com/society/2006/apr/12/longtermcare.comment1

Cantor, N. L. (2017, April 20). Changing the paradigm of advance directives to avoid prolonged dementia. *Bill of Health.* http://blogs.harvard.edu/billofhealth/2017/04/20/changing-the-paradigm-of-advance-directives/

Caplan, A. L. & Quill, T. E. (2016, December 6). Physician-assisted dying: Our society needs it, says MD. *End of Life Washington*. https://endoflifewa.org/news/physician-assisted-dying-society-needs-says-md/

Christakis, N. A. (2008). Too quietly into the night. *British Medical Journal, 337*(7665), 326. https://www.jstor.org/stable/20510532

Cleeland, C. S. (1998). Undertreatment of cancer pain in elderly patients. *Journal of the American Medical Association, 279*(23), 1914–15. https://doi.org/10.1001/jama.279.23.1914

Economist. (2017, April 29). How to have a better death. *The Economist*. https://www.economist.com/leaders/2017/04/29/how-to-have-a-better-death

Gray, R. (1990). The carer's view [occasional book review of *Dementia Care: Patient, Family and Community*, edited by N. L. Mace]. *The Lancet, 336*(8715), 614. https://doi.org/10.1016/0140-6736(90)93404-D

Herald Sun (quoting Bill Silvester). (2015, May 25). Patients kept alive for longer because doctors 'don't know dying wishes'. *Herald Sun*. https://www.heraldsun.com.au/news/victoria/patients-kept-alive-for-longer-because-doctors-dont-know-dying-wishes/news-story/f7fcc7a91d07e0e3c3d5bc37f439ac63

Laurance, J. (2009, November 5.) Hospital staff 'fail patients in dying days'. *Independent UK*. https://www.independent.co.uk/life-style/health-and-families/health-news/hospital-staff-fail-patients-in-dying-days-1814788.html

McMahon, N. (2013, May 4). Life's toughest question: How do you want to die? *The Age*. https://www.theage.com.au/national/victoria/lifes-toughest-question-how-do-you-want-to-die-20130503-2iyey.html

Norwood, F. (2009). *The Maintenance of Life: Preventing Social Death Through Euthanasia Talk and End-of-Life Care – Lessons from the Netherlands*. Carolina Academic Press.

Okie, S. (2011). Confronting Alzheimer's disease. *New England Journal of Medicine, 365*(12), 1069–72. https://doi.org/10.1056/NEJMp1107288

Sachs, G. A. (2009). Dying from dementia. *New England Journal of Medicine, 361*(16), 1595–6. https://doi.org/10.1056/NEJMe0905988

White, B., Willmott, L., & Neller, P. (2016, August 29). Clarifying end-of-life law for doctors. *InSight Plus: Medical Journal of Australia*. https://insightplus.mja.com.au/2016/33/clarifying-end-of-life-law-for-doctors/

Williams, R. (1999, April 4). Old age and dementia [radio broadcast transcript]. *Ockham's Razor*. ABC. https://www.abc.net.au/radionational/programs/ockhamsrazor/old-age-and-dementia/3557290

www.ingramcontent.com/pod-product-compliance
Lightning Source LLC
Chambersburg PA
CBHW072100040426
42334CB00041B/1544